To Sunny

Love & Respect

Dr Ann Marie Evans

Also by the Author:
  1. *Affirmations, Your Passport to Happiness*
  2. *Affirmations, Your Passport to Lasting, Loving Relationships*
  3. *Affirmations, Your Passport to Prosperity/Money*
  4. The Cards of Life
  5. Affirmation/Prayer Cards
  6. Cards of Life Instructional Course
  7. Co-Author of the #1 Best Selling-Series, *Wake up-Live The Life You Love* with Dr. Wayne Dyer, Dr. Deepak Chopra, and Terry Cole-Whittaker

Queries regarding rights and permissions:
  Anne Marie Evers
  Affirmations International Publishing Company
  4559 Underwood Avenue
  North Vancouver, BC, Canada V7K 2S3

  Email: annemarieevers@shaw.ca

  Fax: 604-904-1127
  Toll-Free Phone Number: 1-877-923-3476

  www.affirmations-doctor.com

  ISBN #09680292-X

Learn about the history of Affirmations, as never seen before, with a behind-the-scenes view of how famous authors and people around the world are using Affirmations to transform their lives at www.affirmations-playground.com.

Printed by International Web Express, Coquitlam, BC

Cover Design: Norisa Anderson

Chapter Illustrations from The Cards of Life

Editor: Val Wilson, Ink

I love the lady.
I love the book!

Affirmations Are For Everyone!

♥ ♥ ♥ ♥ ♥ ♥ ♥ ♥ ♥ ♥ ♥ ♥

Anne Marie Evers, with
Reverend Kasem Sapatajaria,
blessing this *Affirmations* book
and The Cards of Life

Debbora Harney Gregor Writes:

"Reverend Kasem Sapatajaria came into my life in the
autumn of 1990. There was an immediate connection, as

somehow we managed to communicate through facial
expressions, hand language, and laughter.

As we got to know each other, I came to learn that Kasem
was a chief monk from Thailand, where he had lived his
entire life. In Thailand, all boys, out of respect for their
parents, must enter the monastery for two weeks. Many
do not become monks, but Kasem made the decision at the
age of 12 because he wanted to travel around the world.

And that he did. He loves Vancouver and would come to visit three times a year. One night, I wanted to visit Anne Marie and introduce Kasem to her. She had just recently lost her husband Roy and I was hoping our visit would help in some small way.

The minute Kasem saw Roy's picture, he asked if that was her husband. She said 'Yes.' He asked if he had passed away. Again, she answered 'Yes.' He then asked Anne Marie if she would mind if he chanted for Roy's soul. He began to explain to her why he needed to do it. It was his duty as a chief monk to chant and offer food to the spirit of Roy for a peaceful heart and for Anne Marie as well. This took some time.

When it was over, Anne Marie told him about the Affirmation work she does. Kasem's face lit up. 'Oh, Affirmations I know very well. I agree with them 100%!!! I do myself many, many times!!!' We spent hours that night in North Vancouver speaking about Affirmations, Buddhism, the Dali Lama, and various other spiritual topics.

Kasem believed in the power of thought and that if we think in a positive way, better things happen in our lives. He believed in kindness, compassion, and love. He also believed that while thinking positive thoughts, peace will follow in your heart. Most of all, he believed in the work Anne Marie has done with her *Affirmations* book series and the Cards of Life.

He wanted to endorse her work in some way, so I took this picture and he was pleased. That evening will forever be etched in my mind. He often mentioned to me how much he enjoyed Anne Marie's warm hugs.

Reverend Kasem Sapatajaria passed away January 5, 2003, at the age of 76. He left behind many wonderful memories and teachings and definitely his own Passport to Happiness! Thanks, Anne Marie, for letting me share this story."
With utmost, unconditional love,
Debbora Harney Gregor

The Author Writes:

I, too, will always remember that evening with Debbora and Kasem. I was so touched with the love, caring, and empathy that Kasem showed me that evening and over the years. I thank Debbora for bringing him to me at a time when I was feeling sad and for touching my life in such a deep, spiritual, special way. Kasem was and still is an important part of my life.

Anne Marie Evers

Prayer

For a Friend

I said a prayer for you today, and know God must have heard

I felt the answer in my heart, although He spoke no word

I did not ask for wealth or fame, I knew you would not mind

I asked Him to send treasures of a far more lasting kind.

I asked that He be near you at the start of each new day

To grant you health, blessings, and friends to share your way

I asked for happiness for you in all things great and small,

But it was for His loving care for you, my friend,

I prayed most of all!

–Author Unknown

Acknowledgements

Special thanks to David Evers for his valuable computer assistance.

I wish to thank Val Wilson for her knowledge, input, assistance, and many hours of work in editing this book.

I would also like to express my sincere gratitude to my daughter Aren Evers and my sister Darlene O'Neill and family members for their interest and loving support.

I am also grateful to Dr. Lee Pulos, Christine Einarson, Debbora Harney Gregor, Glenn Coleman, Caroline Ryker, Shae Hadden, and Wade and Sibella Morlin.

I wish to also thank one of my business associates who helped me define the 51 percent believability factor in business. When you have 49 percent, someone else is in control, when you have 50 percent, it is stalemated, but when you have 51 percent, you have controlling interest. So when doing your Affirmations, you need at least a 51 percent believability factor that the Affirmation will manifest as affirmed.

I am also grateful to all those who use the principles and concepts taught in this book and to the thousands of men and women who have allowed me to guide them in their search for a happier, more fulfilled life. I greatly appreciate your valuable feedback, emails, letters, and telephone calls of encouragement. Thank you for your Affirmation success stories. I am very blessed to have you in my life. Thank you, thank you, thank you.

It is my hope and Affirmation that each one of you will also purchase and use my companion books, *Affirmations, Your Passport to Lasting, Loving Relationships* and *Affirmations, Your Passport to Prosperity/Money*. These books also make great every occasion gifts for that special person in your life. You may also purchase the Cards of Life directly from me or from www.amazon.com.

Please visit my Website at
www.affirmations-doctor.com.

7

Affirmations Doctor

Anne Marie Evers

"I love prescribing affirmations of health, wealth, love, and happiness for everyone!"

Please check out my Website at
www.affirmations-doctor.com

Affirmations When Properly Done Always Work!

Table of Contents

The Building Blocks of the Personal Contract Affirmation Method

part 1 — The Building Blocks

part **2**   **Applying AMCAM in Your Life**

Applying AMCAM

part 3   Personal Growth

Foreword
By Dr. Lee Pulos, Ph.D.

Since the beginning of recorded history, the power of the word has been acknowledged by mystics and shamans as a pathway to personal transformation. King Solomon acknowledged this by saying, "As a man thinketh in his heart, so is he," and 2,500 years ago, the Buddha said, "All that we are is the result of what we have thought." In modern times, we call the power of the word *Affirmations.*

These are bursts of electrical energy consciously directed into our brains to create a positive declaration of what we want to become or achieve. Every minute of our waking life, we are creating Affirmations through our self-talk, at the rate of 150 to 300 words per minute or between 45,000 and 51,000 thoughts per day.

Positive self-talk has been referred to as nutrition for the mind, like planting flowers in the garden of our subconscious, whereas a negative inner dialogue is analogous to planting weeds. Thus, Affirmations constitute positive, controlled, and directed self-talk that gives focus and impact to one's plans and goals for personal growth and fulfillment.

I first met Anne Marie Evers 25 years ago when we were both part of a spiritual development and healing circle. Part of our work included not only verbal but also visual and emotional Affirmations. Since then, Anne Marie has written three books on Affirmations and goal-setting to help thousands of persons realize their dreams. The purpose of Affirmations is simple—to re-educate and re-program the subconscious with desired outcomes or goals.

In this book, Anne Marie has provided a comprehensive, easy-to-follow system for transforming destructive or limiting core beliefs through her *Personal Contract Affirmation Method.*

There are two ways of creating our reality—by consciously programming what we want out of life or by simply accepting what comes our way.

Both work, but only the former will ensure that you get what you want in life. This book helps put you in charge of your programming and, consequently, firmly in control of your life! As you use Affirmations daily and consistently, you will be breathing life into the future of your dreams.

Lee Pulos
Author of *The Power of Visualization* and *Mentally Fit Forever*

Foreword
By The Hon. John Joseph Kennedy

I had the pleasure of "bumping into" Anne Marie in a spiritual book store one afternoon in Vancouver in early 2000. It was one of those rare, magical moments in life that I knew, without a doubt, that the Hand of Providence had swept down and brought us together. It was destiny!

We had so much fun visiting and chatting. I was looking for a special person to help me write a book and trading cards of Affirmations for children for one of my projects, The Royal Critters / Whale Magic Project, and there she was! Anne Marie and I became instant friends and soul mates of sorts; I have had the pleasure of collaborating on a number of events and projects with her since that first "chance encounter."

She appeared as a special guest on one of my television specials, Whale-of-a-Holiday, teaching Affirmations. Together, we taught a third-grade class in Paradise, Washington, about Whales / Ocean Awareness and Affirmations. They were the most adorable group of children and Anne Marie and I were deeply touched by that experience. It was a whale-of-a-day, one I shall never forget.

Anne Marie Evers is one of the most beautiful souls I have ever met. I admire her positive, life-giving work and commitment to mankind, especially children. She is living proof that one person can make an exponential difference in the world. Her cup overflows and everyone who is blessed to know her or impacted by her books, her work, and special gifts is enveloped in this love!

The Hon. John Joseph Kennedy
www.JJKEnterprises.com and www.RoyalCritters.com

Introduction

Affirmations When Properly Done Always Work!

Many people over the years have asked me, "Anne Marie, how did you ever get started on the path of Affirmations?" I tell them it grew out of a very negative situation. My first husband Al was an alcoholic. I decided I had only three choices: drink with him, take the kids and leave him, or find other interests.

I quickly decided that my children already had one alcoholic parent and certainly did not deserve or need another one, so that option was out.

Option two was to take the kids and leave. After spending time checking, I discovered that not one member of my family was in a position to take care of us and, in those days, it was very difficult to find a place that would take a mother and two children.

So I decided to go for the third option: finding other interests. I took up meditation, yoga, reflexology, astral traveling, creative visualization, writing, and much, much more. My quest and thirst for knowledge led me to some positive thinking books and Affirmations. I was so intrigued, I started doing Affirmations, half wondering if they would really work.

I was amazed at what happened in my life. My Affirmations started coming true.

No, my husband did not stop drinking, but I did change the way I viewed him; he sensed the change and some things did improve in our home.

I have used Affirmations in every part of my life and could not imagine life without them.

Out of a negative situation, I learned about Affirmation Power and how to use it. I now feel it is my place in life to help those who wish to learn how to use this extraordinary power.

Now I thank Al for being one of my very important teachers. I believe we are all students and teachers and that we all learn from each other.

When the student is ready, the teacher appears.

When the teacher is ready, the student appears.

About Creation

In the beginning was the word, when God/Creator/Universal Mind affirmed the world into being. This astonishing creative power is still in existence and can be harnessed by individuals to create their own optimal world. Through the use of Affirmations, you can tap into this power to realize your fondest dreams and to generate health, wealth, and happiness. You are the creator of your Universe and a co-creator with God.

The information outlined in this book can be used as your stepping-stones to understanding yourself and realizing the extraordinary power that is within you. You can have and enjoy a loving, lasting marriage or relationship. You can be prosperous beyond your wildest dreams and have anything in the world you desire. You must, however, abide by the Affirmation rules, as follows:

1.   Never hurt or take from anyone.
2.   Ensure that your Affirmations are worded to the good of all parties concerned.
3.   Make sure your Affirmations are realistic, with at least a 51 percent believability factor.

As you read this book, allow the words and meanings to sink deep into your subconscious mind and become a part of your consciousness. Know that you are growing, expanding, and evolving at your own rate. Let the changes occur naturally and easily as you develop and maintain an attitude of gratitude. And remember that you are changed as you decree!

It is my hope and prayer that you will take these golden threads of knowledge and opportunity and weave them together to make your life a beautiful tapestry.

The Power of the Mind

When I was a child, it became quite clear to me how thoughts and the power of the mind affect our lives. At a dinner party one evening, my Aunt Bea served a delicious cream dessert. Everyone raved about it and most of the guests requested a second helping. Four hours later, someone asked Aunt Bea for the recipe. She started to name the ingredients and, when she came to cream cheese, my cousin Alice gasped, put her hand over her mouth, ran to the bathroom, and vomited.

It turned out that Alice was extremely allergic to cream cheese! I could not understand her reaction and asked my mother why it took Alice so long to get sick. Nor could I understand why she became so violently ill when she heard those two harmless words: "cream cheese." My mother said, "It has something to do with thoughts and her mind, dear. Don't worry. She will be okay." The incident stuck in my memory and clearly demonstrated to me the tremendous creative power of the mind. To harness this creative power and manifest things in your life, the *Personal Contract Affirmation Method — AMCAM (Anne Marie's Contract Affirmation Method)* — will equip you with all the tools and understanding you need.

Here are the five building blocks of AMCAM:
- Forgiveness
- Thoughts
- Mind-Power
- Affirmations
- Creative Visualization

This approach is one of the most powerful and effective systems for taking control of your life. It gives you the ability to fulfill your dreams.

Whenever the word God is used here, it refers to the Universal Mind, the Creator, or whatever higher power you believe in. The process of doing Affirmations is not a cult or any form of brainwashing. It is not about black magic. It is a completely real and natural process. You are simply working with the laws of the great Universe. You make your own magic by using your own wondrous, inner creative power.

The information contained in this book is so powerful, it comes with a warning: with everything you do, affirm, say, or think, it is essential that you never hurt or take from anyone and that your objective is *the good of all parties concerned.* This is for your own safety, as well as that of others. Allow these important intentions to permeate your reality and become part of who you are.

I have received thousands of testimonials from people worldwide who have experienced miracles in their lives through the use of AMCAM. Please see the testimonials in this book. One woman told me she takes my book with her everywhere and has greater self-esteem and self-love as a result of doing her Affirmations.

In December 1998, I was interviewed on the David Ingram Show, during which Ingram reported how the well-known singer Rita MacNeil had applied Affirmations in her life to promote her success. In the early years, she would hold a mop handle, pretending it was a microphone, and sing into it. Today, she is a highly successful manifestation of the power of Affirmations and creative visualization.

The Power of This Book in Stories and Letters

The Young Woman

One of the stories that really touched my heart took place at the Barnes & Noble Bookstore in Bellingham, WA. One snowy winter evening when I was conducting a seminar on the Power of Affirmations and doing a book signing, a young girl came to talk to me. Out of her knapsack, she pulled the first edition of my book *Affirmations, Your Passport to Happiness.*

It was tattered and very worn. Each page was marked and underlined in different colours. She said, "Anne Marie, I rode the bus for miles to meet you and to thank you for writing this book. I could not have made it during this past year without it. It goes everywhere with me."

She then told me a story of how she had been viciously attacked when walking home from college. Tears welled up in my eyes and as I looked at her and the copy of my book she was holding in her hand, I just had to ask her where she got it.

She said, "You know, that is interesting. My friend gave it to me several years ago as a gift. I put it away and it turned up last year, just as I was thinking I had nowhere to turn. There it was, right on top of all my text books."

As I hugged her trembling body, I could feel the love and gratitude flowing from her to me. Now when I am spending hours working on my books and the thought runs through my mind if it is worth doing all this work, my mind immediately goes back to that evening and, in vivid detail, I clearly see the face of this young lady with tears streaming down her cheeks and I **know** the results are worth the work! I am so honoured to be a part of her healing journey.

We never know how our words and actions will affect others. This is why it is so important to speak words of loving kindness and encouragement to everyone.

James, The Musician

James Harvey was a homeless young man living on the streets of Vancouver when he started reading a copy of *Affirmations, Your Passport to Happiness.*

He memorized the Short-Form Affirmations at the back of the book. Because he is a musician, he put the words to music, recorded them on tape, and listened to these positive Affirmations over and over. Whenever he needed positive energy, he would listen to this tape, first thing in the morning, at night before drifting off to sleep, and in the middle of the night when he needed to hear some positive reinforcement.

Miracles began taking place in his life. He manifested a place to live with a wonderful 87-year-old gentleman, Richard (Daddy) Babb, and his daughter Marcia. When James called me, he said, "Anne Marie, you will never believe my story." I replied, "Yes, I will." We met and he told me of these wonderful miracles—how he had received clothes, musical equipment, a computer, and many

Richard (Daddy) Babb's 90th Birthday Party: Anne Marie, James, and Richard

other useful things. He now has a job teaching preschoolers in Vancouver and is pursuing his musical career. He asked me how he could give back to the Universe for the blessings he received. I asked him if he thought he could put together a musical CD we could use for our children's anti-violence program, the *Affirm and Learn Enhancement Program.* This program has been taught for the past five years in a third grade class in Washington State and in North Vancouver, British Columbia with excellent results.

James went to work and created the music and lyrics, putting together a positive musical CD. It is children singing songs intermingled with Richard (Daddy) Babb's voice reading Affirmations from this book. Richard passed away in 2002, but his memory and voice will always be with us. The CD was played at his memorial service reception.

Thousands of people have heard and just love this CD. They feel it helps children think positive thoughts and be kinder to one another.

The CD was played for the 89th World Congress of the International New Thought Alliance in Phoenix, AZ in 2003, and at the 90th INTA World Congress in Washington, DC in 2004. It is also featured on a

Radio/Internet Program broadcast that airs the last Monday of each month. This Radio/Internet Program reaches millions of people worldwide.

One day, James invited me to join him in teaching the Power of Affirmations at his school. The children really listened. I feel they learned so much about positive thoughts and how thoughts affect their daily lives. They also learned about "The Ripple Effect" (one of the songs featured on the CD), which explains how showing kindness and passing it on to others creates a positive ripple effect.

Such is the power of Affirmations when you access the power, harness the energy, and use it for positive outcomes.

I am so proud of James and the fact that his Affirmations are not only working in his life, but he is also influencing the next generation in a positive, uplifting way.

New Website

Learn about the history of Affirmations, as never seen before, with a behind-the-scenes view of how famous authors and people around the world are using Affirmations to transform their lives.
Check out my new Website at www.affirmations-playground.com.

Readers' Words Worldwide . . .

- "This book is an easy read and very accessible as a support tool. The author should be applauded for this straightforward and high-impact book. I highly recommend it to people of all ages."
  Tamara, United Kingdom

- "This is the first time I have ever written a letter to an author. It was my purchase of your book that really cemented my foundation for a wonderful life. I have read other books on Affirmations over the years, but I have never found a book as magical as yours."
  Deanna-Anne, Montreal, Canada

- "This book has been a tremendous help for me. My life has become better, richer, and more fulfilling. It is my guiding light."
  Richard Denault, Vancouver, Canada

- "Thank you, Thank you, Thank you. Your book is 'more' than I ever imagined. I am amazed the contents of your book address so many of the issues I have been working on. My heart is full and I am so grateful!"
  Cecilia, US Minor Outlying Islands

- "This is the most comprehensive, complete book on Affirmations I have ever read. Thank you for writing this great book."
  Adrienne, The Netherlands

- "Since discovering your book, my whole world has changed. I am a walking Affirmation. My entire outlook of my future has changed for the positive. I feel so great! Anne Marie, you do make a difference in this life. You have made a huge difference in mine. Your book is on my desk, your teachings are in my mind and heart, and you are in my thoughts and prayers."
  Vernon, Singapore

- "I believe this is the most useful book I have ever purchased for myself. Many of the methods you teach in the book work perfectly for me. Thank you for making it available over the Internet."
  Patty, South Africa

- "We are hooked on Affirmations! My friend came over for a visit and was very concerned about her financial situation and being very negative. I said, 'Have I got a book for you to read!' But I can't part with mine, even for a day, so I need another book! Thank you so much. My Affirmations are working."
  Natasha, Ukraine

- "Our lives have been enriched with the knowledge in your book on how to make our special dreams a reality. Thank you for sharing this wonderful knowledge and yourself. We call it the 'Miracle Book'."
  Sharon and Ted, New Zealand

- "This is a great book—well written and easy to follow. In so many ways, this book has changed my life. I am impressed with your Internet work and Websites."
  Janice, Australia

- "Anne Marie has written a truly miracle-producing book. I have watched repeatedly how *Affirmations, Your Passport to Happiness* finds its way into well-primed hands and hearts at a time when it is most needed or at a time when it is simply welcomed as a friend. In either case, it shines a special light that beams with the gift of inspirational prosperity.

  Through recommending Affirmations to my own clients and through my own personal practice, I have witnessed how Anne Marie's teachings have repeatedly given comfort, hope, healing, and direction. In its humble straightforwardness, this book reminds the reader of a most simple, yet profound truth: that the creator we seek is always with us and within us. Thank you, Anne

Marie, for your gift of guidance, for your true heart, and for the miracles you share in creating!"
Rose Marcus, Evolutionary Astrologer
www.rosemarcus.com

- "I had the privilege and joy of meeting Anne Marie Evers around three years ago in 2001 at a Women Empowering Women seminar. She was one of the main speakers...I can still visualize her standing confidently in front of more than 200 women, speaking passionately about what she truly believed in. What made it even more astounding was that she had lost her beloved husband only five months previous. I thought, 'Wow, imagine that . . . she sure didn't hide or sit somewhere feeling sorry for herself; she practiced what she preached.' I hadn't heard of the Power of Affirmations until that day and bought a book on the spot. I have since bought many to give to friends.

I have been doing Affirmations ever since. And guess what: they have all come true. I am constantly changing them and adding to them. It's a very simple way of asking for what you want. The secret is feeling deeply that you deserve what you want and, in advance, are grateful for all that comes your way. I like to think of them as little acts of faith, hope, and love.

I have also had the privilege of having Anne Marie give workshops right here in my home, where she brings light, truth, and love. I am so grateful for her support and affection. She has made such a difference in my life and I just love her.

Please keep up all your good work. I look forward to a lifetime of your friendship and wish you the continued success you so deserve proclaiming the Power of Affirmations . . . . Thank you, thank you, thank you!"
Lilly Page, Flair Image Consulting
www.flairimage.ca

- "Thank you, thank you, thank you for this wonderful book filled with wisdom and practical tools we can all use in creating our lives into magnificence! *Affirmations, Your Passport to Happiness* not only provides us with the tools for creation, it walks us through the what, when, how, and why behind the whole process. You have covered everything from health, relationships, abundance, fears, and addiction to self-esteem, letting go, judgment, and even parking. I was delighted and a bit relieved to find an Affirmation directed to getting over the fear of dogs (something it has taken me years to work through on my own)!

  Thank you for sharing your personal stories of hardship and success. They make the creation process seem that much more real and attainable for all of us. You truly have provided a complete guide to happiness. I know this is a resource I will use often for my personal growth and as an invaluable gift to pass on to my friends, loved ones, and clients."
  Tanya Harmon, Find Your Marathon Coaching Services
  Author of *Look Who Believes In You: A Guide to Letting Love In*
  www.LookWhoBelieves.com

- "I purchased your book, *Affirmations, Your Passport to Happiness*, approximately seven years ago. Over those years, I have been affirming and receiving things constantly. From affirming a parking spot, to affirming large amounts of money, happiness and health to the people that are important to me in my life, a better job, happiness in my marriage, good health to my children—it has all manifested for me. I believe the only reason Affirmations do not work for people is that they tend to give up on them. Persistence always pays off.

  As you have always said, Anne Marie, Affirmations when properly done always work. I feel that one of the most important things people can do for themselves is learn how to forgive everyone and everything that has ever hurt them.

From there, if you sincerely do this you can open doors to miracles. I know that I have. Thank you for everything you have done for me, my family, and everyone else you have blessed."
Lavone Napier

New Website: www.affirmations-exercise.com

I have created an online affirmations fast-track system at www.Affirmation-Exercise.com to provide an "affirmations playground where people can learn and recall the powerful techniques used in my books that have helped thousands of people transform their lives." It is a fast-track to allow rapid access to ideas on how to overcome different problems.

So if you are stuck trying to remember a certain exercise that you read in my book, you can quickly scan this site and recall those exercises. Or if you just want to brighten your day, you can read stories of how people are transforming their lives with affirmations.

Affirmation-Exercise.com will be continually updated with exciting content and ideas on how to tap into the "magical force" of affirmations.

How to Use This Book

Part 1: The Building Blocks of the
Personal Contract Affirmation Method

This part explains the importance of the five building blocks that make the *Personal Contract Affirmation Method* so effective. In this book, I refer to the *Personal Contract Affirmation Method* as AMCAM (Anne Marie's Contract Affirmation Method).

Chapter 1 discusses the power of forgiveness and releasing and how to use it to prepare the soil of your subconscious mind to plant the seed-thought of your Affirmation.

Chapter 2 talks about the power of thought and its influence on your reality. It also discusses the importance of understanding your own thought process to create effective Affirmations.

Chapter 3 provides information about the dual aspects and characteristics of the mind and shows you how to access the subconscious mind through the conscious mind. You will become aware of the wondrous power that is within, just waiting to be accessed and activated.

Chapter 4 defines Affirmations and explains how they can be used.

Chapter 5 explores creative visualization and gives you sample exercises to perform. It explains the importance of using the five senses when visualizing.

Chapters 6 and 7 show you how to create a Master Affirmation and how to make Affirmations work for you!

Part 2: Applying AMCAM in Your Life

This part covers the practical applications of the *Personal Contract Affirmation Program*. It sets up a contract for you to create good Affirmations and to help you understand relationships, family dynamics, and other key aspects of your life. You will find many sample Affirmations and simple methods and exercises to get you started on the right track. Tap into the wondrous power of your thoughts and mind to make your dreams come true.

Chapter 8 tells how to overcome fear, phobias, and negative habits.

Chapter 9 shows how to boost your self-respect.

Chapter 10 gives you ideas, methods, and Affirmations for happy, successful relationships, marriage, family situations, and more.

Chapter 11 explains how to attract and keep material wealth in your life. It offers ideas, methods, and Affirmations to attract that perfect, successful career or business.

Part 3: Personal Growth
This part deals with attracting and keeping happiness, love and health in your life. It provides information, including methods, tools, and sample Affirmations, to help with retirement issues and deal with death.

Chapter 12 explains methods and Affirmations to attract happiness and love into your life. It also deals with meditation.

Chapter 13 discusses health--the ABCs of health and healing as well as weight reduction and control.

Chapter 14 deals with retirement and what to do next.

Chapter 15 helps you to accept death and gives helpful hints on how to handle it.

This book can be your vehicle for attaining your heart's desires. Please write me a note or email me when miracles begin happening in your life. I am always thrilled to hear from you. You may also order my companion books, *Affirmations, Your Passport to Lasting, Loving Relationships* and *Affirmations, Your Passport to Prosperity/Money*.

The Cards of Life can be purchased directly from me or from www.amazon.com.

Affirmations When Properly Done Always Work!

Love and light,
Anne Marie Evers
Email: annemarieevers@shaw.ca

The Building Blocks

part 1

**of the
Personal
Contract
Affirmation
Method**

Forgiveness and Releasing

The Mechanisms of Thought

Creating Miracles with Mind-Power

The Power of Affirmations

Creative Visualization

Master Affirmations

Making Affirmations Effective

Cards of Life

www.affirmations-doctor.com

1 • *Forgiveness and Releasing*

1st Building Block of the *Personal Contract Affirmation Method:* Healing the Deepest of Wounds

Forgiveness is very powerful. When you forgive, your energy changes the physical structure of your cells and DNA. When you are embroiled in guilt, shame, or depression, you close down the energy systems of your body. All types of negative problems can erupt.

Forgiveness is a process of untangling mental and emotional parts of your being. If you have become tangled up in the negative energy of another person or situation and need to forgive, this chapter shows you how. It gives simple, effective exercises to achieve forgiveness and peace of mind. You will learn how to use the power of forgiveness to heal yourself and get rid of negative people, conditions, thoughts, ideas, and concepts.

Forgiveness is a choice—as is not forgiving. When you do not forgive another person, you remain energetically connected or tied to them. When you forgive others, you break those ties and allow them to move on with their lives—and you to move on with yours.

Gratitude is advanced forgiveness; therefore, it is important to be grateful for your blessings. When you stop blaming others, wishing things were different, or judging something to be wrong, you can truly forgive yourself and others.

Forgiveness reduces stress, lowers blood pressure, increases well-being, and promotes good health. It can also reduce the risk of cancer and other diseases. Forgiveness is private. It is not necessary or advisable to tell people that you are forgiving them. Forgiveness is not ego, although some people say forgiveness is selfish because it largely benefits the person doing the forgiving.

Preventative Mental Health

One of the easiest ways to deal with anger and hurt is to prevent them from forming in the first place. Words from another person cannot hurt you unless you give them power by taking them into your being, accepting them, and making them yours. Just as a computer does not have to deal with material not programmed into it, we have the power to ignore mean, hurtful words.

When someone says something cruel to you, say, "Cancel, cancel, I am happy." Repeat these words silently to yourself. The cruel words are destroyed before they have a chance to enter your being and become your words. Immediately fill that spot with a positive statement such as, "I am happy and fulfilled."

Do some serious thought-watching. Are your thoughts full of fear, anger, and negativity? Are you sending negative thoughts to others? You cannot send any shade of negative thought to others without injuring yourself. If you discover you have been thinking negatively, say to those thoughts, "Cancel, cancel—you are not welcome in my wonderful body. Be gone. I am happy." Do not allow angry words or the anger of another person to interfere with your happiness. Never give your inner, God-given power away! Forgive the negativity of others.

Releasing Negative Emotions

We have all experienced being hurt by another person. When angry hurt is not expressed, it leaves pain inside, which invokes negative energy. When you are full of negative energy, hurt, and bitterness, you can experience emotional and physical pain. You can always search for and find something to feel hurt about. Some innocent, harmless remark or gesture can become a source of deep pain.

When you feel hurt about the actions of another person or a certain situation, you form an emotional attachment to them. Go within and find the original source of the hurt, own it, then release it into the Universe. Ask that it be recycled into divine love.

When someone or something hurts you, you have the choice to forgive and release the hurt or keep it and allow it to fester in your body. With honesty, tell the offending person that he or she hurt your feelings and you do not like it. It is never a good idea to allow hurt feelings and anger to drain your precious life force.

Did you set yourself up for the hurt? When someone criticizes you, really check his or her criticism and see if there is a grain of truth in it. If there is, take that grain of truth, wash it, polish it, and work with it to your benefit.

Forgiveness is putting your thoughts in line with the Laws of the Universe. I speak to many people whose faces show resentment, anger, and bitterness. I know there is a forgiveness problem. Why is it so difficult to forgive? Nature does not have a problem forgiving. The human body is busy all the time, forgiving and healing.

When you cut your finger, it does not stop and say, "No, I am not ready to forgive you; you have been a bad person." Your body immediately begins to repair and heal itself. The doctor sets your leg when it is broken, but it is God or Nature that heals it. When you hold a grudge and do not forgive others and yourself, you are working against the Laws of Nature. When you do not blame, condemn, or judge yourself, others, and circumstances, there is nothing to forgive.

Forgiving is permanent. When you truly and completely forgive an injustice, you never have to do it again.

Practise Forgiving, Forgetting, and Releasing

Betty was unhappy and bitter when I met her. After I heard her story, I could understand why. Her husband Randy had passed on many years ago. Her daughter Cindy had her declared incompetent and institutionalized. Cindy had taken over her mother's financial affairs. She had sold her properties, pocketed the money, and left the country. Betty was working on forgiving her daughter. She told me she would never be able to forget.

When I met Betty, she had just been released from an institution and was staying with a friend. She was homeless, broke, hurt, and very bitter. During our visit, she suddenly exclaimed, "I left some of my valuable jewellery with my niece Wendy. I will get it, sell it, and take the money to make a new start." Her whole appearance and body language changed. She now had the element of hope.

Three years later, I met Betty again. She was a different person—vibrant, happy, and bubbly. She had retrieved her jewellery from Wendy, sold most of it, rented an apartment, and started her own business. The business proved extremely successful, enabling her to purchase a fabulous new townhome in a prestigious area.

As I thought about Betty, it became abundantly clear to me that, whether Betty knew it or not, she was in the process of forgetting. She has filled her mind and life with creativity, purpose, success, and determination.

These days, she does not have time to dwell on the negativity of the past. She does not have time to think about what Cindy did to her, the money she lost, and the unfairness of the whole situation. She has become a fulfilled, self-assured, creative, prosperous, and happy person. Could it be that Cindy unknowingly gave Betty the best gift anyone could ever give her—the gift of herself?

Cindy will have to deal with the hurt and pain she caused her mother. Betty is now enjoying the finer things of life. She recently confided in me that she has now started her search for that special husband. She is living her life with or without Cindy. She cannot change her daughter, but she can change the way she views her. She has done this in a very positive, mature way and has moved on with her life.

Sometimes the intricate process of forgiveness takes time; it usually does not happen overnight. It is important to be patient when doing AMCAM.

Self-Forgiveness

I will always remember the guilt-ridden eyes of an older man who came to see me. Bryant was pleasant-looking, tall, and well-built, but his eyes held misery, grief, and suffering. He told me a sad, tragic story of child abuse and he admitted having sexually abused his daughter, Mandy, over 40 years ago.

Mandy is now married with three children and one grandchild. She was fortunate in that she sought counselling and underwent therapy. Today she is happy, balanced, and well adjusted. Her father, on the other hand, had taken to drinking in an attempt to get some relief from his severe guilt and self-condemnation.

When I spoke to Bryant, he was unable to forgive himself. I urged him to seek out group counselling and therapy, which he did. He also joined a support group and has since stopped drinking. He is now emptying his cup of misery, hurt, and guilt, and dealing with his guilt in a mature manner. (See Cup-Releasing Method on page 37.)

No one would condone this man's former behaviour. We cannot change the past, but we can find the courage to go forward. It serves no purpose to have Bryant walking around with this emotional cancer festering inside him. I gave him a set of exercises on forgiveness to further his healing. He is steadily progressing, one day at a time, and feels as though he is coming out of a deep fog.

He had asked for and received unconditional forgiveness from Mandy and God, but he had not been able to forgive himself. He has now given himself permission to be forgiven and is rebuilding his life on a new, solid foundation of trust and honesty.

Exercises for Releasing and Forgiving

• Hot Air Balloon-Releasing Method

When you desire to forgive and release someone from your life, completely and absolutely, do the following exercise.
Visualize him or her in a hot air balloon securely attached to the ground by two ropes. See yourself standing close to the balloon. As you cut the ropes attached to the balloon, say:

> "I, (your name), now release (person's name) with love (or with God's love). I let you go in peace with loving kindness and detachment from the outcome. I am free. You are free. We are happy to the good of all parties concerned. Thank you, thank you, thank you."

It is important to engage the physical senses.

1. *See* him or her smiling, waving, and being happy.
2. *Hear* the ropes making a snapping sound as the balloon tugs against them.
3. *Feel* the scissors between your fingers.
4. *Smell* the odour of the ropes.
5. *Taste* the brisk, fresh, clean air or bite into a juicy apple.

• Helium Balloon-Releasing Method

I did the following exercise when I was having trouble with a co-worker. I wrote all the cruel and mean things she had done to me on small pieces of paper. I cut them into tiny pieces and stuffed them, together with a photo of her, into the balloon before it was blown up with helium.

In this particular exercise, I could not let go of the string attached to the balloon. I was experiencing resistance. I sat on a bench, tears streaming down my face, clenching the string. Then I mentally went within myself and asked why. I discovered, to my shock, that I actually enjoyed reliving those experiences, with thoughts of negative things that would happen to the person whom I had allowed to hurt me.

Then I felt sorry for her and guilty for thinking that way. I replayed the old tape and changed the ending to a happy one. I was then able to let go of the balloon. As it floated up into the sky, I experienced a tremendous sense of relief flooding my entire being. I immediately filled the empty space with unconditional love. I was free!

The person I released in this manner has never been able to come back into my life in the capacity she once did. Though I still see her occasionally on the street or at social functions, she has absolutely no effect on me. The terrible, negative hurt, anger, resentment, and pain have completely left me.

Caution: It is very important to do this exercise *only* when you are *absolutely certain* you do not wish to have a particular person in your life. It is risky to do this with a former spouse who has child visitation rights or is paying child support for your children. Also, never send anyone away with the emotion of hate, because this negative emotion will surely return to you—multiplied. You can also do this releasing exercise by placing your fears, worries, and phobias in a balloon before it is blown up.

I have since learned that releasing real balloons filled with helium into the atmosphere can prove harmful. *Because of the environmental hazard to wildlife and marine life, we suggest you do the above exercise in your mind, rather than release a real balloon into the air.*

• Cup-Releasing Method

For optimum results, perform this exercise every morning and evening. If possible, get a cup or mug that belonged to the person who hurt you. If you don't have one, print his or her name on masking tape and stick it on the mug. Sit with the cup in your hands and visualize all negative feelings surrounding that person or situation dripping into the water from your eyes, ears, nose, and mouth. When you feel the exercise is completed, take the cup to the sink and pour out that water, saying the following Affirmation.

> "(Name of person or situation), I now pour my negative feelings, emotions, and hurts concerning you and our relationship out of my heart, life, and being. I pour them out with love*. I release you completely and freely let you go. You are free. I am free. You are an individual and I respect your views and opinions as you respect mine. I give you space to live and grow, as you do me. I now release and dissolve any and all negative feelings I have for you. I release any anger, resentment, jealousy, guilt, or hate. As I pour this water down the sink, with my negative feelings in it, I know I can never get it back. I am prepared to live my life without you, should that be your choice. I accept your decision. I am at peace, to the good of all parties concerned. Thank you, thank you, thank you."

*If you cannot honestly feel love, then feel the divine love of God.

When the cup or mug is empty, just say, "Healed heart."

Several years ago, when I needed to forgive my first husband for the perpetual drinking that led to his death, I did the cup-emptying exercise for a period of 21 days. (This is how long it takes to develop a habit.) On the 15th day, I thought to myself, *"This is ridiculous. It is not working,"* but I had committed myself to doing the procedure for this period of time. On the 20th day, my anger and depression started to lift as if by magic. On the 21st day, I felt whole, free, and surprisingly happy. It was an incredible experience.

People asked me how I could be so happy when my husband had recently passed away. I thought about it, felt guilty, then went right back to the sink. I wrote on some masking tape, "My guilt for feeling happy" and stuck it on a cup. I filled that cup with water and did the whole procedure again for 21 days. It was great. After that process, when I was asked that same question, I smiled sweetly and said, without a speck of guilt, "Because I am. End of subject."

One reader, Lisa, described her experience with this exercise.

"I had been seeing a married man for 10 years, but had known for some time that the relationship could not carry on in the same way. I was having a terrible time making any kind of break, because I loved him. I filled a cup with his name printed on it with fresh water every morning and tipped it out for 21 days. I said, 'I let go of my emotional bond to you,' as I poured it down the sink.

The first day, I got butterflies in my stomach and did not want to do the exercise, but I persisted. By the end of the period, it had worked. I saw him in a different light. Gone were the rose-coloured spectacles and that close love bond. We remained good friends, so he is still in my life, but in a different capacity.

Since I made the break, my energy has changed. I have received more attention from men than I have in the last 10 years. It is great! Thank you so much. Your book came into my life for a purpose. Finally, I just wanted to add that I was really scared of letting go. I really did feel he was the one and only love of my life. In one short month, I have found out I was wrong. There is so much out here that I was missing because of my relationship with him. Once again, many thanks."

- **Letter Method**

Another method I use is to write a letter to the person who hurt me. I recommend that you deal with only one person, circumstance, or situation at a time. Write the letter, remembering all hurts, anger, resentments, and injustices. As you put the words on paper, they are removed and released from your being.

See, hear, feel, smell, and *taste* your anger.

Read the letter and feel the pain. Release all negativity surrounding that event, person, or circumstance. Burn or destroy the letter immediately. Burning reduces the anger and negativity to ashes.

You could also shred it or cut it up into tiny pieces and flush it down the toilet. Never leave it lying around so someone can read it and become hurt. It is not the object here to hurt anyone. It is sufficient that you have operated and taken the hurt and negativity (emotional cancer) out of your body by the simple method of the written word. AMCAM works even if the person with whom you are angry is deceased.

One young woman doing this exercise called me late one evening to say, "Anne Marie, I have to stop doing my forgiveness letters because the pain is too great." I advised her to keep doing the process because the pain proved that the exercise was working. It was releasing pain and negativity associated with her situation. She did continue and says today that this simple, effective exercise saved her mental health.

Another exercise is to write yourself a letter of appreciation and encouragement. After I have successfully handled a difficult, delicate situation, I find it very therapeutic to write a letter of self-praise and appreciation and mail it to myself. It is such a treat to receive the letter in the mail, open it up, and read it. I mailed one such letter from Washington State and it was lost in the mail. It was finally delivered several months later. I had completely forgotten about it. When I received and opened it, I was stunned. It certainly had a huge impact on me! Try it and see what effect it has on you.

• Everyday Forgiveness

I feel this exercise is so important to health and well-being that it should be done every morning and evening.

Before you go to sleep at night, say out loud:

> "I, (your name), now forgive everyone and everything that has ever hurt me. I now forgive myself and I am forgiven. I, (your name), now love, respect, accept, and approve of myself just the way I am."

This includes forgiving any circumstance or situation that is unfair to you or that has hurt you. Things you think you had forgotten years ago will come into your memory.

Recognize, own, and deal with them. You cannot give something away unless you first have ownership of it. If too many memories surface at the same time, just say, "One at a time, please."

• Blackboard Forgiving

Creatively visualize a giant blackboard in your mind. On it, write the name of the person or persons who hurt you. Beside each name, write what that person did to you. Look at the blackboard, and read your words, feeling the hurt. Then take a deep breath and let it go completely.

Now take an eraser and rub out everything you have just written. Feel that you are completely forgiving and releasing that person to his or her highest good, with loving kindness. I use an emerald-green eraser brush because green represents change and growth, but you may use any colour that appeals to you.

• Dealing with Negative Memories

When I was doing this forgiveness exercise, an overpowering image flashed into my mind. The image was of a student in school, two grades ahead of me, blocking my way to my locker. I saw her face in my mind's eye and instantly remembered her name. She said, "I will not let you close your locker until you say nobody likes you."

She was taller and stronger than me and I was late for class, so I blurted out the words, "Nobody likes me."

Now, years later, I relived that humiliating experience, felt the searing pain, owned it, forgave her in my mind and heart, and let it go. If you said to me that I was angry with this particular girl for what she had said to me so many years ago, I would have looked at you in astonishment. I was completely unaware of this memory until my forgiveness exercise accessed it and brought it to the surface. This allowed me to accept it, own it, feel the pain, then let it go completely with forgiveness and loving kindness.

Close the doors to your past and keep them closed. Put regrets, bitterness, and unhappiness behind you. When a spouse, relative, or friend hurts you and you cannot hold back the tears, let go and have a good cry. Crying releases pent-up emotions and is actually beneficial to the body.

If it Doesn't Work . . .

Andrew a young man suffering from the AIDS virus had tried to do Affirmations but could not make them work for him. During a consultation with me, he suddenly had a revelation. He said, "Now I know why Affirmations have not worked for me. I am carrying around such negative energy, anger, and guilt. How could they? It would be like my planting a seed in a dry, barren area and expecting it to grow. I know now what I need to do. I must prepare the soil of my mind by forgiving everyone—especially myself."

This is a wonderful analogy. An integral part of the *Personal Contract Affirmation Method* is the process of forgiveness.

I am very grateful to Andrew for his wisdom and for teaching me the importance of preparing the rich, fertile soil of the subconscious mind. As Andrew discovered, this is accomplished by forgiving and releasing all negativity so the positive healthy seed-thoughts (Affirmations) that have been planted can take root, grow, and bring forth after their own kind.

You are the only thinker and manager in your Universe.
Affirmations When Properly Done Always Work!

Cards of Life

www.affirmations-doctor.com

2 • *The Mechanisms of Thought*

2nd Building Block of the *Personal Contract Affirmation Method:* The Nature of Thoughts

What is the greatest power that has ever been discovered? Nuclear energy? The power of wealth or fame? I believe it is the power of your thoughts and mind. Thought is creative and it is the first and most crucial stage in the development of any new idea, invention, business, or other venture that becomes reality.

Thoughts are living things. When thoughts are held in the mind, they form a life of their own and attract other similar thoughts.

We cannot afford the luxury of one negative thought. Thoughts are things. Thoughts are very powerful. Even your smallest, most insignificant thoughts are important and they are influencing everyone and everything around you.

Having thoughts actually creates new brain cells, causing a physical and chemical change in your mind. Through thought, your mind can be programmed at will—and reprogrammed as frequently as required. As the most powerful and transformative tools at our disposal, thoughts must be used wisely if we are to create what we want out of life.

Each thought seeks its own kind.

Like always attracts like. Think about success and you attract successful people. You are a great thought-magnet, whether you like it or not. Mental currents are just as real as circuits of magnetism and circuits of electricity. Each kind of thought has its own rate, degree, and character of motion. You attract your own kind of thought wave to you and you repel your opposite.

Your concentrated thought—when accompanied by a matching clear, colourful mental picture, filled with feeling and belief—always makes an impression upon the subconscious mind and it, in turn, sends that impression to the Universal Mind, which always responds.

The Creative Universal Mind cannot refuse to take the form your thoughts give it. It does not differentiate between so-called good and bad thoughts and it knows only to multiply and return to you that which you have affirmed by your thinking, actions, and Affirmations.

When you pour water into a jelly mold, the water takes the form of the mold. You are always giving life, knowingly or unknowingly, to conditions and situations in your life, whether they are negative or positive. This energy takes the form that we give it. We are all immersed in a thought atmosphere that is a direct result of what we have thought, affirmed, or done.

If you start a new Affirmation stating that you love, respect, and approve of yourself, you may, at first, find it hard to believe. With time and repetition, however, you will come to fully accept this as fact.

Although thoughts cannot be seen by the human eye, the vibrations they emit can be registered by an MRI (Magnetic Resonance Imaging) machine. This device identifies the area of the brain that is being fired when the thought is experienced, allowing doctors to see thoughts as they occur and change in the physical brain. Such technology is enhancing our understanding of how thoughts affect our lives.

The Law of Attraction

Through the Law of Attraction, you have the power to draw to you whatever you focus and concentrate on. The thoughts, feelings, and attitudes held in your mind form a life of their own, sending out a frequency of vibration that attracts more of the same. This gives you the power to create your future.

What is happening in your life *now* actually originated from the ideas, thoughts, and beliefs you have been holding from your life experiences. What you are thinking today is creating your tomorrow.

You attract what you concentrate on, just as surely as a magnet attracts metal. It is therefore important to fill your mind with constructive, positive thoughts. When you associate with negative people, it is possible to graft your mind to their lower thought atmosphere and thought patterns. The mind absorbs the thoughts with which it is most associated.

You can, however, choose what to think, listen to, talk about, and read. You can choose to live in love and light, rather than in fear and darkness. When you become committed to thinking positively, fear and negativity cease to be your jailer.

Fill yourself with positive thoughts and watch miracles occur in your life on a daily basis. When problems (I prefer to call them opportunities) occur in your life, ask yourself, *"What must I be thinking to create this chaos?"* The ability to think is the key to accessing the Universal Mind and realizing your goals.

Thought Transference

Thought transference is the phenomenon whereby one person tunes into and grasps another's thoughts without any evident, visible means of communication. This process is also known as mind-reading or mental telepathy. Your thoughts and desires are actively transmitted to those around you at the subconscious level—beyond your conscious awareness. The resulting force of suggestion is very powerful. We all have this power of suggestion over others through the thought waves and patterns we are continually broadcasting. Our thoughts affect others and the world around us.

Similar to electricity, thought transference requires a sender and a receiver. You may wonder why you receive a particular thought from the thousands of other thoughts being transmitted at that very minute of it. In most cases, you receive *only* those thought vibrations to which you are emotionally attuned at that moment. If you are unhappy or depressed, for example, you will attract this type of thought.

The following example illustrates this very clearly.

Bruce was diagnosed with lung cancer and given six months to live. When his doctor told him the news, Bruce accepted it, resigned from his job, and retreated from life. He did not leave his house and refused to eat properly. He rapidly lost weight, becoming weak and sick.

Five months later, Bruce received a telephone call from the doctor's office, saying it was imperative that he come in immediately to speak with the doctor. When Bruce walked into the office, he looked like a sick, old, dying man. His doctor said, "I do not know how to tell you this, but there has been a terrible mistake. The X-rays I read were not yours. You are not dying of lung cancer. According to your X-rays, you are in good health. I am very sorry and I cannot explain this mix-up."

Bruce was stunned. He asked for proof of the doctor's statement that he was healthy. When he finally accepted the fact that he did not have lung cancer, his whole body and attitude changed. The nurse in the reception area could not believe her eyes. The man who had hobbled into the doctor's inner office was not the same man who came bouncing out of it 30 minutes later. Such was the power of his mind that, despite being healthy all along, Bruce had generated thoughts that actually made him sick.

When the doctor told him it was all a mistake and that he had been healthy all along, Bruce then switched his mind into a mode of good health and transformed himself in accordance with that thought. He started living from that very moment and has since married and started a family.

It behoves each and every one of us to use our thoughts constructively.

How Thoughts Work

Have you ever wondered how thoughts actually work? One thought prompts another and they become a sentence, then a paragraph, then a story, and, finally, reality. When a thought is concentrated, focused, controlled, and charged with feeling, emotion, and belief, it becomes a powerful moving force. Every thought is a force as real as a current of electricity. When you wish to change your life, change your thoughts and create mental pictures of what you desire.

Thought is always attempting to find pathways through which to manifest the picture held in the mind. Examine your thoughts. Are they positive or negative? Thoughts can be stimulated by outside influences, but it is your own mental and emotional reactions to those stimuli that create your beliefs, concepts, and, eventually, your reality.

When you think of yourself as a victim of circumstance, you are narrowing your focus. You could miss out on blessings all around you. When you truly understand how the thought process works, you will discover that you are not the victim, but the creator of your circumstances—whether negative or positive. Even seemingly negative situations often contain the raw material needed to create what you desire.

Never allow the negative thoughts of others to keep you from fulfilling your desires. Let others who choose to be negative live their lives as they wish. You cannot change others, but you can change how you *view* them and thus change your feelings about them. Often that person will sense the change in you and undergo a change as well.

There are different types of thoughts. Some are very deep and cause a definite reaction in the body that could be either negative or positive. These reactions are then stored in the unique, intricate, cellular memory system of the body.

Thoughts with great emotion can create miracles, whereas those with little emotion have little power. Many unimportant or meaningless thoughts pass through the mind and body, creating little or no effect.

Over half of life's experiences take place in your mind, which does not know the difference between a real and an imagined event. With approximately 50,000 to 60,000 thoughts running through your mind daily, hundreds are likely to be insignificant, repetitive, or negative thoughts. Becoming more conscious of the nature of your thoughts or of how many of them are the same as yesterday can help you to focus your mind and transform its endless chatter into positive, consciously directed thoughts.

All answers come from within; there is nothing outside that creates for you. Change your thoughts and you change your destiny. If, with approximately 900 waking minutes per day, you can devote just 10 or 15 minutes toward thinking positive, happy thoughts, you will notice wonderful, welcome changes occurring in your life. The Laws of the Universe always work!

Your negative frame of mind can be changed to a positive attitude through disciplined, controlled, directed, conscious mental action. Your creative mental power is the result of the sum of all your beliefs.

The Law of Cause and Effect

All life is based on the Law of Cause and Effect and there is no such thing as a cause without an effect. What you think and do is the cause; the result of that thought or action is the effect. For every action there is a reaction; something happens as a result of everything you do. If you can recognize and accept the Law of Cause and Effect and work with it, you will have far greater control over your life. If you change the cause (your thoughts, actions, and beliefs), you will experience a different effect or result.

This law can also be powerfully applied to ideas, which are simply thoughts arranged in a particular order. Ideas are the seeds of success and a key ingredient in your imagination. Being open to new, exciting, fresh ideas, while sifting and discarding the old ones, enhances your ability to bring things into effect in your life.

Negative Thinking

Negative thinking can be helpful when it serves as a warning or red flag. When you become aware you are feeling and thinking negatively, you can eject the negative thought—just as you eject a tape or CD—and replace it with a positive one.

Problems have an internal base of operation and always start in the mind before they appear in your life. A mental state always precedes action. If you discover negative thinking, remove that emotional, negative cancer. The only way out of a problem is into the solution.

Getting caught up in traditional negative thinking can freeze your mind and thought processes, blocking your progress. For example, if your father died at the age of 54, your traditional negative thinking might lead you to believe you will also die at that age, even though you are in excellent health. Positive thinking can therefore be very beneficial—and necessary—for most people.

Examine your thoughts to see if they are constantly full of fear and worry. There are really only two emotions—love and fear—and we are always expressing either one or the other. Fear is normally either a call for help or a request for love. If you are fearful, angry, or sending out negative thoughts to others, you are doing yourself a great injustice. Such thoughts and emotions attract more of the same and boomerang right back to you.

If you are confused or bothered about a situation you are facing, ask yourself if you are behaving out of love or fear and adjust your attitude accordingly. Fear is a powerful form of thought; it can paralyze you, often bringing you the very thing you fear.

All conditions and experiences are sent to you for your benefit. Even failures hold blessings in terms of lessons learned and the enrichment of understanding. Difficulties, problems, fear, and obstacles will continue to come until you absorb their lessons and grow from them.

All destructive, negative thoughts toward self and others are deadly toxins in the body, whereas positive thoughts are spiritual food for your mind. Consider what you are feeding your powerful subconscious mind.

New Ways of Thinking

New ways of thinking can be established at any time, since your conscious thoughts control your subconscious mind. In turn, the subconscious mind controls the situations and experiences you encounter—which means you have complete control over your life.

To gain control over your thoughts, however, you first need to be fully conscious of what they are. It may be helpful to write down your thoughts for three days and study them. When you discover whether your thinking process is predominantly negative or positive, you can then change it, if you like.

Your conscious thoughts set creative forces in motion. Focused thought waves burn a definite and lasting impression on the subconscious mind. This is why it is important to practise the art of effective thinking. What you think is far more important than what you say or do because the thought arises first and the words and actions follow.

You choose what you wish to think and believe from the vast, never-ending procession of thoughts that march through your mind. When you totally accept a thought, it becomes part of you and is then added to your reality.

With every thought, you have the opportunity to change your way of thinking. You have the power of thought at your command. Positive, constructive thought gives you the power to create something that is wonderful. When you think, you make an impression on the subconscious mind and it simply responds without distinguishing between positive and negative thoughts.

Exercises in Thought

The following exercises will help you experience the power of your focused thought.

• Eliminating Traffic Jams

When I am in a traffic jam or attempting to catch a plane or ferry, I simply say, with great feeling, "Clear front and back." If I am turning onto a busy street, I say, "Clear side to side." I always add, "To the good of all parties concerned." This exercise has helped me avoid frustration, keep appointments, cross borders, and catch trains, airplanes, and ferries on time.

You can transfer your thought forms from one driver of a vehicle to another. I applied this principle very successfully during a trip with two friends. While driving to the ferry in heavy traffic, we all concentrated and said with great feeling and expectancy, "Clear front and back." The cars around us just seemed to vanish into thin air. One truck actually pulled over to let us go by. As a result, we arrived at the ferry on time.

You can experiment with this technique, applying the same principle when looking for a parking space. By mentally affirming that the perfect parking spot will become available to you—exactly where you want it—you, too, can save yourself a great deal of frustration.

• Mentally Reaching Out

Thoughts are picked up and acted upon anywhere, anytime, and by anyone in the world. Distance is no barrier. Consequently, you can think about—and concentrate on—a certain person and cause him or her to contact you.

When you need to contact someone, try the following exercise. Sit down, close your eyes gently, clear your mind, and take three deep breaths. On the in breath, inhale clarity and focus on your purpose. On the out breath, exhale all doubt and negativity. Focus all your thoughts on that person. Recall everything you can about him or her. Say the following loudly and clearly three times.

> "(Name of person), this is (your name). I need to speak with you. It is very important. Please call. Thank you, thank you, thank you for calling me now."

Then bring in the five physical senses.

1. *See* that person clearly in your mind.
2. *Hear* that person saying, "Hello this is (name of person). I got the feeling that I had to call you."
3. *Feel* how happy you are that he or she is calling you.
4. *Smell* the perfume or cologne.
5. To complete the fifth sense of *taste*, imagine popping a juicy grape, cherry, or tasty mint into your mouth.

Whenever the image of that person flashes into your mind, say silently to yourself, "Thank you for calling me." I often use this simple method, with immediate and startling results.

Affirmations When Properly Done Always Work!

Cards of Life

www.affirmations-doctor.com

3 • *Creating Miracles with Mind-Power*

3rd Building Block of the *Personal Contract Affirmation Method*: Using Your Powerful Mind

The processes of the human mind constitute one of the greatest unsolved mysteries of the Universe, yet most of us take our minds very much for granted. We think, act, and live, rarely stopping to think about how the mind works or how we control it. Affirmations (whereby we repeatedly state our desires so that they become imprinted upon the subconscious mind) represent the key to unlocking the secret door to mind-power. In this chapter, you will learn how to use this unlimited, inexhaustible power to create your heart's desires.

To do this requires consciousness—a state of mindful awareness, alertness, and aliveness in the present moment. You become what you are in life from what you are in consciousness. To be conscious is to think and to think is to give form to thought. With a positive focus, you attract good things and happy experiences to you. When you lower your consciousness, you give away your power and attract thoughts, situations, events, and people that reinforce this lack of power.

The world within creates the world without. Everything you find in your world without was first created in your world within.

Our Many Minds

You have one mind with two distinct yet interrelated functional characteristics.

- One is the conscious, objective, outward, or waking state.
- The other is the subconscious, subjective, inward, or sleeping state.

To understand how Affirmations work through the use of your conscious and subconscious mind, it is necessary to discuss some of the mind's functions and powers.

The subconscious mind is a part of the Universal Mind that is all-powerful and all-knowing. The Universal Mind is the totality of all minds in existence, including God's mind. It is everywhere and within you and its nature is spiritual. The Universal Mind will give you anything you desire, but it does not deliver it to you in a package or by courier. Certain principles and Universal Laws must be applied when generating what is desired; individuals need to be open to receiving whatever gifts are given to them.

There is no object, goal, or Affirmation too small or too big for the Universal Mind to manifest. It acts on people, situations, and circumstances, but you need patience, faith, and perseverance while waiting for your wishes to be granted. You know what you desire and the Universal Mind knows how to bring it to you.

Nothing is impossible. You can control the thoughts you think and transmit them to your subconscious mind which, in turn, is part of the Universal Mind.

Think how honoured we are to have the capability of God's mind within us. Realizing I am a co-creator with God makes me feel humble and full of gratitude and opens a whole new dimension of creative possibility.

The Conscious Mind

The conscious mind is your objective mind and deals largely with the external world. This part of the mind has the power to reason and to decide what is right or wrong. It is the source of all thoughts, concepts, and ideas. The conscious mind's chief powers are reason, judgment, logic, form, calculation, and moral sense. The conscious mind also sets in motion the creative power of the subconscious mind.

The conscious mind is the one and only force to which the subconscious mind responds. It tells the subconscious mind what is required—which is one of its most important functions. The subconscious mind controls the conditions and experiences of your life. Through your conscious mind, you can clearly and specifically tell your subconscious mind what is desired.

For example, when you state you are 100 percent healthy, you are instructing your subconscious mind to prepare conditions in your body to manifest abundant health. The subconscious mind, always willing to oblige, immediately goes to work to create that condition in your body.

Isn't it exciting to know the subconscious mind contains every element necessary to manifest every one of your desires, goals, or Affirmations? You can turn on the switch in your mind, redirecting your mental processes to change from a negative mode to a positive one.

You are made up of billions and billions of beliefs about your body, your material worth, God, sin, life, death, etc. You have taken on some of these beliefs from others and created some yourself, accepting them as the truth. Removing old, negative beliefs and replacing them with positive ones is an essential part of creating what you want in life.

The Subconscious Mind

Your subconscious mind is like a highly sophisticated computer. When you were born, it began to record every feeling, action, thought, or word in your world. You accepted some information from your parents, teachers, peers, and others—all of whom had their own weaknesses and negative patterns.

Your subconscious mind takes in the exact details of every situation. Over the years, it accumulates an astronomical amount of data. It has a perfect memory and stores everything in the present moment. Even though one event in your life may have taken place on July 28, 1982, and another on February 0, 1997, to your computer (subconscious mind), it is all happening now. Your subconscious mind does not differentiate between a real and an imagined event.

The subconscious can also be compared to a bank where you make daily *thought deposits*. These thought deposits grow and become your memory, which represents the basic raw material for new thoughts and ideas.

Your subconscious mind knows more about you than anyone. It can change its viewpoints, often retaining or reverting back to childhood ideas, concepts, and beliefs. It stores your own interpretation of reality. If something very important happened to you at age 14, for example, your subconscious mind may continue to see it from that 14-year-old's perspective.

Your subconscious mind represents the sleeping or subjective state. It is dependent on the information received from the conscious mind and is not normally in direct contact with the outside world. One of its roles is to handle all involuntary functions of the body, such as heartbeat, breathing, circulation, blood flow, and digestion without any instruction from anyone.

This mind is beyond space and time and has many powers, including inspiration, imagination, organization, intuition, emotion, certitude, deduction, suggestion, and memory. It is a part of the Universal Mind, which is also timeless, ageless, and boundless.

My Editor Writes:

"Simply *reading this book* is a powerful experience. I had the privilege of working with Anne Marie as editor for this 6th edition. As I read and re-read her wise and caring words, a funny thing happened. My feelings about a particularly painful part of my life began to change and I became more at peace with the situation and with my truth. My subconscious had already initiated the healing process to help me move forward in my life.

More mind-power at work: As I reached for a delicious ice cream bar (with nuts!) in a corner-store freezer, I was surprised to see my hand suddenly stop. With a grin, I turned away from temptation. . . leaving those calories behind! I am very proud of myself!"
Val Wilson, Ink
Editor

Self-Talk and the Subconscious Mind

Self-talk is very important. The way you speak to yourself about yourself determines your life. The subconscious mind is your humble servant, bringing to you, through the Law of Attraction, exactly what you desire. It takes you at your word. So if you say, "I am broke," it will keep you broke. It simply does the job of manifesting whatever it is programmed to bring forth. As you change your thoughts and mind, you change your life accordingly.

When you do Affirmations, the power contained within your subconscious mind can be consciously harnessed to change your life for the better. By saying your Affirmations out loud, your directions to the subconscious mind are all the more powerful. Once the subconscious mind has fully accepted an idea, it begins to execute it, no matter what it is or from where it came. The scientific order and powerful energy of the Universe go to work to deliver it to you and no power on earth can stop the manifestation.

The Placebo Effect

In an American study, 100 people with an illness received a sugar pill. They were told the pill contained a powerful new medicine that would cure them. As a result, one-third of the patients got better. Their illness actually disappeared without drugs, surgery, or side effects.

A miracle? The simple astonishing reason the placebo worked is that those people *believed* they were going to get better. The subconscious mind sent biochemical messages to their bodies that told the healing process to go full speed ahead—and it did. They were brought back to a state of being 100 percent healthy. Triggered by the doctor's suggestion that they were receiving a new cure, they unknowingly tapped into their subconscious minds to unleash the potent healing ability of their own bodies.

Negative Emotions

Sometimes memories of people, events, or situations from the past lie dormant in the body. They can fester and become what I call "internal boils," which can later manifest in some way in your life.

When something traumatic happens to you, your subconscious mind stores the memory of that event, together with the associated emotions, feelings, and perceptions. Later, this memory may be triggered by someone or something, causing you to have an emotionally charged reaction that may have nothing to do with the present moment.

Operating rapidly and intuitively, the subconscious mind does not wait for the conscious reasoning of the thinking mind. It stores information very subjectively, making many of our feelings unreliable as indicators of what may have actually happened in the past. It is therefore very important to safeguard your subconscious mind from emotional "toxins."

Anger and hatred are deadly toxins in the subconscious mind. If they lie dormant in your body, they can eat you alive. These emotions cause all sorts of physical and emotional problems. You owe it to yourself, others, and the planet to process any unexpressed, suppressed anger. Otherwise you will be polluting the atmosphere. Learn to harness your anger and become totally responsible for it, no matter how uncomfortable it feels. Own it, feel the pain, then release it completely.

When you put a "d" in front of anger, you get *danger*. It can be dangerous for you and your health to entertain negative thoughts. Angry, unhappy people often like to mix with others who are equally negative, enjoying the false sense of power they derive from venting their negative emotions. When I sold real estate, the same little group of "neggies" was always talking about how bad the market was, how high interest rates were, and how few people were buying real estate. I disassociated myself from them, knowing it would hinder my own selling ability.

When someone is angry with you and you feel yourself starting to react with the same negative emotion, stop and count to 10. Mentally place all negativity into a pink bubble and release it into the atmosphere. See it floating up into the sky, out into the Universe to be recycled into divine love.

Always use your creative power for the good of all parties concerned. You can project your thoughts—negative or positive—

onto others, so be certain you do not harm anyone in the process. Whatever you wish upon others, you also receive yourself!

Exercises in Mind-Power

• Programming Your Body Clock

When you wish to be awakened at a certain hour, use your subconscious mind as your alarm clock. Just before going to sleep, tell your subconscious mind to awaken you at a specific time. I use this exercise often; it never ceases to amaze me that I wake up exactly at the time specified. Its accuracy is not affected by the change of time or the clock being slow.

• Asking for Answers

When you require an answer to a question, think of the issue involved and request the perfect solution just before dropping off to sleep. Then say to your subconscious mind, "Please answer," and wait for the answer to appear.

Alternatively, take a glass of water, hold it in your hand, and visualize the question within the water. Drink one-half of the glass of water before going to bed, asking your subconscious mind for the answer by repeating the words, "Please answer." Ask for any relevant information, already stored in your memory bank, to be revealed to you. Ponder your problem before you fall asleep, examining it from all angles and instructing your subconscious mind to come up with the perfect answer. It will automatically provide the solution. Drink the rest of the water upon rising.

Usually, the answer will flash into your mind in the morning or later that day. It can present itself as an event, thought, idea, experience, hunch, words from another person, something you read, a feeling, or a knowingness.

Be certain to say "Thank you" three times, in anticipation of what you will be receiving from the Universe. By emphasizing your gratitude in advance, you are telling the Universe you fully expect your Affirmation to manifest. This expectancy further empowers and reinforces your Affirmation.

• Generating Happiness

I *dare* you to get up in the morning, look yourself square in the eye in the mirror, and say:

> "I, (your name), deserve and now am healthy, happy and wealthy."

Do this exercise for a period of 21 days, saying it with feeling, meaning, and expectancy and see what happens. (Please drop me a line or email to tell me the results!)

One reader changed her whole life by changing her attitude. Every morning she would look in the mirror and say, "Hey, Alma, I love you. You are wonderful. People love and respect you." After several months of doing this, her colleagues commented on her changed attitude and increased self-confidence. She was able to say "No" more easily to things she was asked to do that were not related to her career description and she had a whole new dimension of self-approval. Her colleagues wanted to know what self-improvement course she had taken.

In her home and personal life, Alma asked for and received consideration from her spouse, family, and friends. Her doctor recommended that she stop taking medication for depression because her mood had so greatly improved.

Your Mind at Work

- Simply reading your Affirmations will have a 10 to 15 percent impact on your life.
- Reading and visualizing your Affirmations will have a 55 to 65 percent impact on your life.
- Writing, reading, visualizing, feeling, and focusing on your Affirmations will have a 100 percent impact on your life.

Examine how you are instructing your subconscious mind at this very moment. By taking just five to 10 minutes out of your busy day to do the *Personal Contract Affirmation Method,* you can take control of your life and realize your dreams!

Affirmations When Properly Done Always Work!

Cards of Life

www.affirmations-doctor.com

Affirmations, Your Passport to Happiness

4 • *The Power of Affirmations*

4th Building Block of the *Personal Contract Affirmation Method:* Affirmations—a New Way of Life!

A re you at the point in your life where you are wondering why you are here, what your purpose is, and what more there could be to life? If so, this book is written for you! You will be given tools and simple, effective exercises to enable you to take control of your life and make positive changes.

You are here to learn, evolve, and grow. You are a co-creator with God, with absolute control over your thoughts and, therefore, over your life. No one can think your thoughts for you, nor can you think thoughts for another person. Using the tremendous power of your mind, you can become a magnificent creator and a magnet for all that you desire.

What Are Affirmations?

An Affirmation is similar to a prayer, wish, or goal—only it is more structured, focused, and specific. It is also an order for change, a decree, or statement. Affirmations are based on positive thinking, belief, and faith. To affirm is to *make firm*. Simply put, the basis of all Affirmations is positive thinking. The proper use of AMCAM will allow you to take control of your life, using the five building blocks.

1. Forgiveness and Releasing
2. Thoughts
3. Mind-Power
4. Affirmations
5. Creative Visualization

This powerful process enables you to change your life as you decree.

If you have ever blown out candles on your birthday cake and made a wish, you have done an Affirmation!

Any Affirmation declared with conviction and belief manifests that which it affirms. When you do an Affirmation, you transfer a portion of your life force to that Affirmation and create a magnetic flow of energy. When you affirm, you express the desired experience by way of positive statements. What you genuinely want is already in the area of your subconscious mind or the want would not be there.

A strong desire for something starts it flowing toward you. When used properly, Affirmations are powerful psychological tools for growth. Some people refer to the Affirmation process as "treasure mapping" or "creating a wish list." Affirmations can also be referred to as magic wands or trigger tools.

To produce the desired results, Affirmations must be done repeatedly, with commitment, faith, expectancy, and enthusiasm. This exerts a powerful impact on your belief system, emotions, health, and life. Because of your innate ability to co-create with God, the Universe acts as a gigantic Affirmation machine, awaiting your orders.

When you do Affirmations, you are talking to yourself on paper. It is important to always affirm in the present time because it is the only timeframe in which the subconscious mind operates.

Affirmations Are Natural

Whenever you are goal-setting with powerful, focused intent, you are actually doing a form of Affirmation. Whether or not you are conscious of doing Affirmations, it is a fact that you have done many in your lifetime. You may call it goal-setting, planning, wishing, or praying.

Those of you who have experienced success with goal-setting will be absolutely thrilled with the incredible success you achieve when you do AMCAM faithfully.

Years ago, before I even knew what an Affirmation was, I was doing one—perhaps the most important Affirmation of my life. My son David was born with two crooked feet. His feet were so turned in, he could not walk properly. We were very poor and it would have taken several thousand dollars for corrective surgery to enable him to walk. He seemed doomed to live his life in a wheelchair.

I looked at my baby son and I said, over and over, "You will walk, you will walk." I repeated this statement dozens of times every day and lulled myself to sleep at night, saying, "David will walk, David will walk!" It was my intention that he would walk and I commanded it.

Shortly thereafter, a friend introduced me to a wonderful organization (Shriners) that paid for my son's corrective surgery and hospitalization in Portland, Oregon.

Think back on your life. How many Affirmations have you done that created miraculous results? How many miracles have you experienced?

In the Bible, Jesus taught a form of Affirmation. He said, "Ask and ye shall receive, knock and the door will be opened, seek and ye shall find." These are affirmative, action-packed statements and clear indications of the power within us to make things happen in our lives.

When doing AMCAM properly, you will discover how to do the following:

- Recognize, verbalize, and write out your goals (Affirmations)
- Improve your relationships with self and others
- Attract the perfect, lasting successful career
- Attract that special person (mate)
- Handle and overcome fear and negative habits
- Attract health, wealth, and happiness
- Use thoughts to create miracles
- Use the wondrous power of your subconscious mind
- Forgive everyone and everything that has ever hurt you
- Forgive, love, respect, and approve of yourself
- Believe in yourself
- Meditate and become peaceful
- Reduce your weight and maintain your ideal figure
- Develop self-esteem

- Have peace of mind
- Become more spiritual
- Enjoy optimum health
- Be more patient
- Change your life as you decree
- Face and accept death—the final destination

It is *your* life. Live it to the fullest!

Affirmations When Properly Done Always Work!

Cards of Life

www.affirmations-doctor.com

5 • *Creative Visualization*

5th Building Block of the *Personal Contract Affirmation Method:* Using Your Mind to Create

Creative visualization is a very important part of the *Personal Contract Affirmation Method*. It involves using your imagination to create the manifestation of your desire. We all possess this natural power, whether we are aware of it or not. It is a subjective experience that uses imagery and imagination. The image can be a real event or a totally imaginary one. Both create the same changes in the body.

Creative visualization is structured and directed. The images your mind receives from your mental world are just as real as an event actually taking place. When you practise creative visualization and imaging, you are actually transporting yourself into the future. You put yourself into a situation that has not yet taken place.

Since your mind does not know the difference between a real event and an imagined event, it accepts your visualization as truth.

The instant you visualize in vivid colour the end result of your Affirmation, the energy and power of your visualization take the form of a tiny speck in your consciousness. It is your choice whether to leave it where it is, as it is, or to give it life to grow. Faith is the power and life force that fertilizes it.

To change your world, change the way you picture it and the results follow. You tap directly into the power of the subconscious mind when you visualize, image, and affirm—replacing negative mental images with positive ones. Visualization adds power to everything. It is used by many successful people to create what they want.

Thinking in pictures is one of the basic activities of the human mind. Centuries ago, cave dwellers used creative visualization. They painted pictures of the animals they wished to hunt on the cave walls. They even practised throwing actual spears at the drawings; some of those marks can still be seen on the cave walls. Creative imagery (visualization) is the first language of the subconscious mind. Affirmations (words) are the second language.

When you desire positive changes to occur in your life, use mental images to create the experiences you desire. It is important to speak to your subconscious mind in a language it understands and to which it can respond. This language is imagination and creative visualization. Make your creative visualization pictures colourful and exciting. A specific, vivid, mental picture gives the subconscious mind something definite on which to focus.

Power of Creative Visualization

The practice of creative visualization is extremely powerful. All things come to people according to the pictures they form and hold in their minds. You cannot pick up a pen unless you first have the mental image of picking it up. When you visualize, you get a clear picture or image of the object or situation you desire. Correct mental imaging produces wonderful results.

When you are visualizing what you desire, make it your *intention* to succeed, because intention is a very powerful force.

At first, you are consciously practising and experiencing what you choose to create. Then, by creating pictures in your mind's eye (creative visualization), you turn your experience over to your subconscious mind. Very quickly you will begin to move easily and naturally, step by step, to your goal or the manifestation of your Affirmation. When you visualize the end result, you set in motion a reaction that brings about its manifestation.

A popular television show demonstrated the tremendous power of visualization when they interviewed a teenage girl who was a professional archer. For 15 to 20 minutes before each session, she would simply sit and visualize hitting a bull's eye. The trophies she won certainly proved that it worked for her. It is a known fact that most athletes use this positive form of visualization.

Picture Power

I once read about a soldier in a prison camp who practised his golf game daily in his mind. He visualized it so many times that it became a natural part of him. When he was released and physically played golf, his performance was outstanding. His mind could not tell the difference between the game he visualized in his mind and the one he actually played on the golf course.

This demonstrates the tremendous power of creative visualization. When images in the mind are combined with Affirmations, they greatly enhance the mind's ability to manifest the object of your desire.

Effective coaches also teach team members the art of creative visualization, but this process is not restricted to athletes. People from all walks of life use it every day with fantastic results. Creative visualization empowers and directs your mind to work *for* you, rather than *against* you.

Imagination and Other Methods

Imagination is a form of creative thought. It is the ability to create an idea or mental picture in your mind, but just what it is and where it comes from no one seems to really know. No brain surgeon has ever been able to locate a picture, imagination centre, thought, or idea during surgery.

When you practise the art of imagination, you experience the scene from the inside. This gives you the feeling and experience of it happening at the present time.

There are two types of imagination: spontaneous imagination that comes from the subconscious mind, and willed or guided imagination that comes from the conscious mind.

When doing AMCAM and creatively visualizing, be certain to add faith, emotion, and expectancy because they fuel the imagination of the subconscious mind and make your Affirmations manifest more quickly.

Daydreaming is casual and random. It is the act of involving yourself in fantasy while you are wide awake. It is closely linked to imagination. Children often spend time daydreaming and visualizing what they will be and whom they will marry when they grow up. They also use this process when they play with imaginary playmates.

Daydreaming is a process that takes you away from the present and it can be a time of fantastic, creative accomplishment.

Creative Visualization Exercises

• Using the Five Senses

Find a place where you will not be disturbed. Close your eyes and visualize (see) what you desire to happen.

Make it specific and vivid; see the colours and every detail, engaging the five senses. Really feel the emotion of desire and expectancy in every part of your body.

For example, if you are visualizing a loving, happy relationship, do the following:

1. *See* the outline of him or her.
2. *Hear* your perfect mate saying, "(Your name), I love you."
3. *Feel* his or her arms around you or the ring on your finger.
4. *Smell* either perfume or men's cologne.
5. To engage the sense of *taste*, bite into a juicy apple or pop a tasty mint into your mouth.

Surround your visualization picture in a beautiful pink-coloured cloud and release it into the Universe to manifest as you desire. Colour awakens and excites the subconscious mind and produces quicker results.

Now *step ahead*, in your mind, three to six weeks or months. See yourself in that happy relationship or marriage. See it in vivid Technicolor. You already *have* that happy, loving relationship. It just has not appeared in your reality as yet.

• Preparing the Way

There is always a certain amount of time between the expression of your desire and its manifestation. The exact time depends on both inner and outer circumstances. It also depends on how often you do your *Personal Contract Affirmation Method* and whether you are visualizing the end result with feeling, faith, expectancy, and gratitude.

To further empower your visualizations, visualize a huge ocean liner carrying the manifestation of your desire. Calculate or see in your mind's eye (subconscious mind) just how far away it is from you. Ask yourself if it is 20 feet, 200 yards, one mile, or five miles from you.

Close your eyes and see the manifestation of your Affirmation coming toward you in this huge ship. You can hear the motor running. It is getting closer and closer. You are becoming more and more excited. Make the picture vivid and colourful. How large is the ship? How many people do you see on board? What colour is it? What is the name of the ship? See it carrying the object of your desire, to be delivered to you by the captain.

In this state of visualization, any desire can be carried on this great ship, whether it be a character change, ideal partner, money, or successful career. Your subconscious mind will accept and experience this visualization process as if it were actually taking place. You can make the ocean liner proceed at whatever speed you wish and see it travelling at that speed toward you. Is the water smooth or is it rough and choppy?

If it is choppy and rough, remove the stormy conditions and make the waters smooth as glass. It now has clear sailing to bring about the manifestation of your Affirmation with no interference. You have already obtained your wish, but the ocean liner has not yet arrived at port.

• Cleansing Your Body

This process prepares you for the release of negativity anywhere in your body.

- Sit quietly.
- Visualize that a soothing mist in your favourite colour is gently calming your thoughts and clearing your mind.
- Take several deep breaths, then exhale any negative, unwanted feelings and thoughts.

- Breathe in positive, happy feelings and thoughts.
- Visualize that you have an opening in the top of your head like a teapot does. See your favourite colour pouring into your body through the opening in the consistency of honey. Let the beautiful substance flow throughout your body, down into your arms, your fingers, torso, legs, toes . . . every part of you.

Now completely release all negativity from every part of your body. Fill yourself with peace, joy, love, and happiness. You feel refreshed, invigorated, and rejuvenated.

End the exercise by saying, "Thank you, thank you, thank you."

• Overcoming Cravings

When you crave sweets, paint or sketch a picture in vivid colour of your favourite dessert. Imagine that you are eating that food. Engage your five senses to make a more real and lasting impression on your subconscious mind.

1. *See* the delicious food.
2. *Hear* yourself chewing it.
3. *Feel* your stomach filling up.
4. *Smell* the wonderful aroma.
5. *Taste* the delightful flavours.

Then mentally pick up a giant eraser and rub out the image.

Take a deep breath, relax, release, and let go completely. Notice how satisfied you feel after eating this imaginary food. This visualization works powerfully to satiate any sweet cravings you may have. I do it with butterscotch sundaes regularly. It really does satisfy my craving for sweets. The more real, colourful, exciting, and fun you make it, the more powerfully it works.

• Finding True Self

Visualize your body as a huge block of ice. Imagine chopping and chiselling away at it until you uncover the *real you* hidden deep inside. Focus on forgiving and releasing all negativity, cutting away inside. Focus on forgiving and releasing all negativity, cutting away all that is not really you. Feel the power of discernment fill your body as you imagine yourself being able to say "No" whenever necessary.

As the layers of self-doubt, criticism, and all forms of negative thoughts and feelings about self are chopped away, a beautiful image emerges.

You are special. There is no one else exactly like you. Your heart, mind, and body are filled with self-confidence, self-worth, and love. Your ice carving is complete and you are whole. See this image vividly in your mind and keep concentrating and focusing on it. Think it into existence. Love, respect, and approve of yourself, just the way you are.

In the media, we hear increasingly about alternative healing methods used in the treatment of illness and disease. Doctors cannot explain the cures. One woman, for example, was diagnosed with cancer, which she was told, would require surgery. She visualized her tumour as a huge block of ice inside her body. Then she visualized taking a kettle of boiling water and pouring it over the block of ice every day (just like defrosting the refrigerator).

After several weeks of this concentrated visualization, the block of ice had completely melted in her mind's eye. When she visited her doctor, he reported that the cancerous tumour had miraculously disappeared and that there was no need to operate. Just as negative thoughts can have powerful impacts on our bodies so, too, can positive, healing thoughts.

• The Affirmation Light Bulb: For Self

You may wish to do your *Personal Contract Affirmation Method* in a special place, such as a garden, meadow, treehouse, arbour, or anywhere you feel comfortable and at peace. I enjoy doing my Affirmation Program in my own mental Affirmation "Light Bulb," which helps make my Affirmations more focused and powerful.

To do this, visualize a huge, giant light bulb in front of you. Make it large enough to step inside. It is complete with door and handle.

Open the glass door and go inside. You can see through it in all directions. Just inside the door, there is a panel of push buttons.

When you are working on the relationship Master Affirmation, press the pink button. For a career, press the green button and for healing, press the blue button. The colour you select will then fill your Affirmation light bulb, penetrating the atmosphere and enabling you to breathe in the power of that specific colour.

Imagine putting your Affirmation in a soft, golden cloud and letting it float up and out the large fresh air vent at the top of the Affirmation light bulb. Release it with loving kindness and detachment into the Universe, to manifest as desired.

Now mentally harden the material around the bulb so that no one can come in or see you. Bring in the five senses.

- *See* a huge wicker chair, covered with large coloured pillows in gorgeous pastel colours.
- *Hear* soothing music.
- Sit down in the chair and *feel* your body sink into deep relaxation.
- *Smell* the sweet fragrance of roses.
- Pop a *tasty mint* into your mouth to complete the experience of the five senses.

I use this valuable exercise for a positive pick-me-up whenever I begin to feel discouraged or disheartened. I also sit, meditate, and ask for new, fresh ideas. When you do AMCAM in this wonderful space, it helps solidify, clarify, and empower your Affirmations.

You can also imagine yourself within the Affirmation light bulb when you are in the company of negative people or circumstances.

Create your very own peaceful place. It is a good idea to keep your own individual light-bulb space just for you. This is your secret place. Create whatever you desire. Make it special, unique, and completely safe. Allow your imagination and creative visualization abilities to run wild! Use it when required, but refrain from using it to avoid people who really do need your help and support.

• The Affirmation Light Bulb: For Relationship/Marriage

Invite your partner to participate in this exercise, making a private space together. This can be very romantic, exciting, and fulfilling. One couple who made their own mental Marriage Affirmation Light Bulb swears it saved their marriage. They used it as a safe and sacred place in which to settle disagreements, make love, and talk openly about their feelings. They had a place to run away to, even if it was only in their minds.

The whole procedure was very real to them. They incorporated creative visualization, imagination, and reality. Now that they are in a better financial position, they do the same exercise on the physical plane, joking that their expensive hotel room is their very own mental Marriage Affirmation Light Bulb.

• The Affirmation Light Bulb: For Family

Have fun! You can invite your whole family to participate in the Mental Family Affirmation Light Bulb exercise, making it an exciting learning experience for everyone. Allow each person to provide input and ideas so everyone feels involved. This is a very powerful exercise for families, helping them to communicate and interact more effectively and lovingly. The family that affirms, visualizes, and creates together, stays together.

Affirmations When Properly Done Always Work!

Cards of Life

www.affirmations-doctor.com

6 • *Master Affirmations*

Creating Your World with the Power of Affirmations:
One Affirmation at a Time

In this chapter, you will learn how to create your *own* Master Affirmation. You are a co-creator with God and you can use this marvellous, creative power by doing AMCAM to create your own happy, fulfilled life.

The process of doing Affirmations is completely natural. Using AMCAM, you contact and use your higher power by telling your subconscious mind exactly what is desired. Impressing the image of the desired result repeatedly onto your consciousness causes the Affirmation to seep deep into your subconscious mind and manifest your desire.

Doing Affirmations creates a magnetic flow of energy. What you genuinely want is already in the area of your subconscious mind or the desire would not be there. A strong desire for a thing starts it flowing toward you.

The Law of Attraction is the principle that gives thoughts and Affirmations dynamic power. It states that whatever you put out into the Universe is reflected back to you, making your thoughts act like magnets. Like all natural laws, it is unchangeable and acts with mathematical exactitude. This law is always turned on. In fact, you cannot turn it off.

For this reason, it is important to ensure that you *know* the outcome before you start AMCAM. When you use the principles and Laws of the Universe faithfully, properly, and intelligently, there is no uncertainty as to the outcome. Your Affirmations *manifest!* There is no limit to the wondrous possibilities and miracles that occur in your life. The Universal Laws play no favourites and no one gets preference.

According to the Law of Gravity, when you drop an object, it falls to earth (unless, of course, you happen to be on the Moon). This law, like every other law of the Universe, works the same way for everyone, every time, without fail. No human being has more power than another.

So-called *extraordinary* human beings have simply learned how to attract, master, and utilize this remarkable power from their inner God-consciousness. No one made him or her self. All people operate with the power that was placed in them on the day they were born.

When you do AMCAM in the correct manner—repetitiously, with faith, emotion, and expectancy—you gain complete control over conditions in your life.

Master Affirmation: Seed-Thought

The first step in AMCAM is to create your Master Affirmation. Start dusting off those dreams and let yourself have fun!

This is your order to the Universe—the seed-thought that you plant in the rich, fertile soil of your subconscious mind. Be specific and say exactly what you desire. Your Master Affirmation should be explicit and individual. Don't hold back!

When ordering a dress or shirt from a catalogue, you need to be very specific. If you simply said, "Please send me a dress or shirt," they would probably write back and ask you to state the size, colour, quantity, and price of the article you wanted. This information is necessary if you wish to have your order filled—and to ensure that you get what you want.

Similarly, if you went into a restaurant and asked the server to bring you something he thinks you would like, unless the server knew you very well, he would probably stand there until you gave your order.

Sometimes we give more consideration to ordering from a catalogue or at a restaurant than to God or the Universal Mind. Be precise, specific, and exact. Remember that you get back exactly what you order up or affirm. If your order is vague and uncertain, your answer will be vague and uncertain. Vague Affirmations are seldom realized. Feel the emotion of yearning and anticipation. Your

Affirmations, Your Passport to Happiness

burning desire and deep yearning serve as powerful launching platforms for your Affirmations.

The Master Affirmation is written, printed, or typed on a sheet of paper below the photo, picture or sketch of your desire (see Sample Master Affirmation on page 83). It is then placed in a plastic sleeve to be read every morning and evening. You write your Master Affirmation ONCE, just as you write your Last Will and Testament.

Short-Form Affirmation

- Your Short-Form Affirmation consists of five or six key words taken from your Master Affirmation that are meaningful and most powerful.
- Select those words that have a real emotional charge for you.
- After reading your Master Affirmation, jot these words down three times on a separate sheet of paper at each reading, in the morning and evening.
- You can end your Short-Form Affirmation by drawing a symbol of what you are affirming.

You could use hearts when affirming for love, dollar signs for money, and happy faces for health. You may wish to write your Short-Form Affirmations on 3″ x 5″ cards. You can carry them in your purse, pocket, wallet, or briefcase so you can read them any time you wish. Post them in your vehicle or place them on your desk, mirror, refrigerator, or wherever you desire.

Materials Needed

- Photograph or sketch of desired result (for example, a picture of you and a sketch of your desired mate or a picture of you driving or standing beside that perfect vehicle for you. Put yourself in the picture). If you do not have a photo, do AMCAM anyway. Do not use the lack of a photo as an excuse to procrastinate or avoid doing your Affirmations.
- Coloured felt pen, pencil, crayon, or pen
- Scissors
- Magazines or newspapers from which to cut out pictures and sketches
- Scotch tape or glue

- One 8.5" x 11" sheet of white or coloured paper
- Plastic insert sleeve
- Loose-leaf binder for Master Affirmations
- Loose-leaf binder for fulfilled Affirmations
- Most of all, a burning desire, faith, determination, and sense of expectancy

Let's Set the Scene for Doing Affirmations

Whether this is your very first time doing Affirmations or you have done them many times, it is important to clear your mind of negative self-talk and any upsetting thoughts you may be holding in your head.

Some people may find that a little difficult at first. They might be struggling with some stubborn, old, outdated belief systems that need to be accessed, revised, and changed.

The secret is to apply concentration and persistence to releasing these old, stubborn beliefs, ideas, and feelings. When you do, you will be absolutely delighted with the results.

1. Find a comfortable place to sit where you will not be disturbed. Gently close your eyes and begin to clear out the negative self-talk that may be circulating in your head. Release any thoughts that are bothering you and disturbing your thought patterns.

2. Take a few deep breaths.

3. On the in breath—inhale fresh, loving, healing, prosperous, and peaceful energy. Visualize that the air you are breathing in is a beautiful shade of green.

4. On the out breath, exhale hurts, anger, bitterness, disbelief, and all negativity—past and present. Visualize all the negative feelings leaving your body inside a dark cloud.

When you have done this exercise several times, visualize that you have just released all the negativity that was hindering you.

When you feel fresh, alive, energized, enthused and excited, it is time to do your Master Affirmation!

Know that **Affirmations When Properly Done Always Work!**

Your Sample Master Affirmation

Your Firm and Binding Contract

(For Affirmations to be truly effective, you must appeal to your five senses and the Affirmation must engender a positive, emotional state.)

*(**Picture or Sketch.** This gives the subconscious mind something on which to focus.)*

I, (your name), deserve and now have or am:

_____

(Write your desires.)

_____

_____

to the good of all parties concerned. Thank you, thank you, thank you.

I Fully Accept:

Your signature: _____

Witness: _____

Date of Acceptance: _____

Note:
Use words that trigger feeling and emotion in your body.

Now you have made a firm and binding contract with your Higher Self, God, Universal Mind, or the entity in which you believe. Make your Master Affirmation colourful, because colour wakes up and excites the subconscious mind.

Affirmations When Properly Done Always Work!

Master Affirmation Checklist

- Is it specific, stating exactly what you desire?
- Is it heartfelt and emotionally charged and does it resonate with you?
- Do you feel it in your body?
- Did you release negative feelings and beliefs?
- Is your heart and mind in agreement with your Affirmation?
- Have you added the words "deserve and now have"?
- Is it colourful, exciting, and interesting?
- Is it designed not to hurt or take from anyone?
- Is it to the good of all parties concerned?
- Is there at least a 51 percent believability factor that the Affirmation can manifest?
- If visual, did you put yourself in the picture?
- If auditory, do you hear your Affirmation and its manifestation (hear the applause)?
- If kinesthetic, do you feel your Affirmation?
- If gustatory, do you taste your Affirmation? Was it a delicious experience?
- If olfactory, do you smell your Affirmation—the sweet smell of success?
- Did you say "Thank You" three times?
- Is it dated?
- Is your Acceptance Statement signed and witnessed?
- Did you say "Yes" to the Universe?
- Did you have fun?

If you answered "Yes" to all the above questions, congratulations! You have just completed your first Master Affirmation in your *Personal Contract Affirmation Method.*

The 3 Ps to Creating an Effective Affirmation

1. Personal
2. Positive
3. Present tense

Some people find that doing Affirmations in the first, second, and third person work well for them.

1. **1st Person:**
   I, Mary Smith, deserve and now have a happy, loving relationship.

2. **2nd Person:**
   You, Mary Smith, deserve and now have that happy, loving relationship.

3. **3rd Person:**
   Mary Smith deserves and now has that happy, loving relationship.

Ladies: You may use your maiden name, if you desire. Some women use their maiden name together with their present, legal name when doing their Master Affirmations.

One reader found it very beneficial to use both names when affirming for her perfect, lasting, successful career position after years of training and studying. She said that when she started her education, she was single and now that she is married and uses that name, putting both names on her Master Affirmation made it clear for her. It worked! She now has a great position as a Professor at a prestigious university in her city.

One divorced woman also used this process with great results. She felt that using her married name hindered the manifestation of her Affirmation for a new husband. Three months after she added her maiden name to her Affirmation, she met her husband.

It is your choice whether to use your legal name or the one that you use to sign cheques and legal documents or to *add* your maiden name.

My Master Affirmation for Marriage:
How it Worked for Me

My first husband, Al, died in 1984. After three years of grieving, I decided I wanted a full, happy, married life. I began affirming for the perfect man for me. Of course he would not be perfect, but he would be perfect for me! I wrote my Affirmation as follows.

> "I, Anne Marie, now have a loving, lasting, happy marriage with the perfect man for me."

I did the *Personal Contract Affirmation Method* conscientiously for seven months and nothing happened. I became depressed. One evening I said to my subconscious mind before retiring for the night, "I cannot teach this material if it does not work for me. What is wrong?"

The next morning I awoke to one word ringing over and over in my mind. The word was *"deserve."* This word was the missing piece of the puzzle. I sat down and really thought about myself. I was a good wife, mother, and person. I really deserved a happy marriage. I began to *feel worthy and deserving.* I changed my Affirmation to read as follows.

> "I, Anne Marie Evers, **deserve** and now have a loving, lasting, happy marriage with the perfect man for me."

I began to feel I was a good person and really and truly deserved a good husband and happy marriage. I lulled myself to sleep nightly, saying, "Happy marriage, happy marriage." I developed the marriage consciousness and brought it into my being. My subconscious mind had all night to work, find, and assemble the ingredients to make my Affirmation manifest as affirmed.

I met my husband Roy three weeks later. When I was doing my Affirmation without adding the word *deserve* and without *feeling* worthy, my conscious mind was cancelling out my Affirmation. It did this with thoughts such as, "You already had one marriage and there are not enough men to go around," or "Men in your age group are looking for young chicks." With all these statements surfacing in my mind, my Affirmations were negated by these negative thoughts.

In AMCAM, I affirmed that my new husband would love to cook (my first husband, Al, was a well-known chef). Roy, who passed away January 22, 2002, was also a wonderful cook and did most of the cooking, canning, and baking in our home. He brought me coffee in bed every morning. I also affirmed he would be about 6 feet tall. Roy was 5 feet 11 ¾ inches. I certainly did not complain about a quarter-of-an-inch!

Be specific and say exactly what you desire. But be careful what you wish for or affirm, because it happens!

Action Affirmations

Even though he was completely unaware of it, Roy was also doing an Affirmation before I met him—an action Affirmation. On one of my first visits to his home, I spied a room with a Do Not Disturb sign hanging on the doorknob. When I asked him what was in that room, he rather reluctantly opened the door. I gasped. The room was absolutely beautiful and completely out of keeping with the rest of the house.

Roy had been a widower for some years and his home was definitely that of a bachelor. As a sports enthusiast, he had decorated his home with deer and moose antlers. Golf clubs, fishing rods, nets, wading boots, and other outdoor equipment were also lying around.

This one room, however, was like a photograph right out of a designer magazine. It contained the most gorgeous brass bed I had ever seen and plush wall-to-wall carpeting, custom drapes with matching bedspread, and pillows, pictures, and furniture. He had actually prepared this room for his special lady *before* he met her. This room was our bedroom. By taking action, Roy blew breath into his Affirmation, physically creating the environment in which his dream could manifest. It worked!

One reader created the Master Affirmation that she was married to the perfect man for her. Eight months before she met her husband, she purchased her wedding dress, wrote out her wedding invitations, and planned her whole wedding in vivid detail—right down to the wedding cake.

That was a powerful, action-packed affirmation that manifested exactly as she had visualized and affirmed. She blew breath into her affirmation in a very real and effective way.

You will reap great results when you do AMCAM regularly and faithfully. It is the law!

The Personal Contract Affirmation Method

Before embarking on your Personal Contract Affirmation Method, clear your mind and put yourself in a positive, receptive mode. Make sure your heart and mind are in agreement with your Affirmation and that it resonates with you.

Step One: Soil Preparation
Forgiving, Forgetting, and Releasing

Prepare the soil of your subconscious mind by forgiving and releasing everyone and everything that has ever hurt you. Then forgive yourself. The forgiveness exercises can be done by physically writing—saying them out loud—or visualizing them in your mind. Once you have done this, the freshly prepared soil of your subconscious mind is ready to receive the seeds.

Step Two: Seed Selection and Planting
Selecting What You Want and Writing Your Master Affirmation

Decide what you want, being very specific so your Affirmation is tailored to suit your individual needs and desires. Clear your mind and concentrate on your desire. To help you focus and get clear about your desire, ask yourself the following questions.

1. Is this Affirmation realistic for me?
2. Do I want it with all my heart?
3. Is this merely what someone else wants for me?
4. Do I have at least a 51 percent believability factor that it can manifest?

5. Whose voice am I hearing?
6. How do I really feel about it?

When you have the answers to these questions, you will know if you truly desire what you are affirming.

If your Master Affirmation is longer than one page, tuck the extra sheets in behind the first one in the plastic sleeve. Mentally plant the Master Affirmation (seed-thought) into the rich, fertile soil of your subconscious mind. The mind knows only to reproduce what is planted in it (what you are affirming). These words become Your Master Affirmation—your order to the Universe.

Step Three: Watering and Fertilizing the Seed
Reading Your Master Affirmation Twice Daily

Take out your Master Affirmation every morning and evening and read it over, knowing that your subconscious mind is taking in every detail and storing it for all time. Jot down your Short-Form Affirmation three times on a separate piece of paper. (You can either dispose of this paper or keep it). Reading your Affirmation puts it on the front burner in your mind.

Step Four: Anticipating the Harvest Taking Delivery of the Manifestation of Your Master Affirmation

Mentally step ahead three to four weeks or months and creatively visualize yourself obtaining your goal. Engage the five senses. When affirming for that special partner, do the following.

1. *See* the outline of that person.
2. *Hear* him or her speaking to you.
3. *Feel* how happy you are together.
4. *Smell* a flower, perfume, or cologne.
5. For the sense of *taste*, imagine taking a bite of a juicy apple.

Know that you already have that perfect, loving, lasting relationship; that successful career; or whatever you desire. *It simply has not physically materialized yet!*
Lull yourself to sleep saying your Short-Form Affirmation. You may wish to record your personal Affirmations and listen to them

Lull yourself to sleep saying your Short-Form Affirmation. You may wish to record your personal Affirmations and listen to them as you fall asleep. Your own voice has a powerful effect on your subconscious mind.

Give yourself permission and credit for being capable of changing negative feelings about yourself, your life, and the past.

Step Five: Tending your Affirmation Garden
Anticipating the Harvest

AMCAM is similar to planting a garden. In Step One, you prepared the soil of your subconscious mind by forgiving everyone and everything that has ever hurt you. The gardener carefully prepares both the soil and the seed. The method of doing Affirmations (creating the object of your desire) is the same process that takes place in the planting of a seed. The Master Affirmation is the seed. The growing takes place in the darkness below the surface.

Writing formalizes the Affirmation process. When you write out an Affirmation, you are talking to yourself or thinking on paper. The way you form your letters, words, and paragraphs tells a story about your personality type and character. It reveals a wealth of knowledge about you.

The moment you write out your Affirmation, it is on the way to happening for you. Written words are a step closer to the materialization of your Affirmation. When you write down a thought on paper, your full attention is automatically focused on it. The written word exists for all time.

By writing down your thoughts, you anchor them to the Universe and engrave them on your mind. Writing or typing an Affirmation uses a larger part of the brain than mere thought and places your Affirmation in the area of reality, transforming the intangible into the tangible.

To confirm your willingness to accept the outcome of your Affirmation, write on the bottom of the Master Affirmation, "I fully accept," and sign your name and fill in the date.

Total acceptance is a very important part of AMCAM. (A cheque is not valid unless it is dated and signed.) Your Master Affirmation is a firm, binding document with yourself, your subconscious mind, and God or the Universal Mind. Ask someone to witness your signature on your Master Affirmation.

In Steps Three and Four, we read the Master Affirmation and creatively visualize the end result, allowing it to sink deep into the subconscious mind. It will take root, grow, and manifest what is affirmed.

After you do an Affirmation, feel it as real. *Know* it is already existing in your mind and that it will manifest. Start affirming small things in the beginning, then move on to larger things.

It is a good idea to keep a record of what you have achieved through your Affirmations. I recommend having a Fulfilled Master Affirmation Book that you can fill with numerous, completed Affirmations. Keeping track of the positive results increases your faith to move on to new and larger goals. When even your smallest Affirmation manifests, you will experience a feeling of excitement and amazement.

Sample Master Affirmation for Relationship

"I, (your name), deserve and now have a loving, happy, lasting relationship (that turns into marriage) with the perfect man or woman for me. He or she is kind, loving, generous, healthy, attractive, about my age, unattached, and (specify height and colouring). He or she is financially independent, prosperous, and finds love and happiness with me. I am kind, loving, generous, and I give and receive freely and unconditionally. God or Divine Intelligence knows where this person is and the great wisdom of my subconscious mind now brings us together in its own way. I love, respect, approve of, and accept myself just the way I am. I believe in myself. I make good choices. We deserve each other and enjoy a long, lasting, happy, healthy relationship, to the good of all parties concerned. I now release this request, with faith, to my subconscious mind, knowing that it has manifested. I give thanks to God for the perfect answer to my prayer. Thank you, thank you, thank you."

Sample Short-Form Affirmation: **Perfect life-partner for me or happy marriage**

Sample Master Affirmation for Career

"I, (your name), deserve and now have the perfect, lasting, successful career for me. I earn in excess of $_____(monthly, yearly, net, or gross). My employers and clients are very pleased with my excellent work and reward me accordingly. I am fulfilled. I enjoy my work. I easily take advantage of career advancements. I am thrilled and excited with my career. I am balanced and have time for my family, social activities, and myself. We are all happy to the good of all parties concerned. Thank you, thank you, thank you."

Sample Short-Form Affirmation: **Perfect, lasting, successful career for me**

Affirmations When Properly Done Always Work!

Cards of Life

www.affirmations-doctor.com

Affirmations, Your Passport to Happiness

7 • *Making Affirmations Effective* .

Creating Affirmations that Work!
Tailor Your *Personal Affirmation Program*

Keep it Short

Debbie, a busy housewife with two teenagers and two part-time jobs, was upset that she could not devote enough time to doing her daily Affirmations. When I asked her how long they took, she replied, "I am doing five of them and I spend more than one hour in the morning and the same or more in the evening."

I discovered that Debbie had been preparing her Master Affirmations over and over every single day! She spent time searching for pictures or sketches of her desires and pasting them beside each of her five Master Affirmations. Then she wrote out that specific Affirmation under the pictures or sketches. What a lot of extra, unnecessary work! Remember, your Master Affirmation is only written **once!**

Your preparation work is finished once you do your Master Affirmation. That particular one never has to be done again. The only work left to do is the watering and fertilizing process (reading your Master Affirmation, jotting down your Short-Form Affirmation three times, then proceeding with the "stepping ahead" process).

It is rather like writing your Will. It can be altered by the attachment of letters or codicils, but the preparation of the Will itself is performed once.

A Master Affirmation can be modified, updated, or discarded. When it manifests, it is placed in the Fulfilled Affirmation Book.

I decided to time my own Affirmation Process. It took approximately one minute to take out my completed Master Affirmation and read it over three times. It took less than one minute to jot down my Short-Form Affirmation three times and about one or two more minutes to do the creative visualization stepping-ahead process, bringing in the five senses. The total time it took me to do one Affirmation was approximately three minutes. So if Debbie were doing five Affirmations in this manner, it should take no longer than 15 minutes in the morning and the same in the evening.

AMCAM should only take a few minutes out of your busy day—all that is required to generate powerful, positive results!

Stay Positive

At times, your Affirmation may seem to be delayed or just not happening. Not achieving the manifestation of your Affirmation in your particular timeframe, however, could be the best thing that ever happened to you. When you look back over your life, you may thank God for some unanswered prayers, wishes, or Affirmations. What you are affirming may not be to your highest good at this particular time in your life. It is always a good idea to affirm divine timing and divine order.

There could be a tendency to become discouraged when there are no immediate results from your Affirmation. At times you may fail to recognize them. The answers or results may appear as a sign, awareness, problem, feeling, thought, new opportunity, or even an overpowering hunch.

Some people feel it is important to put a certain timeframe on the Affirmation manifesting.

Timing

Keep on doing your Affirmations even when you are discouraged or depressed. One of my readers told me that, since he started doing AMCAM, he has not had any of his usual feelings of depression or discouragement. The program itself created and caused an uplifting experience even before any of his Affirmations manifested. Recently, he had at least three Affirmations manifest in one month.

A delay in manifestation could also be a sign or warning that you may be overly attached to the outcome of your desire. If this is the case, you could be hindering its manifestation. It is a good idea to detach yourself from the outcome. Even though you may not realize it, your Affirmations are working for you through the precise Laws of the Universe. It is very important at this time to keep on affirming.

Should your Affirmation not materialize as you think or feel it should or in the timeframe you stipulated, be calm, relaxed, and remain in the flow of the great, divine energy. Know that Affirmations always do manifest, but sometimes not when you think they should. Affirm divine timing repeatedly. Know there are even greater blessings for you just upstream.

Many of your Affirmations come true but are not recognized. The results of your Affirmation appear the moment the mind fully accepts and believes that the Affirmation is true. Invent ways to prime the pump of your mind to believe and accept that the Affirmation is true and always has been. Tap into your innermost feelings and emotions and ask when the time is right to take action. Also ask what type of action is appropriate.

Learn from the Lowly Seed

The lowly seed puts its roots and tiny tendrils down into the rich, fertile soil of the earth. It takes root and grows. At the same time, it sends sprouts up toward the light. When it encounters any obstacles, as it undoubtedly does, it is not discouraged. Instead, it simply goes around them, always stretching toward the life force of the sun and the air.

The little seed shows no lack of faith, nor does it question the length of time it will take to manifest as a plant or tree. It simply acts, trusting in God and the Laws of the great Universe. A seed of faith, once planted, never dies. The tiny seed is programmed. It puts all its energies into bringing its inherent blueprint into materialization. It knows, trusts, and acts. It produces without question, fear, or delay. Affirmations, like seeds, have a timetable of their own.

The process of doing Affirmations is a growth process. The knowledge of how to produce and create loving relationships, health, wealth, and happiness in your life was placed in you before you were born. This knowledge is activated through practising or doing AMCAM.

If your thought, desire, or Affirmation arises at the instant when there are no conflicting thoughts present to nullify this power, the mind throws its great force behind that one desire or Affirmation. The power of the mind is not divided among other thoughts, so that particular Affirmation manifests immediately, as if by some form of magic.

Words are thoughts expressed. They carry the message and energy of your Affirmations with them. Some words are neutral, but most words are either negative or positive and charged with the emotion of fear or love. When you do word Affirmations, you speak the words out loud. Verbal Affirmations manifest what is affirmed by declaration. Every word filled with the positive emotions of faith and expectancy brings forth after its kind, in body, mind, and spirit. Whether shouted or whispered, your words have power.

Never minimize the power of a softly whispered Affirmation filled with love and expectancy. You convey your innermost thoughts to others through language (words). Your words are powerful tools and have an energy all of their own. Words can convey love and cause peace and harmony between and among people and nations or they can convey hatred, creating wars and enmities.

Words are creative and you create with every word you speak. Affirmations convince the mind of the spoken and written word. Watch your words, because they are very powerful. They have the power to injure or heal others. Keep track of the words you use in everyday conversations. Write them down and study them. Consciously replace the negative ones with positive ones.

The Law of Attraction is constantly bringing to you what you believe and accept. It is a perfect mirror, reflecting back to you your thoughts, feelings, desires, beliefs, and the truth.

Empowering Your Affirmations

The power of creation is always present in the now and you are always creating and re-creating. If you have a problem, you created it and you can uncreate it. Always affirm in the present time. Saying and decreeing, "I deserve and now have" makes it present tense. If you say, "I deserve and will have," you are putting the manifestation off into the future—perhaps some future lifetime.

Your subconscious mind will honour the postponement inherent in this statement. You cannot live in the past, present, and future at the same time.

Avoid Using Negative Terms

When structuring your Affirmations, refrain from using "not" and "non." For example, "I, (your name), deserve to be a non-smoker and do not smoke." Your subconscious mind could cancel out the negative words, so your Affirmation would then read "I, (your name), deserve to be a smoker and do smoke," which, of course, would be reinforcing the fact that you smoke. Instead, structure your Affirmation as follows:

> "I, (your name), deserve to be and now enjoy being smoke-free."

Laura told me she was disappointed in the Affirmation process. Even though she was faithfully doing her Affirmations, she was still depressed and unhappy. In fact, it was even getting worse! I asked her to read what she had written in her Master Affirmation. It read, "I, Laura, am not depressed." When she was affirming over and over that she was not depressed, her mind was cancelling out the word not, and she was actually affirming *she was depressed*.

As in the above example of smoking, her mind had been trained not to recognize the word "not". She changed her Affirmation to read:

> "I, Laura, deserve to be and now am depression-free. I am happy, peaceful, and free of depression."

Today, I am so happy and peaceful.

The *Modus Operandi*

When doing Affirmations, never worry or concern yourself about the *modus operandi* (the way it happens). You know the what and God, Universal Mind, or whomever you believe in knows the how. Get out of the way and trust the Laws of Mind and Creation to take care of the manifestation as affirmed!

Never Use Another's Name

Refrain from doing any Affirmation to control another person or specify that another person commit to you. It has to be that other person's own choice.

One woman who was doing an Affirmation for a happy marriage complained to me that her Affirmation was not working. We examined it and discovered that, at the end of the Affirmation, she had actually named the person with whom she desired marriage. I explained to her the reason her Affirmation was not working was that it was an improper Affirmation.

You must never affirm (or order up) a specific individual, because it may not be to the good of all parties concerned. In this case, the person named in her Affirmation was already married to someone else. She changed her Affirmation accordingly and has since met the man of her dreams, who is unattached and perfect for her. They are now engaged to be married.

An improper Affirmation never works to your highest good. Although the married man could have left his wife and married her, negative results could have occurred because of her interference in that man's free will.

One beautiful young woman's married lover did just that. He divorced his wife, married her, and now both of them are absolutely miserable. She has since taken a lover. She felt, among other things, that she could never trust him. Her wish did manifest, but proved disastrous to her lover, his family, and the woman herself. Where will it all end?

To the Good of All Parties Concerned

This is one of the most important clauses in AMCAM. You must use this clause in every Master Affirmation, because it is your safety net. When you say, "To the good of all parties concerned," you eliminate the possibility of negative interference. Also, when you use this phrase, your Affirmations will not manifest unless they are to the good of everyone involved and this, of course, includes **you!**

You could add to your Affirmation, "This or something better now manifests for me." Think big and expect and enjoy delicious *Cosmic Affirmation Cookies* from the Universe.

I refer to the following story as my $100,000 lesson! On one occasion, when I was a party in a lawsuit, I affirmed that the judge would rule in our favour. I sat in the courtroom staring at the judge, projecting this thought at him. I did this procedure for the entire duration of the trial. To everyone's surprise, the judge did rule in our favour and awarded us a sum of money. This led to my investing additional money to open a restaurant in Ferndale, Washington— which turned out to be the worst possible thing that could have happened. It caused me much worry, work, grief, heartache, and the loss of US$100,000.

I truly believe that, if I had added to my Affirmation the safety clause, "To the good of all parties concerned," the judge would have decided differently, which would definitely have been to my highest and best good. This was a very expensive, yet valuable, lesson.

When teaching Affirmations, I am very careful to stress the importance of always adding this very essential clause.

Being Grateful in Advance

Be thankful. Adopt an attitude of gratitude. It is easy to give thanks after you have received your blessings. Give thanks before. Write "Thank you" three times after every Master Affirmation. When you give thanks, you obligate the planet to bring you more. Have and maintain an attitude of gratitude and watch miracles happen in your life.

One day, my daughter Aren told me of something she just had to do for someone, right then. She was insistent. When I asked her why, she said, "I have to, Mother. They thanked me in advance and now I feel so obligated."
Gratitude is the willingness to be thankful for what you have and a celebration of lessons learned from life's experiences. Concentrate and focus on the things you have, rather than on the things you are lacking.

Long-Term Affirmations

You may wish to do some long-term Affirmations for projects or goals you wish to realize in six months, one year, or five years from now. As an example, you may wish to affirm that, in five years, after you retire, you live in a beautiful home on the beach. This may not be possible at this time due to career demands in your life, but will be later, when you retire.

Be prepared, however, to change and update your Affirmations as you change. Another example of a long-term goal would be that of a student affirming his or her successful career as a doctor, after finishing professional training. He or she could affirm a particular location to set up practice and so forth. You can affirm anything you desire, as long as you add the safety clause, "To the good of all parties concerned."

Many people do long-term goals or Affirmations for careers and other things, then put them away in a drawer and take them out years later. It proves very interesting to see how many of them have materialized. I wrote out some long-term goals five years ago. When I took them out recently and read them, I was truly amazed. All but two had manifested!

To obtain successful results, it is most important to accompany your desire with a viable, well-thought-out plan (AMCAM). The five building blocks of forgiveness, thoughts, mind-power, Affirmations, and creative visualization are crucial to success. It is also important to "blow breath" into your Affirmations by taking the appropriate action.

FAQs

• Can I Do Affirmations for Others?

You can do Support Master Affirmations for others, but only if they desire exactly what you are affirming. Every person has been given free choice.

• Where Can I Do My Affirmations?

You can do Affirmations anywhere, anytime. You can do them in the privacy of your own home, vehicle, while waiting at traffic lights, in a doctor's office, bathing, or while exercising.

• When Should I Do Them?

You can do Affirmations any time, whether you feel anxious and discouraged or happy and fulfilled. When you are happy, do Affirmations for continued happiness. If you are discouraged or feeling negative, do the appropriate Affirmation to lift your spirit.

The best time to do AMCAM is first thing in the morning and the last thing at night. You can do Affirmations any time you think of them and as many times as you wish. Say them over and over in your mind. You cannot overuse this incredible power. The more you use it, the more there is available for you to use.

• Who Can Do Affirmations?

Everyone and anyone, from a very young child to a senior citizen, can do Affirmations. I know a young child and a great-grandmother who are doing Affirmations. The great-grandmother changes her Affirmations weekly and most of them now are for her continued health and that of her loved ones.

• Why Is it Important to Do Affirmations?

Affirmations can reveal any negative blockages. You can then recognize, overcome, release, and forgive them. In their place, put loving kindness, peace, joy, and happiness. Now you are free to live the life you choose. Do Affirmations to make your fondest dreams come true.

Helpful Hints

- Take several deep breaths—*exhaling* negative, unwanted feelings and thoughts and *inhaling* positive, happy feelings and thoughts.
- Make a point of doing Affirmations at the same time each day.
- Clear your mind of all cares, worries, and burdens.
- Make certain you feel you deserve what you are affirming.
- Be specific and accurate.
- Utilize the physical senses.
- Keep it a secret, at least in the beginning.
- Speak your Affirmations out loud whenever possible because the spoken word drives images deep into the conscious and subconscious mind.
- Add to your Affirmations, "This or something better now manifests in my life."
- Be aware of and work with the Law of Cause and Effect (what you do is the cause and what happens as a result of that action is the effect).
- When you desire an effect, affirm for the cause, which brings about that effect.
- Make your Affirmations a win/win situation for all concerned.
- Make certain you have at least a 51 percent believability factor that the Affirmation will manifest.
- Never hurt or take from anyone.
- Affirm balance (strive for equanimity).
- Never compare yourself to others.
- Use descriptive words that trigger emotion, such as lovingly, joyously, easily, etc.
- Inject your Affirmations with love and say "Thank you" three times.
- Never concern yourself with how your heart's desire will manifest. Leave that up to the Universe.
- Develop and maintain an attitude of gratitude.

- Refrain from affirming *abilities* because you already have them. For example, you would not affirm, "I, (your name), deserve to be and can be happy." You already have the ability to be happy. If you did affirm in this manner, it would not make any difference in your life. Instead say, "I (your name), deserve to be and now am happy."

Whatever you choose, do it with enthusiasm and excitement. Luke-warm Affirmations or goals do not produce effective results.

One Step at a Time

Every journey begins with the first step—one step at a time, one miracle at a time. Be aware that every goal or Affirmation consists of several steps, each one based on the previous one. The first step of any journey or program is of prime importance. Once the steps are clearly formed in your mind like a picture, they are easy to follow.

These steps are the Master Plan (AMCAM) that carries you to the materialization of your goals and Affirmations.

One of my students told me that her Affirmations were coming true in stages or baby-steps. I advised her to put Step One, Step Two, and Step Three on her Master Affirmations and check off each step as it manifested for her. This is a faith-builder.

Everything in life is like a progression of steps. If you swallowed a large apple whole, you would choke. If you cut the apple up into bite-size pieces and ate one at a time, you would accomplish the task of eating the apple. A baby first crawls, walks, then runs. It is so important to do the first step, which is deciding what you really desire, then to do the appropriate Affirmation that produces the desired result.

Tackle one task at a time, one step at a time and one grain of sand at a time.

Once you have done your Master Affirmation, analyze it and break it down into steps. Number the steps in a way that is logical to you. If necessary, break it down into even smaller steps. Check out each part. Is it reasonable? Will it work?

Be flexible. Change and revise your Affirmations as often as necessary. As you change, your Affirmations change. Make adjustments and allow room for the unexpected. Welcome new ideas and be self-disciplined and persistent. Perseverance means hanging in there when all the odds appear to be stacked against you.

The Importance of Repetition

Repetition accelerates the energy and vibration already present to make your Affirmations manifest more quickly. We all know repetition is the mother of learning. When you repeat Affirmations, thought patterns are impressed on your subconscious mind. You are transforming your previously held beliefs, opinions, ideas, and concepts about that statement.

When you say Affirmations over and over, the words become a living presence in your awareness. Later, you become the words in the Affirmations. It is important to then turn it over to a higher power—God—for materialization. Repetition reinforces the belief system and convinces the mind that it is true. The Laws of the great Universe take care of the rest.

Repetition is accepted in every culture. Some forms of prayer are repeated many times. When people chant in rhythm, it helps them achieve a reflective state. In some types of meditation, the mantra is chanted. The process of doing Affirmations is not a one-time procedure or event. It requires constant repetition.

To make an Affirmation concrete, think, write, feel, and say it out loud with great feeling. Convince yourself of its truth and reality. There is no quick fix or spiritual fast-food method of doing Affirmations. It takes work, effort, and concentration. The results are well worth the effort.

Check Your Attachment to the Outcome

Could you be overly attached to the outcome of your goal or Affirmation? If so, release it and let it go with loving detachment into the Universe. You have now set free the mind-power you activated. Your subconscious mind can then support the image and make the desire of your Affirmation a reality. When you fret, worry, or feel too attached to the outcome of your Affirmation, you only hinder the process of manifestation.

Many people delay the completion of their desires by being rigidly attached to the exact outcome. Affirmations can manifest in a different manner than expected. Release your completed Affirmations into the Universe with loving detachment.

Assure your thoughts and Affirmations that they will find the perfect answer and return to you. Another way is to bless your Affirmations as you send them out into the Universe to manifest.

Blow Breath into Your Affirmations!

Affirmations are further empowered when you take action in accordance with your desires. For example, in addition to doing Affirmations when seeking that perfect relationship, blow breath into your Affirmations by accepting invitations, seeking out other single people, and going places where they are likely to be. Be conscious of other single people when shopping and travelling. Tell friends and relatives you are interested in meeting that special person.

Many people have found their partners and spouses on the Internet. It is important to exercise down-to-earth common sense when meeting new people. Make it happen! You can stand in an elevator all day and affirm, state, or demand that it rise to the third floor. But until the appropriate action is taken and you, or someone else, pushes the button for the third floor, it will not move.

Revising Your Affirmations

Affirmations should never be set in concrete. They should be updated, amended, revised, and changed as your life and circumstances change. When you change, your Affirmations change.

I remember doing one Affirmation for perfume, which worked so effectively that I ended up with 72 bottles of perfume. Everyone I knew and others I did not know gave me perfume as a gift. I said, "Please stop. I have enough perfume." Immediately, the perfume gifts stopped coming. If the occasion ever arises where I run out of perfume, I will simply start another Master Affirmation to bring it back into my life.

Never force Affirmations. Allow them to grow and unfold like a rosebud. You may wish to modify, erase, scratch out, start over, or change your Affirmations. Avoid allowing yourself to be locked into any Affirmation in which you have lost interest or for which the excitement has disappeared.

Negativity and Positivity Are Important

How can you know what it feels like to be positive if you have never experienced how it feels to be negative? When doing AMCAM, at times you may feel negative and think that your Affirmations are not working.

Negative thoughts can be red flags warning you to stop, slow down, change direction, or re-think. It is normal to have some negative thoughts. Everything in life is seeking a balance. The Universe is built on the principle of duality, which gives us choice in all things.

Everything that exists is balanced by its polar opposite. Light is balanced with darkness, male with female, hot with cold, failure with success, and disappointments with happiness.

When you feel negative, say, "Cancel, cancel. I am happy." It is important to add that you are happy, because nature abhors a vacuum and will rush in to fill the emptiness. When I am cancelling a thought, I usually clap my hands or stamp my foot to create energy and make my statement more powerful.

Learning to be positive takes time. Keep on practising a positive mental attitude. It will soon become an important part of your life and daily routine.

Do a quick check right now to see what frame of mind you are entertaining. If your thinking is in a negative mode, consciously change it into a positive one.

- Think of things you are thankful for.
- In your mind, create a sense of gratitude that you have already received those blessings.
- Enjoy the positive, peaceful feelings you are now experiencing.

It is so important to create and maintain an atmosphere of faith, peace, and happiness when doing AMCAM. This acts as extraordinary fertilizer for your fragile new seed-thoughts (Affirmations).

If you have a sour taste about anyone or anything, accept it, take responsibility for it, then get rid of it immediately. A sour taste can block you from your blessings.

Be patient with yourself. Positive people are in control of their lives. Positive thinking is not appropriate at all times. Refrain from being too rigidly attached to being absolutely positive all the time. If you are, it can be limiting and somewhat dangerous.

If you have a medical condition that needs attention, simply being positive may not be the total answer.

Affirmations of Denial

Old negative patterns can become so ingrained in your consciousness, it may be necessary to do some simple exercises to rid yourself of them. At times, it is important to do Affirmations of Denial. An Affirmation of Denial is a declaration of rejection, whereas a positive Affirmation is a declaration of acceptance.

Affirmations of Denial are used to free one's self of lack, limitations, false beliefs, and erroneous concepts.

Affirmations of Denial are powerful toxin cleansers and releasers. They are helpful in assisting us to uncover and unravel hidden blockages. Be prepared for some surprising, unexpected, disturbing feelings and memories from the past to surface when doing Affirmations of Denial. This process may uncover previous negative programming and work to diffuse it.

When you examine your denial statements, you can readily see where your blockages are, and then you can go about releasing them. Speak with authority. Tell negativity it has to go immediately. Affirmations of Denial will also show you with great certainty how deeply you desire the manifestation of your Affirmation. Learning is a matter of uncovering and discovering. Do the following exercise to discover where you have blockages.

• Accessing and Overcoming Blockages

Beside each of your Affirmations, write any mental objection that comes to mind.

My Affirmation: the Blockage

Affirmation	Objections
I am lovable.	No, I am not. Tom left me for a younger woman.
I am a good wife.	Tom said I was sloppy.
People love me.	No, everyone hates me.

Continue this exercise until there is no negativity left. Record and release all negativity in the right column and let it go completely. You will be happy to note that soon your right column will become more positive and will start to agree with your Affirmations.

In this manner, you are recognizing your negative feelings by writing them on a piece of paper. Examine each one of these statements, then take a deep breath and release them. Ask yourself how long you have held these thoughts and beliefs and how deeply they are ingrained. Where did they come from and do you still want them to be part of your being? If the answer is "No," release them today.

Now it could look like this.

My Affirmation: the Truth

I am lovable.	Two, kind, interesting men asked if I was single.
I am a good wife.	I am an excellent cook and housekeeper.
People love me.	I was invited to two parties this week.

Every one of us has, at one time or another, experienced blockages that keep us from loving self and others. Some of these blockages can actually prevent you from attaining your heart's desires.

Decide exactly what you desire. It is important to be specific. To make up your mind is a wondrous thing. It directs you toward your mental image and sets you on the path. Decision is an important part of everyday living. Every moment of every day, we are all making big and small decisions.

When you decide to accomplish something, you mentally toughen yourself to make it happen. It is important to know the meaning and spirit of your Affirmations. Look up the meaning of any unfamiliar words you use in your Affirmation, to ensure that you use powerful, descriptive words that you totally understand.

The Importance of Faith

Faith is the action of mind and heart that takes an idea, goal, or Affirmation as truth, accepts it, and acts upon it. When you have faith, you live in the mental and emotional state that would be yours if your desires were already fulfilled, even when sense perception gives evidence to the contrary. It is very important to add the element of faith to all your Affirmations. Develop faith and expectancy because they go hand in hand. Feel and accept the Affirmation as a completed reality.

Affirmations Work, Even if You Don't Believe!

Affirmations can manifest even when you doubt they can. The process of doing Affirmations is unique and individual. You can tailor AMCAM to suit your individual needs. After you do an Affirmation, feel what you are affirming as real and already existing in your mind, where all true cause resides.

Know that your image will manifest as you keep it sharp and clear in your mind's eye. Get the feeling you are not making something happen, but merely accepting and watching it happen.

Several years ago, I was doing an Affirmation about being a guest or speaker on a television program talking about the power of Affirmations. This idea was certainly far-fetched in my mind. At that time, I had no connection with anyone in the television business. I thought this one would never work, but I did it faithfully and repetitiously, using the exact procedure outlined in this book. I worked with the laws of the Universe and was careful to add, "to the good of all parties concerned." When I was visiting a bookstore in Bellingham, Washington, the owner of the store introduced me to a young man in search of an interesting topic for a television program. The four-hour, non-stop show I consequently hosted on the Power of Affirmations was divided into three segments. This program proved so much in demand that each segment was shown twice.

When people tell me they cannot do Affirmations because of their negative belief system or limited faith, my mind goes back to the television story. I have learned to expect the unexpected!

Focusing

If you hold a magnifying glass over a small portion of a newspaper outdoors on a sunny day, the paper will burn if the sunlight is strong enough. This is an example of focused energy. Nothing will happen if you hold the magnifying glass at a distance from the newspaper or move it quickly back and forth, because you are scattering the energy and power.

It is the same with Affirmations. You can work on many Affirmations at one sitting, but you must deal with one Affirmation at a time, so that you do not scatter the power of the focus. Should you place several Affirmations on one page, it can become confusing and you may dilute and scatter your focus.

When you do an Affirmation, focus and concentrate on what you desire. The results are powerful.

Monitoring Your Success

When my Affirmations manifest, I put a big check mark on the Master Affirmation with a felt pen, together with the date it actually happened. I place it in my Fulfilled Affirmation Book. To expand and increase my faith when I begin a new Affirmation, all I have to do is look back at all the Affirmations that have successfully manifested. It brings them to my attention and consciousness and also increases my faith. I have many huge, loose-leaf books containing Fulfilled Affirmations from all phases of my life. The good news is that you can have the same results.

Reinforcing Affirmations

Several of my students have reported great success from reinforcing their Affirmations in personal ways. One student found that, after she recorded her own Affirmations for a week or so, miracles began taking place in her life. Another student said she puts one of her daily Short-Form Affirmations under her pillow every night, then thinks about it and lulls herself to sleep saying it. She does the same one for seven days and then goes on to another Affirmation. Many people have reported exciting results with this Affirmation Pillow Method.

When you are in a state of sleep, forces (your thoughts) are still active. They are working on and with other minds, situations, and events. Your thought processes work on your desired Affirmation all night, prompted by your last thought before going to sleep. Use the same process with anything you desire—a new vehicle, money, more friends, or any material object.

Saturation Affirmation Program

In this procedure, you write out your Short-Form Affirmation 77 times for seven days consecutively. If you miss a day, start the whole procedure again. If your Affirmation is delayed, take another look at it. Is your Affirmation based on truth? Most of all, is it true for you? You may discover you need to re-write the Affirmation or stop for a period of time to allow it to manifest. Sometimes Affirmations materialize immediately after the Affirmation process is stopped.

Experiment with the process of writing with your dominant and then your non-dominant hand. This is a very powerful, useful exercise and can be used to release any deeply held emotional issues or fears. Using this process, I wrote out 30 Affirmations with the dominant hand—my right hand. Then I wrote 10 with the non-dominant hand (left hand), and the rest with the dominant hand. This process uses both sides of the brain.

When I did the Saturation Affirmation Program for releasing fear of claustrophobic conditions in my life, tears started rolling down my cheeks. This occurred when I was writing with my left hand (non-dominant hand). I began sobbing and a deep sense of pending danger encompassed me. A picture from my childhood flashed into my mind. I was seven years old and I heard the doctor telling my mother I was suffering from a burst appendix and that gangrene had developed. He also said there was not much hope for my recovery because it was too advanced.

I recalled, in vivid detail, the doctor and nurse strapping me down on a hospital bed, pouring chloroform on a cloth, and placing it over my mouth and nose. I relived that horrible feeling of losing control and consciousness. Could this be where my fear of closed-in spaces originated? The negative feeling of fear and terror quickly subsided when I reverted back to writing with my dominant hand. I later learned that using the non-dominant hand accesses old hurts, unpleasant issues, memories, and situations from childhood years.

Team-Effort Affirmations Manifest (TEAM)

Masterminding

Team-Effort Affirmations Manifest (TEAM) that which they affirm. This is where groups of people of like mind get together and affirm for a specific goal or mutual desire. This could be to raise funds for a new hospital, church, or school or find a cure for a disease or help feed starving children. It could also be a company's project or sales goal. Some people refer to this type of group affirming as master-minding. Collective, positive energy—focused and concentrated on a single goal with single-mindedness, faith, and determination—does manifest.

I suggest that people start their own Affirmation Group with friends, to affirm positive, collective goals for making a difference in the world.

11:00 pm Daily Affirmation/Prayer Group (In our minds)

At 11:00 pm (Pacific Time), we do a Group Affirmation/Prayer with people from all over the world. We have developed an Affirmation/Prayer Card. These Cards are ideal reminders for those who wish to join our nightly Affirmation/Prayer Group. Reverend Eva Grace Johnson and I started the Affirmation/Prayer Group in Washington State in 1989.

We join in our minds and affirm for divine wisdom and divine order to our world leaders, peace in the world, healing, love and respect to Mother Earth, and a cure for Cancer, AIDS, and other diseases.

We join with anyone—anywhere in the world—who, at that moment, is thinking thoughts of peace and love. We send peace and love to every corner of the world. Many thoughts joined together are magnified tenfold.

We have been doing this Affirmation/Prayer for the past 16 years every night, without fail. Thousands of people worldwide join us every night. It is very powerful. Many miracles have been reported.

Please join us in your mind whenever you wish.

Do email me at annemarieevers@shaw.ca with your individual prayer/Affirmation requests. We will add them to our nightly list.

We look forward to affirming with you.

Be Consistent

If you keep on doing your Affirmations when things are wonderful in your life, you stay on track—and you may not have to experience the bumps, potholes, detours, etc., that may be needed to keep you on track.

There are three important keys to the success of the manifestation of your Affirmations.

1. Burning desire
2. Focused imagination
3. Excited expectancy

Keep on doing AMCAM, properly and repeatedly, and your Affirmations will succeed. It is just a matter of time. Remember how the lowly seed, when planted in the rich, fertile soil of the earth, brings forth after its kind. When you plant potatoes, you do not dig up turnips. You will reap what you sow. It is the Law! Walk in your Affirmations on a daily basis.

Keep an open mind, reminding yourself that closed minds do not inspire belief and results. An Affirmation is a decree, command, or a demand of the Universe. According to its nature and structure, it has no choice other than to fulfill that demand, according to what is desired and affirmed.

Now that 95 percent of my Affirmations have materialized, I have started a whole new set this year. Most of these are for other people. I affirm continued health and happiness for my family, friends, others, and myself. I am also affirming having the perfect vehicle for transmitting my message about the power of Affirmations to all those people worldwide who are open and ready to enhance their lives.

The greatness of your Affirmations will be reflected in the greatness of your life!

Affirmations When Properly Done Always Work!

Heart Song

I listened to my inner voice
Sing its melody of love,
Revealing a wonder-filled vision of life
Filled with peace, light, prosperity,
Joy.

Holding on tight,
I cast myself into that turbulent sea of work.
After all, it was only a vision—time now for me
To strive, push, exert.

But something was wrong,
Or at least not quite right.
For no matter how hard I tried (and I tried!)
My goals and dreams seemed unreachable,
Elusive illusions
Existing only at the border to my subconscious.

What magic secret lies
At the heart of life's success?
A seed-thought of an answer:
You create what you believe is true.

I'd believed myself not worthy
Not deserving of God's love or hope,
Or a clear vision of my purpose.
And then a realization of the Power of the Mind:
I'd manifested exactly what I chose.

A change in belief, then a change in thought.
An affirmation of my personal truth
Reinforced consistently, regularly
Brings success now to what I do.

Acting as if
My life is meant to be
The way I envision it,
Miracles happen.
I give of myself without stress.
Universal Mind responds
In divine order
To the highest good of all.

My heart sings ... with joy.

Shae Hadden

Applying AMCAM

part 2

**in
Your
Life**

Overcoming Fear, Phobias, and Negative Habits

Boosting Self-Respect

Relationships: Marriage, Family, and Others

Material Wealth & Career and Business

Cards of Life

www.affirmations-doctor.com

Affirmations, Your Passport to Happiness

8 • *Overcoming Fear, Phobias, and Negative Habits*

A. Overcoming Fear and Phobias

Fear Born of Worry

When you allow worry to get out of control, it turns into fear.

When I was on holiday, driving across Canada, my daughter Aren became concerned about my safety because she had not heard from me for several weeks. She began to worry and paint negative pictures of me in an accident, injured, or in the hospital.

Then she remembered what I had taught her and immediately changed her negative thoughts to powerful, positive ones. She visualized that I was driving safely, seeing fantastic scenery, enjoying myself, and having a wonderful vacation. She then relaxed and stopped worrying.

The next time someone you love is late coming home, start thinking positive, powerful thoughts. Know that your loved one is safe, happy, and protected. Visualize that person surrounded in God's love, peace, joy, and protection.

If you spend too much time worrying, write down everything that is worrying you. Date your list of worries and file it away in a drawer for a year. When the year is up, take out the list, read it over, and see how unimportant most of your worries turned out to be. You will realize that approximately 90 percent of what you worried about never happened. The other 10 percent that actually did happen was not the least bit affected by your worry. So why worry!?

Casting Out Fear

Divine love casts out all fear. It penetrates and destroys all negativity. I read somewhere that humans are like tea bags; they do not know their strength until they get into hot water. Do what you fear the most, over and over again, and it will lose its power over you.

Uncontrolled fear is a negative emotion. It is the greatest cause of the life force becoming blocked, stagnant, or unbalanced and is often at the root of poverty, lack, and failure. Fear is caused by being separate from God or the Universal life force.

It can also be the result of giving your power away. Your power is always present in the now; you can change your state of being by focusing your attention on positive, happy, loving thoughts and emotions.

Give yourself permission to be happy if you did not receive it from important people in your childhood or life. If you did not receive approval from your parents, you may wish to write yourself a letter from either your mother or father or both.

In this letter, you say how much the parent loves you and how proud he or she is of you. Then write a letter to that parent, thanking him or her for their love. This exercise is purely for you. The letters are never mailed or given to the parent.

The Many Faces of Fear

Fear is a natural emotion as we grow and challenge ourselves with new situations and environments. Structured, controlled, normal fear can be used to your advantage. Fear causes you to sit up and take notice and to make decisions and discriminating choices about your actions and life. If fear is kept in its rightful place, it can be a helpful, positive tool.

Uncontrolled, negative fear, however, can create negative conditions and warp and distort your vision. It can generate negative Affirmations in your mind, leading to negative outcomes. It can also cause constriction of the blood vessels and make you physically ill. It inhibits the immune system and the regeneration of cells and creates poison that can be injurious to your organs and general health.

When you feel the emotion of fear and bless it, it can be transformed and eventually become peace. We have all heard the meaning of fear—False Evidence Appearing Real. I personally refer to fear as Find Enlightening Answers Readily.

Sometimes, fear can be a warning that should be heeded. In these cases, it protects you. Strive to make friends with your fear. Accept and understand fear and write out your feelings about it.

You were born with only two fears: the fear of noise and the fear of falling. All other fears are learned from your parents, environment, teachers, friends, peers, and anyone who influenced your early years. Fear—the greatest enemy—is behind sickness, failure, low self-esteem, broken marriages, poor human relationships, poverty, lack, and negative actions.

Some people even suffer from fear of success, health, and happiness. Others fear everything—living, loss, dying, beginnings, endings, change, being stuck, people, commitment, loneliness, and the unknown. Face what you are afraid of until you are no longer afraid of it. When you understand the situation surrounding your fear and can face and deal with it, it loses its power over you.

Fear of Loss of Relationship

When people experience fear over losing their spouse, it is rarely the spouse that they are afraid of losing. Usually, they fear the loss of their own feelings of being loved, cherished, and protected by that person.

Look at and examine fear. If you fear losing your happiness, you never really had happiness at all. What you have is simply a false security based on familiar scenes, situations, and thoughts that have become habit. Real happiness comes from within. What you really desire is self-acceptance and self-love.

One of the best cures for overcoming fear is to learn to laugh at it. You are the only decision-maker in your Universe! You have the choice to control your fear and choose happiness!

Phobias

A phobia is an exaggerated, inexplicable, and illogical fear of people, animals, objects, or situations. Phobias affect millions of people, preventing them from being their true selves and fulfilling their potential. As a result, these people become servants to their fears.

A phobia could be a conditioned reflex set up by some frightening past experience, usually from childhood. When you are unable to release a phobia, you may require professional help.

Most Common Phobias

Acrophobia	Fear of heights
Ailurophobia	Fear of cats
Agoraphobia	Fear of open spaces
Bacteriophobia	Fear of germs
Claustrophobia	Fear of crowded or confined spaces
Cynophobia	Fear of dogs
Erythrophobia	Fear of blushing
Hematophobia	Fear of blood
Llyssophobia	Fear of rabies
Mysophobia	Fear or dirt and contamination
Nyctophobia	Fear of dark
Xenophobia	Fear of strangers
Zoophobia	Fear of animals

Daniel's Fear of Dogs

Daniel was a young realtor who suffered from severe cynophobia (fear of dogs). It was affecting his career. Part of his business as a realtor was practising the art of door-knocking. While this phobia might not interfere with the earnings of a person in another occupation, it did interfere with Daniel's.

He told me he had to limit his real estate activities to apartments, townhouses, and condos, where he felt safe from dogs. This was limiting his income and keeping him from his heart's desire of being top salesperson. Ironically, whenever Daniel was in the vicinity of a dog, that dog would head straight for him, growling and snarling. It was as if the dog sensed Daniel's deep, real fear. His fear was attracting to him the very thing he most feared.

After doing an Affirmation for two months to overcome his phobia (see Daniel's Master Affirmation in this chapter), Daniel noticed a marked improvement in his attitude toward dogs. He was actually drawn to them and they responded accordingly. When he went knocking on doors and ran into dogs, not one attacked him. They barked and bared their teeth, but Daniel's confidence shone through and the dogs posed no threat to him.

Daniel is doing another Affirmation to become top salesperson. He refuses to let dogs control his life. Now, Daniel is back in control.

Tanya Harmon Writes:

"I was delighted and a bit relieved to find an Affirmation directed to getting over the fear of dogs, something it has taken me years to work through on my own!"

Watch Your Self-Talk

Do not allow negative thoughts of fear and worry to enter or to stay in your mind. Stop beating yourself up with statements like "I should have—Why didn't I?," "I wish I had," "I messed up," etc.

Instead, say: "It is okay. The next time I will do it differently."

When you do your Affirmations faithfully and talk to yourself gently with loving kindness, your whole attitude toward life changes. You begin to act differently.

Hold a strong belief that your wish is manifesting now. Step out of the way and allow it to take place. Be totally willing to receive and accept the manifestation of your Affirmation and all it brings with it. Expect miracles on a daily basis.

Be aware of the self-talk of your friends, family, and associates. If they dwell on fear and negativity, cancel their words in your mind, repeating, "I am healthy, prosperous, happy, and loving.

Change your negative thoughts to happy, positive, loving thoughts and you will be absolutely thrilled with the incredible results!

Banishing Fears

• The Fear Dragon Exercise

Fear can be a block that keeps you from doing something you wish to do. For example, a fear of flying could prevent you from experiencing many wonderful travelling experiences.

Imagine your fear in front of you; see it in the form of a *fear dragon*. How big is it? What colour is it? What shape is it? How close is it? Can you feel its breath? How hot is it? Do you feel uncomfortable? Now *mentally* take a club and place it in one of your hands and push the *fear dragon* away from you. You do not wish to burn yourself. You are stronger than any *fear dragon*.

Ask it to speak to you. Say, "Have you anything to say to me?" Listen with your inner ear. Now be firm with the *fear dragon*. Inform it that it has no place in your body or around you and that it has to go.

If the *fear dragon* tries to hang around, say again, "You must go. You are not welcome in or around my being." Say, "*Fear dragon*, you have no power over me. You are helpless. I am the powerful force here and you must obey me. I am the boss." Be firm and the *fear dragon* will vanish completely. Now, in its place, create an image of what you wish to accomplish.

For example, see yourself on an airplane embarking on some exciting adventure. See yourself surrounded by a pink, soft bubble—being safe and content, enjoying the flight to wherever you desire.

This technique is very effective in banishing any limiting fears, and helping you achieve what you want.

• The Fear Zoo Exercise

You might wish to put your fears into proper perspective by forming your own fear zoo—a place where you can put all your fears. You may fear a wild tiger in the jungle but would you fear a tiger in a cage in a zoo? My own fear zoo is where I place all my fears.

I visualize my fear of closed-in spaces as a ferocious tiger, my fear of rejection as an angry gorilla, and my fear of dying as a giant giraffe. I visualize my fear of poverty and lack as two grizzly bears and any other smaller fears as cantankerous, quarrelsome monkeys. I visit them as often as possible. I look forward to our conversations and discussions! I consider them great, valuable teachers and learn from my experiences with them.

At times, I just sit quietly among them, feeling their presence and allowing them to feel and experience my presence. When you give fear a name and form and speak directly to it, its hold over you is lessened and its power is scattered.

What is your greatest fear? Name it, give it form, and speak directly to it in a controlled, safe atmosphere.

What animals will you choose? Your fear becomes manageable when you do this exercise. As long as you continue to grow and learn, fear will be your constant companion. Isn't it better to manage and control fear than to let it control you?

When we taught the Fear Zoo Exercise to a third grade class, one student visualized her fear of heights as a huge giraffe. After doing this exercise, she discovered to her absolute delight that her intense fear of heights had completely vanished.

Become *phobia-free* by doing the following Master and Short-Form Affirmations.

Master and Short-Form Affirmations

Overcoming Fear

"I, (your name), deserve to be and now am happy. My life is full, rich, and rewarding. I live in the now. Any and all negative, unwanted fear leaves my body and I am 100 percent healthy. I enjoy being calm, peaceful, and phobia-free. I thank God daily for all my blessings and fully accept them. I enjoy being abundantly wealthy and successful. I am completely free of fear and safe. I am happy, to the good of all parties concerned. Thank you, thank you, thank you. "

Short-Form Affirmation: **Free of fear, happy, peaceful, and thankful**

Daniel's Master Affirmation (for a fear of dogs)

"I, Daniel, deserve to be and now am a friend of all dogs. I like and respect dogs and they like and respect me. I am safe. Any fear of dogs now completely leaves my body. I radiate loving kindness, peace, and joy to everyone and every dog. I am free of any fear of being attacked by dogs. I am 100 percent safe and I door-knock with ease. I go about my business door-knocking in the secure knowledge that I am safe, protected, and happy, to the good of all parties concerned. Thank you, thank you, thank you."

Short-Form Affirmation: **Happy, harmonious dogs**

Overcoming Phobias

"I, (your name), deserve to be and now am completely in control of my life. I am calm, peaceful, and relaxed in every situation. Whenever a feeling of panic appears in my body, I immediately release it and fill myself with the peace of God. I am safe and I give myself permission to be happy. I am calm, peaceful, and 100 percent healthy. Fear is powerless over me. I am phobia-free. I love being in full control of my body. I am happy, to the good of all parties concerned. Thank you, thank you, thank you."

Short-Form Affirmation: **100 percent healthy, calm, and peaceful**

Overcoming Claustrophobia

"I, (your name), deserve to be and now am free of any fear of closed-in spaces, elevators, airplanes, and crowded rooms. When I get in an elevator, I take a deep breath, breathe out all negativity, take another deep breath, and breathe in God's peace and tranquillity. I bless, love, and respect the elevator. I thank it for taking me safely and peacefully to the floor I desire. All fears of darkness are completely dissolved. I am safe, peaceful, and secure everywhere. I am peaceful, to the good of all parties concerned. Thank you, thank you, thank you."

Short-Form Affirmation: **Safe, calm, relaxed, and peaceful**

B. Overcoming Negative Habits

You have the Power

You are a powerful lighthouse that withstands the storms of life. You can overcome the waves of negative habits and emerge strong, steadfast, and bright. By shining your light into negative habits, you can make them evaporate before your eyes.

Addictions are among the most destructive negative habits, representing a dependency on some substance, person, or activity that causes harm or interference in a person's life. Most addicts suffer from psychological reversals that block or sabotage their potential. Breaking their addiction requires a positive outlook, personal commitment, and an awareness of the factors motivating the destructive habit. When blockages are recognized, they can be removed.

The following Affirmations, if practised regularly, can help you overcome a range of negative habits and emotions.

Master and Short-Form Affirmations

Alcoholism

Some people become alcoholics because they have an unconscious wish to punish or destroy themselves. Excessive alcohol suppresses fear, anger, frustration, and many other emotions, blocking a person's ability to experience unresolved issues. A drink of whisky, to some, is a shot of courage. The children of alcoholics can suffer enormous emotional trauma and psychological damage. Some experience the need to be perfect, are very self-critical, and have low self-esteem. They may be unhappy, but do not know why. They exhibit the need to be people-pleasers and may have an addiction to one or more negative habits. They are also prone to long periods of depression.

If alcohol is interfering with your life and the lives of your loved ones and if you want to eliminate your unhealthy addiction and regain control of your life, you must first admit you have a problem. When you decide to become and remain alcohol-free, doing Affirmations can help you achieve your goal, if you are determined to take positive action to overcome the problem (such as joining an AA group).

"I, (your name), deserve and now enjoy sobriety and peace of mind. I give myself permission to be alcohol-free. I am safe and have full control over my tastes and desires. I am still powerful. Any desire for alcohol leaves my body. I do all things that promote my well-being. I believe in myself and my future. I enjoy being, and now am alcohol-free. I am free from the dependency of alcohol. I actually dislike the taste of alcoholic beverages. My body heals and I am 100 percent healthy, to the good of all parties concerned. Thank you, thank you, thank you."

Short-Form Affirmation: **Alcohol-free, self-control, peace, and happiness**

Anger Control

Anger is a negative emotion that can cause all types of health problems. It is a deadly toxin in the body. Your body will be a lot healthier if you can learn to recognize anger, become aware of it, release it, and let it go completely. Anger could be an "internal boil" or prompter from negative people, situations, or circumstances from your past. We all enter this life with agendas, filled slates, and things to experience. Refrain from becoming involved in another's anger. Use Affirmations to help you deal with this dangerous emotion in healthy, positive ways.

"I, (your name), deserve to be and now am in full control of my feelings and emotions. I am balanced and happy. When I become angry, I find natural ways to vent my feelings. I am safe. I trust and believe in myself and others. I live and let live. I enjoy being in control of my life. I am peaceful and happy, to the good of all parties concerned. Thank you, thank you, thank you."

Short-Form Affirmation: **Balanced, wonderful control of my emotions**

Affirmation Avoidance

Do you find it a chore to do your *Personal Contract Affirmation Method* daily? You have approximately 900 waking minutes per day. Can you not take even five to 10 minutes to concentrate on what you wish to create in your life? You change your life as you decree. Write your own story.

"I, (your name), deserve to do and now enjoy doing my *Personal Contract Affirmation Method* daily with patience, feeling, belief, and faithfulness. I totally accept the manifestation of all my Affirmations. I am happy, to the good of all parties concerned. Thank you, thank you, thank you."

Short-Form Affirmation: **The wonderful power of Affirmations is mine.**

Blood Pressure Imbalances

Reducing your salt intake, dropping 10 to 15 pounds, and exercising regularly all help in lowering blood pressure. Minimizing negative stress, anxiety, and worry also helps, particularly in conjunction with a positive Affirmation program.

"I, (your name), deserve and now have and enjoy normal blood pressure. I am calm, relaxed, and peaceful. I am at ease in all situations and handle them in a peaceful, relaxed manner. I desire fresh fruits and vegetables in place of salty, fried food. I give my body permission to be 100 percent healthy. I meditate each morning and evening. I enjoy and participate in an exercise program tailored especially for me. I live every day to the fullest, to the good of all parties concerned. Thank you, thank you, thank you."

Short-Form Affirmation: **Normal, healthy blood pressure**

Caffeine Addiction

Many of us enjoy coffee and feel we cannot start the day without it. Caffeine is a powerful drug that does not appear to be harmful when used in moderation. But if you are addicted to coffee, colas, and chocolate, rather than merely enjoying them, you may wish to look at how your addiction is affecting your life and your health. When you drink coffee, you get a lift. This is simply the result of stored sugar being released from your liver, which puts stress on the adrenal glands and other organs. Many doctors feel caffeine is a factor in hypertension and heart disease, while other doctors feel it is a key to staying younger and is actually good for you.

"I, (your name), deserve and now enjoy drinking fresh fruit juices in place of coffee products containing caffeine. I am wide awake, alert, and 100 percent present. I drink coffee in moderation. I crave fresh, sparkling water, and fruit juices. I have strong, steady nerves. I am healthy and happy, to the good of all parties concerned. Thank you, thank you, thank you."

Short-Form Affirmation: **Coffee and caffeine products in moderation**

Cell Phone Addiction

Cell phones have become commonplace in our society and, in some cases, are a necessity. It has been reported that extensive use of cell phones can be detrimental to health.

"I, (your name), deserve and now use my cell phone in moderation. When driving, I exercise courtesy to other drivers and the public by limiting my calls or pulling off the road to talk. I am thankful for this wonderful communication tool and I treat it with respect. I am peaceful, to the good of all parties concerned. Thank you, thank you, thank you."

Short-Form Affirmation: **Respectful use of cell phone**

Computer (Internet) Addiction

The subconscious mind is similar to a computer hooked up to the Internet. The Internet is a great tool and has the latest information, procedures, and data on virtually every subject of interest. On the Internet, you can meet people, do advertising, purchase merchandise, or research an issue. It is like being in the largest library in the Universe and having thousands of books at your fingertips. Some people, however, allow their minds to become totally absorbed with the Internet. Others cut themselves off from society and become obsessed with it. If you find yourself in this position, a positive Affirmation can help you regain a healthy balance in your life.

"I, (your name), deserve and now use my computer and the Internet to my highest and best use. It is my friend. I respect it and use it to glean information on any subject I choose, to increase my business, communication, and writing. I am perfectly balanced. I exercise moderation in all phases of my life. I still have time for family, friends, recreation, exercise, and everything I choose. I am happy, to the good of all parties concerned. Thank you, thank you, thank you."

Short-Form Affirmation: **Safe, balanced, informative use of computer/Internet**

Concentration-Challenged

Do you experience problems concentrating on your Affirmations, goals, and desires? If so, you may be scattering and wasting your energy, rather than focusing it on achieving your goals. Concentration involves putting all your thoughts on one particular subject or object until an idea is developed. This enables you to focus on what you want and how to get it.

"I, (your name), deserve and now have fantastic concentration powers. I focus all my energies on whatever I choose and this ability increases daily. I am very powerful and use my tools and gift of concentration to the good of all parties concerned. Thank you, thank you, thank you."

Control Issues

When you attempt to control or dominate another person, you are simply demonstrating your own insecurities. Watch how hard you have to work at controlling another. The only person you can control is yourself. Release that feeling of attempting to control others.

One of the most vicious acts a person can do is to place another human being under the threat of fear. Never allow yourself to be placed or kept in that position by anyone. You are never responsible for any situation that you have neither the power nor the authority to change.

"I, (your name), deserve to have and now take control of every situation in my life. When I cannot change the situation, I simply change how I view and feel about it. I am assertive in my desires, yet kind, considerate, and loving. My opinions and ideas are valuable. I believe in me. I am strong, positive, and full of self-confidence. I am happy, to the good of all parties concerned. Thank you, thank you, thank you."

Short-Form Affirmation: **Complete control of my life and situations**

Couch-Potato Syndrome

- Are you a couch potato?
- Have you lost your interest in life?
- Do you come home from work and position yourself on the couch and remain there all evening?
- Are you too listless to exercise?

Change your outlook today and start creating the kind of life that will bring you joy and excitement. Become actively involved in making things happen and infusing your body with energy and vitality.

"I, (your name), deserve and now enjoy optimum health. I am vibrant, happy, and involved in life. I have loads of positive, pure energy. I enjoy doing the exercises that are tailored to my lifestyle, age, mind, and body. I involve myself in outside activities that interest and stimulate me. I am happy, to the good of all parties concerned. Thank you, thank you, thank you."

Short-Form Affirmation: **Full, active, involved, healthy life**

Creativity Suppression

Is there a creative genius lying dormant in you, just waiting to be set free? We all have hidden talents that, for many reasons, we ignore or overlook. You may be a budding artist, a talented musician, writer, or super seamstress, but unless you give your creativity some expression, you may never know just how talented you are. Realize your creative abilities today.

"I, (your name), deserve and now have a great creative genius inside me, who is always creating new, fresh, innovative ideas. I tune into the Creative Universal Mind from whence all knowledge comes. Great ideas come to me easily and effortlessly. I believe in myself and my abilities. I am safe. I give myself permission to release my creative energy and I use it now to the good of all parties concerned. Thank you, thank you, thank you."

Short-Form Affirmation: **Fresh, new, creative, interesting ideas**

Criticism

Criticism is a reflection of one's own insecurities and is a negative, unhealthy habit. To understand a person's mind, you first need to understand your own mind. When you are criticized, stop and ask yourself whether it was constructive criticism. If your mind is clear and free of cobwebs, you will know instantly if the criticism is centred in truth. Refrain from indulging in hurtful criticism of others and self.

The Sandwich Method

When it is absolutely necessary to give constructive criticism, sandwich it with praise.

For example, if your daughter has a very messy room, you might say:

1. "Holly, you are such a wonderful daughter." (one slice of bread)
2. "Your room is quite disorganized and messy." (the sandwich ingredient)
3. "You always pride yourself in being such an organized, clean person, so I know you will clean up your room." (the other slice of bread)

You have sandwiched your constructive criticism with praise, which is very different from simply saying, "Holly, your room is a mess. It looks terrible, so clean it up right now!"

"I, (your name), deserve to love and now love myself. I accept constructive criticism and use it to my benefit. I am not locked into other people's opinions. I am balanced, happy, and peaceful. I believe in myself. I love and respect myself, to the good of all parties concerned. Thank you, thank you, thank you."

Short-Form Affirmation: **Centred, balanced, and happy**

Depression

Depression has biological and impersonal roots. It can also be "frozen rage," whereby strong negative emotions are suppressed and pent up inside. It is important to get to the root of depression. Do you feel everything is hopeless, that there is no point in getting up in the morning or no light at the end of the tunnel? Do you see only the dark side of life, make mountains out of molehills, feel that you are drowning, and that everyone is grabbing for a piece of you? If you answered "Yes" to these questions, you need help. When suffering from depression, consult your doctor, health practitioner, and/or a counsellor. Find out about the many new vitamin supplements and exciting treatment programs now available.

> "I, (your name), deserve to be and now am happy. I take time to stop and smell the roses. I am safe. I give myself permission to be happy. I handle every situation with enthusiasm, efficiency, and loving kindness. I see clearly the positive end result. I make the right decisions easily, at the right time, with the right people. I am worthy. I enjoy being free of depression and illness. My body enjoys happy, healthy, positive thoughts. I am important. I am peaceful, happy, and relaxed, to the good of all parties concerned. Thank you, thank you, thank you."

Short-Form Affirmation: **Happy, peaceful, healthy**

Driving Irresponsibly

Driving is stressful enough without the added stress of talking on a cell phone. Instead, use the time to listen to positive audio tapes in the car.

If you find yourself getting overtired when driving, pull over to the side of the road or go to a restaurant for a cup of coffee or tea. Many people are killed in road accidents because of drivers who fall asleep at the wheel.

If you end up driving the wrong way down one-way streets, you need help. Contact a defensive driving school to learn about courses that will improve your driving skills.

Do your driving Affirmation faithfully.

> "I, (your name), deserve to be and now am mentally alert and wide awake while driving my vehicle. When driving, I always wear my seat belt. My driving is defensive and confident. I am safe. I give myself permission to be an excellent driver. I am courteous and considerate on the road. I limit talking on my cell phone or I pull off to the side of the road to talk. My senses are clear and alert when I get behind the wheel of my automobile. I react quickly and accurately to any situation that may arise. I love driving and it gives me a sense of power that I respect and

use to the good of all parties concerned. Thank you, thank you, thank you."

Short-Form Affirmation: **Safe, confident, protected driver**

Drug Addiction

Are harmful drugs adversely affecting your health or the lives of your loved ones?

The first step in overcoming drug addiction is usually the hardest. It involves acknowledging the problem, then deciding to take action to overcome it. Unless the individual concerned decides to stop using drugs, no program, doctor, or medicine will be effective. The decision has to come from the person using the drugs. The following Affirmation can help.

"I, (your name), deserve to be and now am honest and truthful. I make wise and healthy decisions. I easily refuse all harmful drugs. I am happy with my life and am in complete control of it. I believe in myself. I am safe. I know it is my decision and mine alone to get off and stay off of harmful drugs. My body is now drug-free. When I attend parties or social gatherings, I easily refuse any form of drugs. I take only medication prescribed by my doctor. I am forever free of any dependency on drugs. My eyes are bright, clear, and focused. I am happy, to the good of all parties concerned. Thank you, thank you, thank you."

Short-Form Affirmation: **Drug-free, happy, fulfilled life**

Empty Nest Syndrome

Have your children left home to pursue their own careers and lives? Many parents, especially mothers who have spent their lives as homemakers, feel the pain of loss when this happens. This should, however, be a happy time for all. You now have the opportunity to pursue your goals and wishes and to do all the things you dreamed of doing! Live each day to the fullest!

"I, (your name), deserve to have and now have happy free time for myself. I now pursue all my unfulfilled dreams. I enjoy and savour memories from the past, but I refrain from dwelling on them. I live in the now and enjoy life today. I think of exciting new ventures to fill my days and ways to help others. My family is safe, secure, and happy. I release them with loving kindness to their highest good. My spouse or friends and I now enjoy our quiet time together, to the good of all parties concerned. Thank you, thank you, thank you."

Short-Form Affirmation: **Happy, fulfilled, exciting life**

Envy

Envy is an indication of self-doubt. It is not a healthy emotion. If, for example, you envy someone with a beautiful home, you doubt your own ability to acquire such a home for yourself. Strive, instead, to genuinely admire others' possessions and accomplishments.

Rather than thinking that the grass is always greener on the other side of the fence, why not fertilize and care for the grass on your side of the fence? Being envious is a waste of valuable energy. Learn how to rejoice in others' happiness and prosperity, thus ensuring happiness for yourself. When you wish and affirm positive thoughts for others, happiness flows to you.

"I, (your name), deserve to be and now am happy for my friends and their good fortune. It is wonderful that they are so successful. They deserve health, wealth, and happiness. I am so happy they won money, dropped all that weight, or got that promotion. I believe in myself and live in the now. I am safe. I wish them greater and greater success, health, and happiness. I deserve and now have health, wealth, and happiness, to the good of all parties concerned. Thank you, thank you, thank you."

Short-Form Affirmation: **Peaceful, fulfilled, happy, and envy-free**

Fear and Worry

Do fear and worry control your life? Is your mind filled with thoughts of terrible things that have never happened? Do the Fear

Zoo Exercise; put your fears into your own Fear Zoo and make friends with them.

Write down everything you are worrying about, date the page, and put it away in a drawer. Then take it out in a year's time and read it. You will discover that 90 percent of what you worried about never happened and that the 10 percent that did happen was not the least bit affected by your worry.

"I, (your name), deserve to be able to and now handle all situations of life. I am confident, calm, safe, and secure. Faith, belief, and confidence radiate from my being. My mind is busy replacing negative thoughts with positive ones. I give myself permission to be happy. I enjoy being free of worry and fear. I believe in myself. I love life and living in the present. I look forward to wonderful things taking place in my life. I am happy, worry-free, and peaceful, to the good of all parties concerned. Thank you, thank you, thank you."

Short-Form Affirmation: **100 percent peaceful and worry-free**

Friendships

Friendships are very important and true friends are precious gifts. All friendships, however, require work and commitment. To have a friend, you must first be a friend.

"I, (your name), deserve and now have many loyal, supportive friends. I respect and understand my friends as they understand and respect me. I now magnetize the right friendships into my life. I am popular. I have happy, lasting, worthwhile friendships, to the good of all parties concerned. Thank you, thank you, thank you."

Short-Form Affirmation: **Loyal, trusted friends**

Gambling

Usually money won through gambling does not bring happiness. Although people may win money at slot machines, bingo, lottery tickets, or through the stock market, we do not hear about how much was paid to win. Make up your mind today to control your gambling. Gamble in moderation and with money you can afford to lose. When you feel the urge to gamble, stop and think about what you could buy with the money you will spend. Then do your Affirmations with that goal in mind. In this way, you bypass the money and go right to the object of your attention.

"I, (your name), deserve to be and now am free of the uncontrollable urge or desire to gamble. I spend money wisely. I do everything in moderation and that includes gambling. I am completely balanced and peaceful. I am in control of my life, mind, body, and my spending. I am happy and peaceful, to the good of all parties concerned. Thank you, thank you, thank you."

Short-Form Affirmation: **In full control of my life and spending habits**

Gossip

Gossip is "thought poison"—a negative habit that is best avoided. If you do listen to gossip, be careful to avoid spreading it. Do not engage in gossip or judgment of others. Instead, focus on the good qualities in individuals, situations, and circumstances.

"I, (your name), deserve to respect and now respect others. I never involve myself in gossip in any form. I search for and focus on the good qualities and characteristics of others. I respect and honour my friends. I keep secrets and never betray their confidence. I am happy and fulfilled, to the good of all parties concerned. Thank you, thank you, thank you."

Short-Form Affirmation: **Respect and confidentiality**

Impatience

We are living in an impatient world. Are you impatient waiting for that perfect partner to appear? The impatient state of mind will either drive your desires away from you or delay them. Could this be the reason your Affirmation has not yet materialized?

Do one thing at a time. Longing infers impatience because things do not come as quickly as desired. Do you absolutely detest standing and waiting in long line-ups or waiting for traffic lights that never seem to change? Do you feel your blood boil while waiting for that person who is never on time? Learn to change what you can and accept what you cannot change.

"I, (your name), deserve to be and now am calm and patient under stress. I am a very patient person. I know patience is a virtue and I am a virtuous person. I am balanced and peaceful. I accept circumstances that cannot be changed and change those situations I can, with ease. I believe in myself and my decisions. My nerves are calm and relaxed. I love being patient, to the good of all parties concerned. Thank you, thank you, thank you."

Short-Form Affirmation: **Patient, peaceful, happy self**

Inability to Say "No"

Do you have trouble using the simple word "No"? It is your God-given right to say "No" when you please. Do you go places, do things, or visit people you are not interested in because you are unable to say "No"? Think of the person you are disappointing the most—you! You are the only decision-maker in your Universe. Use "No" whenever you choose not to do something or go somewhere. Say "Yes" only when you choose to do so. Be in control of your life.

"I, (your name), deserve to be able to and now say "No" when I choose. I realize the power is within and is my God-given right. I can and do say "No" whenever I choose. I have faith in myself to make the right choices and I choose wisely. I call upon this great power whenever I choose. I am creating my own reality now. I enjoy being guilt-free and filled with love and respect for myself, my opinions, and my divine right to say "No." I am peaceful and happy, to the good of all parties concerned. Thank you, thank you, thank you."

Short-Form Affirmation: **Saying "No" easily without guilt**

Inactivity

Do you put off exercising, even though you know it will enhance your well-being? Make a conscious decision to take control of your life today and begin an exercise program tailored just for you. When doing so, take into consideration your age, weight, health, and lifestyle.

> "I, (your name), deserve to do and now enjoy doing my exercise program, tailored just for me, regularly. It is beneficial for my mind, body, and spirit. Exercise helps my heart and strengthens my muscles, organs, bones, and body. I enjoy exercising and, with each step I take, I say my Affirmations. My body thanks me for creating and maintaining perfect health. I am happy and healthy, to the good of all parties concerned. Thank you, thank you, thank you."

Short-Form Affirmation: **Enjoyable, healthy exercising**

Indecision

Indecision simply means you have decided not to act or make a decision. You are in a state of flux. Decide to begin doing the *Personal Contract Affirmation Method* today and enhance your ability to make timely, wise decisions.

> "I, (your name), deserve and now take action. I make good, solid decisions. Once I decide on a course of action, I never allow others or circumstances to hinder or block my progress. I am divinely guided every day in every way. I believe in myself and my life. I am happy, to the good of all parties concerned. Thank you, thank you, thank you."

Short-Form Affirmation: **Decisiveness and divine order**

Inferiority Complex

A complex is an emotionally charged group of feelings, ideas, memories, or impulses that are working in the subconscious mind. An inferiority complex usually develops in the early years, due to the high demands or overprotectiveness of a parent. Careless, negative remarks made by parents, peers, and others can also be picked up by a child's subconscious mind.

To overcome an inferiority complex, do a complete self-assessment. Write out what you think of yourself and why. What led you to the image of yourself that you are now holding? Have you ever been rejected by your parents, peers, teachers, or others? Were you overprotected as a child or punished for your failures? How did you get along with your siblings?

With AMCAM, you can learn a great deal about yourself. This valuable information will show you how to concentrate on your strengths and build up any weaknesses. It will constitute your own internal balance sheet that can prove very helpful in developing self-esteem.

> "I, (your name), deserve to release and now let go of all past and present negativity. I forgive my parents, peers, teachers, myself, and all others for any negativity. I am worthy and I count. I love, bless, and thank everyone for their influence in my life. I know they did the best they could with what they had at the time. It is easy for me to be non-judgmental. I love, respect, and approve of myself, to the good of all parties concerned. Thank you, thank you, thank you."

Short-Form Affirmation: **Self-love, respect, and approval**

Irresponsibility for Life

If you do not take responsibility for your life, you are not really living. If you cannot have a good relationship with yourself, how can you expect to have one with others? Do not blame others for your problems. Give yourself a heaping serving of good, old-fashioned self-respect and loving kindness. Accept responsibility for your problems and immediately find ways to deal with and solve them.

> "I, (your name), deserve to take and now take responsibility for my life and opportunities. I make the best of every situation. I take responsibility for my faults and mistakes, saying, 'The next time, it will be different or I will do it differently.' I am

happy and relaxed, to the good of all parties concerned. Thank you, thank you, thank you."

Short-Form Affirmation: **I am happy, relaxed, calm, and in complete control**

Jealousy

Jealousy represents a desire to own another person—which is impossible. Jealousy is a strong, unhealthy, negative emotion that can control and destroy you. When you learn to truly love, respect, and approve of yourself, you will discover there is no need or place for the emotion of jealousy. It will vanish!

"I, (your name), deserve to be and now am happy and free. I know I am important. I believe in me. I give unconditional love to myself and everyone I meet. I celebrate my life and accomplishments. I rejoice in the happiness and success of others. I never attempt to own or control another person. I enjoy being free of all jealousy and negative conditions. I am fulfilled, confident, peaceful, and happy, to the good of all parties concerned. Thank you, thank you, thank you."

Short-Form Affirmation: **Complete happiness, peace, and security**

Judgement

Sometimes people fall short of our expectations of them and we may judge or criticize them for it. But if we reject people because they are not exactly what we think they should be, in some particular aspect of personality, we might be shutting out some very successful, happy relationships. Accept the goodness of friends, family, and co-workers—with all their faults. You may not always be able to understand why people behave the way they do, but practising acceptance will greatly enhance your relationships. Live and let live!

"I, (your name), deserve and now accept my friends and all others, just the way they are. I live and let live. I freely and completely let go of all thoughts of how they should act, feel, or talk. They are free to be themselves, just as I am free to be me. I accept them with their faults and they accept me with mine. It is wonderful to be free of judgement and envy. We are all happy and peaceful, to the good of all parties concerned. Thank you, thank you, thank you."

Short-Form Affirmation: **Total acceptance, non-judgement**

Junk Food Addiction

Are you a fast food junkie or sweetaholic? Do cravings for salty chips and sweets control your life? Do you eat your way through every shopping excursion? Do you regularly sleepwalk to the fridge, hungrily devouring the last half of that double-chocolate fudge cake? If you answered "Yes" to any of any of these questions, it is time to take control of your life.

"I, (your name), deserve to be and now am in complete control of my body. Any desire for sweets or junk food now dissolves and disappears. I know excess sweets are unhealthy in the nourishment and beautification of my body. I feel free and wonderful. I am safe. I am happy and healthy, to the good of all parties concerned. Thank you, thank you, thank you."

Short-Form Affirmation: **Food that is 100 percent healthy**

Lack of Self-Respect

It is very important to respect yourself. How can you expect others to respect you if you don't? When you respect yourself, you give yourself permission to be yourself.

"I, (your name), deserve to and now truly love and respect myself. I am at peace with the world and myself. I give myself permission to be me. I am safe. I am the only decision-maker in my life and I respect my own decisions. I believe in me. I love being me. My self-respect is my gift to myself. I love, respect, and approve of myself and all others and I am happy, to the good of all parties concerned. Thank you, thank you, thank you."

Short-Form Affirmation: **Unconditional love and self-respect**

Lack of Willpower

You can learn to cultivate and use willpower to your advantage. Make up your mind to do something and have a strong desire and will to accomplish it.

Make it your intention to use your willpower to do your highest good.

> "I, (your name), deserve and now have fantastic willpower. Once I make up my mind to do something positive and constructive, no force can stop me. I have a strong determination to succeed and I am successful. I easily and quickly accomplish all tasks I set out to do. I have extraordinary strength and willpower; I only use this wonderful power wisely and to the good of all parties concerned. Thank you, thank you, thank you."

Short-Form Affirmation: **Determination, strength, and willpower**

Listlessness

Are you tired, listless, and bored with life? Do you drag yourself around, overwhelmed by even the simplest task? Energy is depleted by stress, worry, overwork, and other negative factors. Unresolved issues can also cause energy depletion. Strive for balance in all that you do—and treat yourself well.

> "I, (your name), deserve and now enjoy a powerhouse of natural and spiritual energy. I am happy and thrilled to greet each new day and all that it hands me. I am safe and balanced. Pure, spiritual energy flows through every cell, tissue, and muscle of my body. I am surrounded by loving energy. I breathe it in now. I am happy, to the good of all parties concerned. Thank you, thank you, thank you."

Short-Form Affirmation: **Pure, divine, wondrous energy**

Loneliness

Loneliness is an attitude of mind. When you truly understand and love yourself unconditionally, you are no longer lonely. Loneliness to many people means being without that special person, not having friends, or just being bored. One can be lonely in a room full of people or in an unhappy relationship or marriage. Fill your mind with curiosity and passion for a subject that interests you. Move out of your comfort zone. Fall in love with yourself and you will never be lonely. Become involved in life and living. Focus on good news, positive people, and happy events.

"I, (your name), deserve and now have and enjoy many friends. I am invited to numerous, exciting social gatherings. I am popular, fulfilled, and happy. Others find me interesting and exciting. I am a love magnet to the right people and situations. I love, respect, and approve of myself just the way I am. I have many interests and activities to keep me busy, involved, and happy, to the good of all parties concerned. Thank you, thank you, thank you."

Short-Form Affirmation: **Popular, interesting, exciting life**

Male Climacteric Syndrome (Especially for Wives)

This can be referred to as the foolish 40s, frenzied 50s, or the male climacteric. In this syndrome, the male experiences all sorts of symptoms, such as self-doubt, worry, depression, forgetfulness, and declining sexual interest.

Men may suffer from short-term memory loss, weight gain, frequent urination, indecisiveness, irritability, and depression. Some foolishly look for immortality by searching for younger partners, not admitting to themselves that they are afraid of getting older. This is why many men, after years of marriage, go searching for and have affairs with younger people. What they are searching for they already have within. They are often looking for validation of their attractiveness.

"I, (your name), deserve and now love my husband. He is the greatest and we have a fantastic, enjoyable love and sex life.

He is a great provider. I am happy to have him as my partner. He is very important to me and my life. I enjoy giving him loving, tender care during this difficult period of his life. I love and respect him and I know he loves and respects me. We are happy, to the good of all parties concerned. Thank you, thank you, thank you."

Short-Form Affirmation: **Marital harmony and bliss**

Menopause

Has the change of life got you down, then up, then down, then up again, and almost out of control? Are your family and friends on the verge of disowning you? Does your doctor cringe at the mere sight of you? Do you suffer from hot flushes, mood swings, or irrational behaviour? Menopause marks the third stage of a woman's life and it usually takes place between the ages of 40 and 50. It can happen to younger or older women, however. Some women have little or no stress, whereas others experience hot flushes, chills, heart palpitations, dizzy spells, insomnia, and an increased or diminished appetite.

"I, (your name), deserve to be and now am totally relaxed and stress-free. I enjoy being free of hot flushes and mood swings. My hormones are completely balanced and functioning perfectly. I am safe. I give my body permission to be completely relaxed and at ease during this phase of my life. I know it is a natural part of my life, leading toward greater personal freedom. I sail through menopause, problem-free. I handle all situations with ease, grace, and dignity. I give myself permission to be me and I am happy, to the good of all parties concerned. Thank you, thank you, thank you."

Short-Form Affirmation: **Easy, healthy, balanced menopause**

Menopause (Especially for Husbands)

"I, (your name), deserve and now appreciate and love my spouse. She is very attractive to me. I understand she is going through a normal changing process. I am safe. She is safe. I am tolerant and patient as I remember all our anniversaries and important dates we shared together. I enjoy being supportive of my wife and helping her through this part of her life. We are happy, to the good of all parties concerned. Thank you, thank you, thank you."

Short-Form Affirmation: **Loving kindness, patience, and understanding for my wife**

Negativity in Others

We all know people who drain our energy. They are "energy robbers" who leave us feeling exhausted, drained, or as if we have been punched in the stomach. These individuals, having no strength of their own, suck strength and energy from others. It is important to avoid such people and to choose to spend time with those who are positive and happy.

To contain your energy when dealing with negative people, simply cross your ankles and place your hands together. This helps keep your energy intact. Say to yourself, "My energy is completely contained within me." You can do this when you are speaking on the telephone by propping the phone against your ear so that your hands are free. (This uncomfortable position will also help you end the conversation more quickly!) I find it very effective to stick two words, "Divine Order," on my telephone to ensure I only receive calls from people who need to call and people from whom I wish to hear. That really cuts down on the number of people who call.

""I, (your name), deserve to have and now enjoy private time with my family and selected friends. My energy is vibrant and bright. I fill myself with positive thoughts of health, happiness, and peace. Other people's problems are theirs and everyone is responsible for themselves and their lives. My own wonderful, healthy energy is intact within me. I breathe in peace and joy. I support people when they go the distance, but I refuse to go the distance for them. I am balanced, safe, and happy, to the good of all parties concerned. Thank you, thank you, thank you."

Short-Form Affirmation: **Conserved energy, happy, peaceful, and fulfilled**

 Affirmations, Your Passport to Happiness

Nicotine Addiction

There is no longer any doubt that smoking causes all sorts of physical problems, disease, and death. Tests indicate nicotine can also cause blood vessels to contract. Children can suffer physical defects and emotional problems if their mother smoked while she was pregnant. Second-hand smoke is harmful to those breathing it in.

Do cigarettes or tobacco control your every waking moment? Does your breath reek of smoke? Are your fingers yellow and stained?

Be honest.
- Have you ever desperately searched through ashtrays in a frenzied attempt to find a butt worth smoking?
- Every time you wash your walls, windows, or drapes, do you cringe at the sight and colour of that ghastly, greenish-yellow nicotine?
- Do you huff and puff, walking up a flight of stairs?
- Do you wish to live longer?

You can change all this with a sincere desire to quit smoking and by taking action and using AMCAM.

"I, (your name), deserve to be and now am completely happy. Any desire for nicotine has completely left me. I am free, healthy, and happy. I enjoy being nicotine-free and maintaining my ideal weight. Every cell, nerve, tissue, and muscle of my lungs and my whole body is now healing and becoming 100 percent healthy. I enjoy being and now am smoke-free. I believe in me and my ability to be smoke-free. I easily refuse cigarettes or any form of tobacco, to the good of all parties concerned. Thank you, thank you, thank you."

Short-Form Affirmation: **Healthy body, nicotine-free**

Parking Spaces

Do you ever experience difficulty locating a parking space and find yourself driving around and around in frustration? By doing the *Personal Contract Affirmation Method* regularly, you can mentally affirm to yourself that you have the perfect parking space in front of the place you are about to visit. Whenever I do that, someone usually vacates a space just as I arrive and I drive right into it.

"I, (your name), deserve and now have the perfect parking space for me within the next few minutes in front of (place) to the good of all parties concerned. Thank you, thank you, thank you."

Short-Form Affirmation: **Perfect parking space, easy access**

PMS (for Women)

Women who experience PMS may be lethargic, irritable, and depressed, and have feelings of tension and aggression. The physical signs may include bloating, headaches, pain, and other problems. Dozens of different symptoms are attributed to pre-menstrual syndrome.

"I, (your name), deserve to be and now am calm, relaxed and happy. All my hormones are balanced and healthy. They are working. I am peaceful and happy. I know my body is healthy and reacting in a healthy manner. I am free of irritability, headaches, bloating, and any other discomfort. All is well and balanced in my body and I am happy, to the good of all parties concerned. Thank you, thank you, thank you."

Short-Form Affirmation: **100 percent healthy, happy, and peaceful**

Procrastination

Procrastination is a half-brother to indecision. At the root of procrastination, you will discover feelings of inadequacy. You are better off making mistakes than not making decisions. Procrastination means postponing action. Just hoping, without action, can also be postponing. It takes more effort to start a job than to keep it going. It is a fact that we can never finish a job unless we first start it. Decide what you wish to do, how to do it, then dive in and do it. Reach your goals. Start overcoming procrastination today.

"I, (your name), deserve and now enjoy life in the now. I am a self-starter and enjoy getting things done now. I easily do what I need to do today. I complete all tasks with ease. I love doing my work now. I live in the now. I enjoy today and look forward to miracles and happiness in the future. It makes me feel good and gives me a sense of accomplishment. I complete all tasks quickly and efficiently. I am happy, to the good of all parties concerned. Thank you, thank you, thank you."

Short-Form Affirmation: **Well-organized, self-starter**

Rejection

Do you ever feel rejected by people and life? In reality, no one ever rejects you. They simply reject what they think is you, based on their observations of your external appearance and behaviour. It is not actually you they are rejecting.

Overcome the fear of rejection today and be the strong, self-reliant person you desire to be. Every one of us, at one time or another, has suffered the pain of rejection. It is always painful, but we have the inner power to dissolve this pain or any other negative condition in our lives.

Learn from children. Watch them play. How many times is a child rejected? Kids may be told, "I don't like you; you can't play in this game" or "You can't play in my yard." Does the rejected child take this rejection to heart? In most cases, the child will withdraw temporarily, then, very quietly but surely, make his or her way back into the group or game.

Refrain from dwelling on rejection of any kind. The next time someone attempts to reject you, say "Cancel, cancel. I am happy." Never allow this type of negative talk to seep into your being. If you do not allow this rejection to enter your computer (subconscious mind), you will not have to deal with it.

"I, (your name), deserve and now radiate positive inner strength. I believe in myself and accept myself wholly, just as I am. I am rejection-free. Any and all rejection dissolves when it comes into contact with me. I have good ideas and my opinions are important. No one ever rejects me; they only reject what they think I am. I believe in myself. I reject all negativity easily and quickly. I am happy, to the good of all parties concerned. Thank you, thank you, thank you."

Short-Form Affirmation: **Healthy, happy, rejection-free**

Scatoma

A scatoma is a blind spot, obscuring your vision and preventing you from seeing something. Circumstances and situations can become excuses for "blind spots" to be created so that the reality of the problem does not have to be seen.

"I, (your name), deserve to see and now see things clearly. I see where I need to change my thoughts and actions. I am aware of how I am living my life. I call upon and use my inner wisdom and power. I am happy and fulfilled, to the good of all parties concerned. Thank you, thank you, thank you."

Short-Form Affirmation: **Seeing things clearly**

Sex Addiction

Is your sex addiction or that of your partner destroying your life? Is it unbearable? Any negative addiction can become destructive and may require professional counselling. It is wise to use balance and common sense in the bedroom, as well as in every other aspect of your life. Sex is an expression of caring. It is also the result of love shared by two responsible, mature individuals. It is a vital, basic need of humanity.

"I, (your name), deserve and now enjoy having sex or making love with my partner. It is a beautiful, loving, healthy act. We exercise the desired control and balance in our love-making and enjoy safe, healthy, normal sex. Any extreme or uncontrollable urges now fade out of our lives and we respect and enjoy each other. We are happy, normal, and balanced, to the good of all parties concerned. Thank you, thank you, thank you."

Short-Form Affirmation: **Safe, healthy, exciting sex life**

Shopaholic or Spendaholic

Many shopaholics and spendaholics suffer from feelings of inadequacy, low self-esteem, and low self-worth. They feel it is important to dress up the outside because the inside is an empty void. Go inside and change the picture. Attack the root of the problem inside yourself. Remember always that your self-worth is far more important than your net worth!

> "I, (your name), deserve and now feel love and respect for myself. My self-respect and self-worth grow daily. I enjoy making wise decisions, I use money wisely and I shop efficiently. I stop and really think about the article I am about to purchase. I know money is important in my life, however, my self-worth, self-respect, and self-control are more important. It is unnecessary to compete with anyone or to measure up to anyone's expectations. I have powerful control over my desires and feelings when spending money. I am happy with my self-image. I concentrate on what I can spend and refrain from dwelling on what I cannot buy. I am debt-free. I am complete, whole, healthy, and at peace, to the good of all parties concerned. Thank you, thank you, thank you."

Short-Form Affirmation: **Normal, healthy spending habits, debt-free**

Stress

Some forms of stress are actually good for you, providing the fuel (energy) that spurs you on to get things done. But negative, excessive stress is not healthy and should be eliminated.

> "I, (your name), deserve to be and now enjoy being free of negative stress. I know that some stress is a good motivator for me. I perform all my obligations and duties successfully in the allotted timeframe. I am relaxed, efficient, confident, and happy, to the good of all parties concerned. Thank you, thank you, thank you."

Short-Form Affirmation: **Stress-free, healthy, and happy**

Taking Life Too Seriously

Having fun and laughing is very important to your health and well-being. Do you take life too seriously? Why not take time to stop and smell the roses or enjoy the thrill of a ride on the roller coaster? When was the last time you played for the sheer fun of it? Release, play with, and be a loving, caring parent to that inner child in you.

"I, (your name), deserve and now see and appreciate the humour in all aspects of life. I have a great sense of humour. People laugh with me. I enjoy laughing, playing, and having fun. I am safe and I give myself permission to enjoy life and have fun. I love to romp and play. Smiling, laughing, and playing come easily to me, enabling me to release negative energy. I allow my inner child to come out to play, laugh, and have fun. I extend happiness to all I meet, to the good of all parties concerned. Thank you, thank you, thank you."

Short-Form Affirmation: **Filled with fun and laughter**

Tardiness

It is very important to be on time for appointments and when meeting others. Being punctual is a sign of respect—for yourself and others. Use your time wisely.

"I, (your name), deserve to be and now am on time for all my appointments. I enjoy being punctual. My life is balanced and well organized. I have all the time there is. I respect others and their time and others respect me. Being on time shows respect for the other person. We are happy, to the good of all parties concerned. Thank you, thank you, thank you."

Short-Form Affirmation: **Punctual, well-organized person**

Temper

Are you a volcano just waiting to erupt? Does the slightest annoyance send you into a fit of rage? Vent your anger by punching your pillow and thereby releasing hostility toward a person, situation, or self. When you become uncontrollably angry, you can actually change the colour of your skin and raise your blood pressure. Your pupils dilate with strong emotions of anger, worry, fear, jealousy, and hostility. Outbursts of temper can adversely affect your health.

One of my friends, a hairstylist, has four words written on his mirror: "I am handling it." When anger begins to rise up in him from the bottom of his feet, he looks at those four words, concentrates on them, and takes a deep breath. He breathes in the statement, "I am handling it." He says the powerful negative energy is diluted and then becomes manageable for him. These powerful words have been on his mirror for the past 12 years and have helped him control his temper.

"I, (your name), deserve to and now accept others as they are. I can only change myself and the way I view that other person. I release all anger, frustration, and hurt from my life now. I believe in me and my ability to control my temper. I am serene and relaxed and can handle any stressful situations with loving kindness. I am in complete control of my emotions and I enjoy being in control of my body. I am happy, to the good of all parties concerned. Thank you, thank you, thank you."

Short-Form Affirmation: **Happy, healthy, and even-tempered**

Time Management

Make time your friend. You have all the time there is. Time stands still for you. Manage time wisely and it will serve you well.

"I, (your name), deserve and now have time for all my projects. I spend quality time with my family and friends and in social activities. I enjoy my successful time spent in my career or business. I have all the time there is. Time truly does stand still for me. I complete all my projects at the appointed time with ease and efficiency. I love my new, successful, balanced time schedule, to the good of all parties concerned. Thank you, thank you, thank you."

Short-Form Affirmation: **Well-organized, balanced time schedule**

Workaholic

Do you live to work or work to live? Do you plan your work, then work your plan? Work smarter, not harder. We all know people who take piles of work with them on vacation. You can spot them sitting on white, sandy beaches, in a bathing suit with a briefcase nearby or using a calculator, laptop, or minicomputer.

Some people perform business transactions on their cell phones while shopping for groceries. How do you think their inner child feels? Trapped, depressed, and frustrated, I would imagine.

Learn to balance, delegate, and take vacations from your career. Have fun! Put on a happy face and greet each day with enthusiasm and joy!

> "I, (your name), deserve to be and now am balanced and happy in all I do. I enjoy delegating and organizing my work schedule. I say 'No' easily to overwork. I have time for myself, family, and loved ones. I enjoy social activities. I am clear, happy, and balanced, to the good of all parties concerned. Thank you, thank you, thank you."

Short-Form Affirmation: **Balanced in work and play**

Worry

Chronic worry is abnormal. A person who worries that he or she has nothing to worry about is a worrywart! Worry is such a wasted emotion. The main basis of worry is negativity and apprehension. It could be the expectation that the worst will happen. Tension results from worry and brings on more worry, so that it becomes a vicious circle.

I read somewhere that worry is like a rocking chair—it gives you something to do, but gets you nowhere.

Decide to limit worries. Worry is interest paid on trouble before it becomes due. Worry is like a boil coming to its painful head—which is fear! Worry becomes fear if you allow it to or do not control it. Fear short-circuits the cosmic energy that flows throughout your body. It inhibits your cells and creates poison that can be injurious to your organs, tissues, and every part of your body. Any negative thought, if fertilized, can develop into a real fear monster that can tear you down. Conquer fear by putting it into proper perspective. Worrying about things that we cannot control dissipates energy faster than we can accumulate it.

"I, (your name), deserve to be and now am worry-free. In my mind, I place all my worries into a balloon and release them into the atmosphere to be recycled into divine love. I am in control of my life. I concentrate on my blessings and the positive things in my life. I live in an attitude of gratitude. I enjoy being worry-free. I am happy, to the good of all parties concerned. Thank you, thank you, thank you."

Short-Form Affirmation: **Positive, worry-free**

Affirmations When Properly Done Always Work!

Cards of Life

www.affirmations-doctor.com

Affirmations, Your Passport to Happiness

9 • *Boosting Self-Respect*

Loving Yourself:
Discovering the Real You

Self-respect is very similar to self-esteem and is determined by how highly you regard yourself, how much faith you have in yourself, and your sense of personal dignity and independence.

A healthy level of self-respect brings self-reliance, regard for oneself, and an awareness of who you are and how you feel about yourself. When you have self-respect, you respect yourself and your abilities and you expect others to respect you accordingly. You do not allow others to run your life and you do not overextend yourself or play the role of a people-pleaser. You are able to say "No" to the demands of others and to anything that is not in your best interest.

Healthy, divine, unselfish love, and respect for self increase your self-esteem. When your self-esteem goes up, so does your popularity. What you think and how you feel about yourself is very important because it sets the mode for how others react to you.

It is never too late to heal your self-image. Begin today to see yourself in a different light and accept your perfect place in life. Become aware of who you really are. How can you expect others to respect you if you cannot respect yourself?

You have the power within you to create your dreams, increase your income and improve your self-image. Through the power of your subconscious mind, you can develop a positive mental attitude and attract lasting relationships, career, and money.

When you learn to love, respect, and approve of yourself—just the way you are—wonderful things happen in your life. Make a habit of forgiving, nurturing, and loving your self and focusing on health, wealth, and happiness in your life. Your self-worth is much more important than your net worth.

As with all new habits, this usually takes at least 21 days to develop. By constantly, consciously changing negative thoughts into powerful, positive thoughts, your self-respect and self-esteem automatically increase.

Increasing Self-Confidence

Have confidence in yourself and expect the best. When you know you are a winner, you make things happen and you make your dreams come true. Self-talk is very important—how you speak about yourself determines your life experiences.

In one of my workshops, a participant said, "Anne Marie, why don't you write a book?" That statement caused a light bulb to explode in my mind. I recalled telling family members years ago that, when I grew up, I would write a book.

But numerous negative, hindering thoughts immediately came to mind at the idea of actually doing it.

- You can't do that.
- Who would read your book?
- Where would you get the money to publish it?
- You do not know any publishers.
- You are not well known enough.
- You do not have any letters after your name.
- Who would buy it?
- What if you lose money and end up with boxes of unsold books?
- Why would you waste all that time and energy? You would be moving out of your comfort zone into the unknown territory of book writing, publishing, printing, and marketing.

I listened to every negative statement, idea, or thought, wrote them down, and studied each one individually, as follows.

a. I can't do that.

My answer was "Why not?" Many ordinary people have written books and successfully published and marketed them. I have spent my whole life studying, teaching, and using these principles and methods, so why shouldn't I impart my acquired knowledge and methods to others?

b. Who will buy my book?

I thought about that statement very hard, then I realized that my work was already in demand because students were signing up for my courses! Students in my previous workshop would buy it. That would be a good start.

c. How will I finance a publishing project?

My answer to that was that I would save money for as long as necessary. Also, I could put my own teachings into effect and create money that way—positive proof that my methods really worked!

d. How will I market my book?

I was not in the advertising business. But I had been Director of Public Relations for a large recreational project and, through my office, we had sold over $3 million in recreational property in one year. I realized I could use the same principles and methods to market my book.

e. I am not well known enough.

Every successful writer has to start somewhere. I certainly did not mind starting at the bottom and working my way up the writer's ladder. The participants at my workshops and seminars obviously felt I was well-known enough for them to pay money to attend my events. I now receive many invitations to appear as a guest speaker on numerous radio and television talk shows to discuss the Power of Affirmations.

f. What if the book is not successful and I lose money?

Nothing ventured, nothing gained, I reminded myself. Life is full of surprises. It is better to do something than to do nothing at all—in any area of life.

g. I do not have letters after my name.

It was true that I did not have the traditional degrees, but I did have some credentials of my own—certificates from three counselling courses. I recall Anthony Robbins being asked, during an interview, if he had any degrees or psychology training. He replied, "No, but I have never had anyone who was threatening to commit suicide ask for my degrees." I do have some degrees of my own: Anne Marie Evers, P.H.D.

(perseverance, hard work, and dedication)! I have earned the title 'Affirmations Doctor.'

It worked! Thousands of copies of my book have been sold throughout the world—that's Affirmation Success!

I am so glad I moved out of my comfort zone and into creation and the unknown. The way to grow is to keep moving forward, experiencing and learning.

Learning to do Affirmations properly creates miracles. When AMCAM is used properly, it opens up a whole new way of life for you. I have proven this wonderful power in my own life. I also have thousands of testimonials from readers around the world, telling of miracles taking place in their lives when they use this process properly.

Ask yourself what is hindering you from reaching your goal or dream. If I can do it, you can, too! It is important to remember that experiencing fear when moving out of your comfort zone is very normal. Stretch your imagination to new heights. You can if you think you can! I know you can!

Expanding Time

If you find yourself wishing there were 25 hours in every day, you may need help managing and organizing your time effectively. In reality, we have all the time there is and it is a good idea to frequently remind yourself that you are timeless. And that time stands still for you.

Managing time efficiently is a great esteem-builder. Make friends with time. Remember: the mind knows no past or future. There is only the present moment. There is no rush hour in heaven and tomorrow may never arrive. We need to author our moment of happiness and love for ourselves and others in the moment. Living "in the moment" helps us appreciate and make more effective use of our time.

Self-Esteem and Friendships

When you have healthy self-esteem, you tend to have many friends. You are magnetic; people naturally gravitate to you. But to have friends, you must first be a friend. And, most important, you must be your own best friend. It is very important and valuable to help others but, in the final analysis, you are on your own! No one else can do your living for you.

Love, respect, and approve of yourself, just the way you are. Some people consider this selfish, but it is not. The most selfish people are those who do not take care of themselves and end up in hospitals or long-term care facilities where they have to be supported by government and taxpayers' money.

To assess the kind of friends you have, ask yourself the following questions. Are your friends and acquaintances helping to build you up or are they tearing you down? Are they giving you something of value or taking something of value from you? Choose your thoughts and friends with careful consideration. Weed out the so-called friends who overwhelm you with negativity or their own self-worship.

Self-esteem comes from healthy self-love.

Get in touch with yourself and your own voice. Whenever you think you have to do something, ask yourself, "Whose voice is saying that? Is it my parents, peers, or is it my voice?" When you spend time alone, remind yourself that you are visiting the most important, interesting person you ever had the pleasure of meeting. Say often during the day, "Hello, self, I love you!"

Avoiding "Doormatitis"

Refuse to be a doormat! We all know people who suffer from doormatitis. They will do almost anything to gain approval and be liked and accepted.

Unfortunately, they do not possess the qualities of healthy self-esteem. These people usually suffer from some tension-related ailment, such as high blood pressure or ulcers. They never do what they want to do.

When you take on the role of doormat, you give yourself a large helping of self-poison. You belittle yourself and your capabilities and you give your power away. Only by learning to love and respect yourself can you expect others to respect you.

You can use the cup-emptying exercise to eliminate any doormatitis in your life. Stick a label marked "Doormatitis" on a cup, then fill the cup with water and visualize all the negative feelings of living the role of doormat going into the water. Then empty the cup of water, imagining all those feelings draining away. Repeat the whole process every day for 21 days. You will experience various emotions associated with releasing and letting go of the past.

Following this procedure, take another cup and label it self-love, respect, and approval. Fill it with water and drink it, repeating this process every day for 21 days. The results are absolutely unbelievable; you will find yourself filled with peace, joy, and fulfillment.

Affirmations When Properly Done Always Work!

Cards of Life

www.affirmations-doctor.com

10 • *Relationships: Marriage, Family, and Others*

Making All Your Relationships Work:
Cherishing Relationships

All relationships are instruments for growth and, with growth, come problems (opportunities). Attracting that special relationship is similar to putting a jigsaw puzzle together. Problems are only a piece of the larger puzzle. You may need to find solutions to each part of it. Even the smallest piece of the puzzle is important; if it is missing, the whole puzzle is incomplete. Working on solving the whole puzzle involves other people and situations.

Successful, loving, happy relationships do not just happen! They take loving kindness, work, and respect. I feel respect is the most important ingredient in any successful, happy relationship or marriage.

This chapter will show you ways to attract and keep that special person in your life. That perfect relationship or marriage is just waiting for you to call it to you through the power of the *Personal Contract Affirmation Method.* You will also learn how to release, forgive, and let go of relationships and marriages that do not fit your puzzle or are no longer working for you.

Everything in life involves relationships. You are in relationships with yourself and everyone and everything—your car, your computer, even your pencils.

But the most important relationship you will ever experience is the one you have with yourself. A great two-person relationship can enhance your life, but it cannot make it complete on its own. Any unresolved emotional issues will need to be dealt with before you are ready to engage in a healthy, balanced, loving relationship with another person.

If you are looking for a partner out of need—for example, because you are lonely or have a fear of living alone—it is important to first focus on healing yourself, rather than searching for someone to fill that need.

Everyone has basic needs for food, clothing, shelter, and living necessities, but a need in a relationship indicates a gap in your own life. Such needs can only be filled by you.

If it is not, your relationships will be unhealthy, unfulfilling, and probably short-lived. A needy love is a false love. To overcome and heal such needs, do a Master Affirmation to love, respect, and accept yourself.

Making it Work

Differences of opinion are a normal part of any relationship. Everyone thinks differently and there are always opposing views. There is no right or wrong view, only the chosen view. It is important to openly discuss any issues of concern with your partner and to own, take responsibility for, release, and heal any personal wounds you may have prior to entering into a marriage or relationship.

Consider how much effort and work you are prepared to put into your *Personal Contract Affirmation Method*. Affirmations are powerful tools for helping you retrain the mind and deal with all aspects of relationships.

When affirming for the perfect relationship, ask yourself these questions.

- What you are willing to give?
- Are you willing to change?
- How much effort and energy are you prepared to put into the relationship?

No other person can meet all your needs or requirements, nor can you please everyone. No relationship is perfect, but it could be perfect for you.

Sustaining Relationships

Once you have met your special someone—your prince or princess— it is time to rejoice and give thanks. Some people start worrying immediately that the relationship or marriage will not last; they are afraid of abandonment or rejection. They have a fear of loss. Control such fears with positive, healthy self-talk.

Expect your relationship or marriage to last a lifetime when you have planted your Master Affirmation (seed-thought), fertilized it, and taken care of it. Now it is time to reap the glorious results— a solid healthy, wealthy, happy, lasting, loving relationship or marriage.

You can choose to make your marriage a healthy, loving, lasting, happy one by focusing on and magnifying your partner's good points and giving loving kindness. Nurture your marriage. Remember what attracted you to that person in the first place. Rekindle that interest and love.

Do your *Personal Contract Affirmation Method* to maintain that happiness, even when you are happily married. It is a small investment of time that pays off in great dividends.

Master and Short-Form Affirmations

Cultivating a Relationship

"I, (your name), deserve and now have a loving, lasting relationship that turns into marriage with the perfect person for me. We enjoy each other's company and have similar interests. We accept one another. I give my partner space and I receive space in return. We love, respect, and approve of each other, just the way we are. There is no need to change. We are happy, fulfilled, and peaceful, to the good of all parties concerned. Thank you, thank you, thank you."

Short-Form Affirmation: **Loving, lasting relationship/marriage**

Note: When you have children, especially young children, it is imperative that you add that this person accepts and respects your children and that they accept and respect him or her and that they have and enjoy a healthy relationship.

Attracting that Special Person

"I, (your name), deserve to have and now am led to the right places to meet my life partner. The power and intelligence of my subconscious mind draw the right person to me now! We enjoy caring and sharing. We have a happy, committed marriage or relationship, to the good of all parties concerned. Thank you, thank you, thank you."

Short-Form Affirmation: **Drawn to the right places**

Releasing Relationship or Marriage that is Not Working

"I, (your name), deserve and now am resolved to let you (name of person) go with loving kindness. I forgive you for leaving me, our relationship, family, or home. I give you space to grow and you give me space to do the same. I accept the fact that we are separate at this time. I close the doors to the past and open new, exciting doors to the future. I will live my life without you, should that be our mutual decision. I am at peace, to the good of all parties concerned. Thank you, thank you, thank you."

Short-Form Affirmation: **Release with loving kindness**

Attracting the Right Date

"I, (your name), deserve and now attract the perfect date (partner) to me. My children (family) accept him or her. We spend quality time together, getting to know one another. We are safe, happy, fulfilled, and relaxed, to the good of all parties concerned. Thank you, thank you, thank you."

Short-Form Affirmation: **Perfect date for me**

Releasing Negative Emotions

"I, (your name), deserve to be and now am at peace. I release anger and negative emotions that are in my body surrounding the break-up of our relationship or marriage. I know that if I release a beautiful bird, it will return to me if it was meant to be with me. If it does not return, it was not meant for me. I know that if our relationship is meant to be, you will return when the time is right for both of us. If we decide to part company permanently, I know I can go on and meet another mate when I choose. It is my choice. I surrender all negativity around our relationship. I dissolve all pain, fear, and rejection in my body, mind, and spirit. I release you and let you go with loving kindness. I am peaceful to the good of all parties concerned. Thank you, thank you, thank you."

Short-Form Affirmation: **Total release and surrender of feelings**

Continued Happy Marriage

"I, (your name), deserve and now have and enjoy, a loving, lasting, healthy, happy marriage with the perfect partner for me. Our marriage continues to grow in love, trust, and companionship. We enjoy sharing our life together. We both thank God for the wonderful gift of marriage and each other. We love, respect, and honour each other. Our love grows deeper every day and we are happy, fulfilled, and peaceful, to the good of all parties concerned. Thank you, thank you, thank you."

Short-Form Affirmation: **Happy, lasting marriage**

Remember to accept, date, and sign your Master Affirmations, making them firm and binding contracts.

Food for Thought

Forgive more than you can forgive
Then do it!
Love more than you can love
Then show it!
Attach your relationship to a star
Hold on tight
And there you are!

For more information, please read my companion book, *Affirmations, Your Passport to Lasting, Loving Relationships*.

Family and Other Relationships

Affirmations for Children

Teaching your children to use the power of Affirmations at a young age is one of the best gifts you can ever give them. Although we start life with simple, childlike faith, we become programmed by limited, negative thinking.

By making positive, affirming statements to your children, you program and encourage them in a positive way, enhancing their self-esteem and their faith in themselves.

Start encouraging your young children to make small choices and decisions. For example, allow them to decide what dress or shirt to wear. When they get older, they will have the basic decision-making framework in place to make big, important decisions.

During the first years of school, children are concerned mainly with how they feel. Teach your children to use the power of Affirmations and affirmative thinking to assist them in creating healthy relationships with others while they are still young.

Say Affirmations directly to them. A child's inner talk does not just happen; it is born of what children hear from other people. Children absorb words, feelings, actions, and beliefs from you and others and they internalize them.

When children hear words of praise and encouragement, they learn to love, praise, and respect themselves. If they hear words of criticism and blame, they learn to feel ashamed and worthless and they blame themselves. Affirm and validate the positive qualities and unique talents in your child.

You can teach your child to watch his or her thoughts, words, actions, and manners, and use positive Affirmations to help them love and respect self and others. Affirmations of unconditional love go right to the core of children; they thrive on words of encouragement about how smart they are and what good marks they get on their report cards.

Children can be programmed negatively in subtle ways. When you tell your children to be careful, for example, you may be implying that the world is full of great big boogiemen lurking around every corner and tree. It is extremely important to talk to children about the real dangers, such as speaking to strangers or taking rides or candy from people they do not know. Do refrain from filling their innocent minds with thoughts of doom and fear.

To further enhance your child's positive outlook, be careful to avoid using the word "but." For example, if you say to your child, "I love you, but you are lazy and untidy," you are affirming your child's negative behaviour and cancelling out the positive statement of love. Affirm the child's special attributes, saying, "You have a great smile, your skin is silky, or your teeth are so perfectly formed." You can always find something positive to say to your child.

Affirm your children's worth non-verbally, with a hug, a loving look, and by spending quality time with them. Words are important, but the need to be mothered by the action of love is of utmost importance. When you have congruence with words, feelings, and actions, your Affirmations ring true. Affirm positively on a regular basis and your child will internalize the words you say.

Most parents experience challenges and difficulties with child-rearing. Realize this fact, accept it, and work out the answers to your problems. Your powerful tool is the daily use of the *Family Personal Contract Affirmation Method.*

Family Personal Contract Affirmation Method

Children who do Affirmations on a regular basis are more independent and responsible and they experience greater self-confidence and self-esteem. It is easier for them to know what they want and achieve their goals, desires, and wishes. They are able to say "No" more easily to negative situations and people. They attract, develop, and enjoy greater optimism for the present and future.

A simple method of introducing Affirmations to your children is to ask them to identify some personal goals or challenges in their life. These could be making friends, being accepted, becoming popular, liking school/teachers, or getting good grades. Reflect the child's feelings back to him or her.

Before you can help a child with an Affirmation, it is important that you acknowledge, understand, and validate the child's feelings and thoughts about that Affirmation. Help the child formulate an empowering Affirmation in a positive self-statement, written in the first person, that the child can understand and say to him or herself.

The earlier you begin teaching your children Affirmations, the sooner you see positive results. Never force children to do Affirmations. Make it an exciting, imaginative journey or fun-filled adventure.

Making Affirmations Fun

One mother, Marie, made an interesting Family Affirmations Game. She printed Short-Form Affirmations on small pieces of cardboard (small flashcards) and placed them in a box on the kitchen table. Each of her three children picked one card every morning. The child repeated the Affirmation three times, then turned the Affirmation over to his or her subconscious mind to attract other similar thoughts.

Because the children were too young to understand the process, Marie suggested that they think about the meaning of the Affirmation. They all got very excited about the Family Affirmation Game. Marie reported it had an astonishing, positive impact upon the family.

Marie used vivid, brightly coloured cardboard for the Short-Form Affirmations, which included the following: "I like school. I get good grades. I am honest. I am popular. My teacher likes me. I have many friends. I feel happy and I am smart. I am on time. I like learning and it is easy for me to learn." She added happy faces, hearts, stars, and stickers to make the cards more attractive to the children.

Eleanor, a young mother of three—teenager Judy and two younger ones—is another inspiring example of how powerful a positive approach can be. Judy seemed full of anger and hate for her mother; Eleanor did not know what she had done to deserve this negative treatment. I helped Eleanor work out a plan whereby she would take Judy out for a grown-up lunch and they would each write gripe sheets about each other.

When lunch was over, they would enter into a discussion about how to improve their own relationship. They would talk out their hurts, emotions, and misunderstandings. They wrote an agreement setting out their expectations for each other and establishing healthy boundaries. They both signed and dated it. Now they had a basis from which to work.

The first lunch did not go too well, but Eleanor persisted; the second lunch was very successful.

Now both mother and daughter have a better understanding of each other. Eleanor says, "It is a miracle!" She realized the only person she could change was herself. She could and did, however, change the way she felt about and viewed her daughter.

When I was teaching Affirmations to a grade 3 class, Donald, the known class bully, said to me, "Anne Marie, I used to fight a lot." I said, "Oh, you did?" With his hands on his hips, he replied, "Yep, but that was before I learned about Affirmations and the ripple effect."

If you expect respect, trust and love in return, treat your teenager and all your children with respect, trust, and love. You can still be that loving, caring parent while adding a whole new dimension— that of a trusted friend.

Don't worry about the small details. If you are sensitive and someone says hurtful things to you, simply say to yourself, "Cancel, cancel, I am happy." In this way, those hurtful statements will not be able to enter into your consciousness (your inner computer) and you will not have to deal with them.

Master and Short-Form Affirmations for Family Members

General Family Relationships

"I, (your name), deserve and now lovingly accept (person's name) as an exceptional human being. We now enjoy a rich, rewarding relationship with each other. We love and respect each other. We recognize we are both different. We are surrounded by a loving, healthy atmosphere. We learn from each other, to the good of all parties concerned. Thank you, thank you, thank you."

Short-Form Affirmation: **Happy family relationships**

Adoptive Parent

"I, (your name), deserve to and now release my child in love to search for their natural parent. I give my love, understanding, and support. I keep my emotions under control and am free of jealousy. I believe in myself and my parental abilities. I am secure in my love for my child. We love and respect each other. I assist in any way possible to make the search easier. We are all happy, to the good of all parties concerned. Thank you, thank you, thank you."

Short-Form Affirmation: **Unconditional love, happiness, and support**

Step-Parent

"I, (your name), deserve and now have a healthy, happy family life. My stepchildren now accept me and the family unit, and I accept them. I enjoy being a friend and I know it is not my role to replace the previous parent. I gain love and respect in my own right. We talk about problems, challenges, opportunities and we genuinely like one another. Our home and family are relaxed and happy, to the good of all parties concerned. Thank you, thank you, thank you."

Short-Form Affirmation: **Accepted, loved, and respected step-parent**

Children's Affirmations

• Grades 1 to 6

"I, (student's name), deserve to have and now make friends easily. I am cheerful, popular, and happy. I feel good about my teacher, friends, and myself. I am totally accepted and do well in school. I am safe and protected. I like attending school to the good of all parties concerned. Thank you, thank you, thank you."

Short-Form Affirmation: **Acceptance, happiness, and good education**

• Grades 7 to 9

"I, (student's name), deserve to be and am now accepted by my peers. I am happy, positive, and popular at school. I get good grades and enjoy doing my homework. I have a balanced, happy time, both at school and in my social life. I say 'No' easily when I wish to. I am safe, happy, and protected, to the good of all parties concerned. Thank you, thank you, thank you."

Short-Form Affirmation: **Happy, accepted, good student**

• Grades 10 to 12

"I, (student's name), deserve and now like school and do very well in all my assignments. I get excellent grades. I feel good about life, other people, and myself. I enjoy my many friends. I say 'No' easily and firmly, when I choose, without guilt. I love, respect, and approve of myself. I enjoy attending school because I know it is training me for my desired vocation. I graduate with honours or at the top of my class. This valuable training enables me to be a successful, productive, happy adult. I am peaceful, to the good of all parties concerned. Thank you, thank you, thank you."

Short-Form Affirmation: **Solid foundation, good education, and acceptance**

• University

"I, (your name) deserve and now complete all my courses successfully. When I need to remember something, I close my eyes and say, 'Clear, search, and retrieve' and the correct answers for exams come to me easily and effortlessly. Studying comes easy to me. I love studying and preparing for my life career. I am happy, peaceful, and secure, to the good of all parties concerned. Thank you, thank, thank you."

Short-Form Affirmation: **Completed university studies**

Parents of School Age Children

• Grades 1 to 6

"I, (your name), deserve to be and now am happy that my child likes attending school. I give thanks for my child having healthy, well-adjusted friendships and for being accepted by his or her peers. I am becoming more involved and interested in their school and individual activities. I am so pleased to see the wonderful creative abilities developing in my child's life, to the good of all parties concerned. Thank you, thank you, thank you."

Short-Form Affirmation: **Well-adjusted, healthy, happy child/ children**

• Grades 7 to 9

"I, (your name), deserve to be and now am a caring, balanced parent. I love and respect my children. They grow every day in love, honesty, and happiness. They get excellent grades and do well in all their schoolwork. I surround them with God's love, my love, and the love of nature. They grow into responsible young adults who love to share with others. I instruct my children about life's dangers in a manner that does not frighten them. I teach them awareness and common sense. They choose healthy, well-adjusted, interesting friends. They are accepted totally for who they are. They are secure, happy, and fully protected, to the good of all parties concerned. Thank you, thank you, thank you."

Short-Form Affirmation: **Safe, protected, happy, healthy child/children**

• Grades 10 to 12

"I, (your name), deserve to be and now am a loving, balanced parent. I love and respect my children and give them freedom to grow. I trust them to make their own decisions within reason, which prepares them for difficult adult decisions. They surround themselves with a circle of healthy, happy, productive, balanced friends. They are totally accepted and respected for who they are. They do well in school and make the right decisions and graduate at the top of their class or with honours. We are happy, to the good of all parties concerned. Thank you, thank you, thank you."

Short-Form Affirmation: **Well-adjusted, healthy, happy young adults**

Other

Expectant Mother

When you do family and personal Affirmations, you build solid foundations that help the family learn, grow, and develop in a positive manner. It is never too late or too early to start doing AMCAM. This program can be started during pregnancy. Hold your hand over your tummy and say:

"I, (your name), deserve and now am blessed with a perfect, healthy, happy child. I enjoy, love, and nurture my baby. My baby grows in health and happiness every day. I adapt easily to motherhood. My baby is colic-free and 100 percent healthy. It is protected in all waking and sleeping moments. Childbirth is very natural and easy for me. My body heals normally, quickly, and naturally. My body now reverts back to my normal ideal weight. I affirm divine order in our lives and our home. My spouse and I are happy, peaceful, and calm, to the good of all parties concerned. Thank you, thank you, thank you."

Short-Form Affirmation: **Healthy baby, happy, loving home**

Releasing Married Daughter

"I, (your name), release and let go of any control issues surrounding my daughter. She is free to live, learn, and grow at her own speed in her own space. I encourage my daughter to spread her wings and fly. I give unconditional love, support, and understanding. I am aware that my role has changed and that my daughter's primary commitment is to her spouse. I accept this changed role willingly, with loving kindness. My life is full and happy. We are all happy, to the good of all parties concerned. Thank you, thank you, thank you."

Short-Form Affirmation: **Freedom, support, and unconditional love**

Releasing Married Son

"I, (your name), release and let go of any control issues surrounding my son. He is free to live, learn, and grow at his own speed in his own space. I encourage him to spread his wings and fly. I give unconditional love, support, and understanding. I am aware that my role has changed and that my son's primary commitment is to his spouse. I accept this changed role willingly, with loving kindness. My life is full and happy. We are all happy, to the good of all parties concerned. Thank you, thank you, thank you."

Short-Form Affirmation: **Freedom, support, and unconditional love**

Adult Relationship between Two Partners

"I, (your name), deserve and now have a loving, lasting, happy relationship with the perfect mate for me, who accepts my family and me. We communicate freely on a daily basis. We share common interests. We are happy and enjoy harmonious family outings. We are mutually kind, loving, and respectful. We enjoy private adult moments as well as happy family moments and have a healthy, fulfilled sex life. We are happy, to the good of all parties concerned. Thank you, thank you, thank you."

Affirmations, Your Passport to Happiness

Forgiveness for Betrayal of Trust

"I, (your name), deserve to and now really and truly forgive my mate for betraying my love and trust. I release all feelings of hatred, hostility, hurt, and anger toward him or her. I know keeping these negative feelings inside my being only hurts me. I am relaxed, calm, poised, and in control of my feelings. My spouse and I now build on a solid foundation of renewed trust and love for each other. We overcome any problems of the past and realize that they are history. We let the past go. Today is another new, glorious day. We are happy living in the now, to the good of all parties concerned. Thank you, thank you, thank you."

Short-Form Affirmation: **Forgiveness, renewed trust, and love**

Rewarding Friendships

"I, (your name), deserve and now have many long-lasting, happy friendships. We trust, love, and respect one another. We enjoy companionship and look forward to spending time together. We encourage and help one another through difficult times. We respect each other's individuality. I hold a space for my friends. I am not in their space. I enjoy harmonious, healthy, rich, and rewarding friendships, to the good of all parties concerned. Thank you, thank you, thank you."

Short-Form Affirmation: **Trust, unconditional love, and friendship**

All successful relationships are the result of people sharing, caring, and working together. If there is someone in your life with whom you just cannot communicate, you may wish to use the following two exercises.

Spiritual Disinfectant Exercise

On a piece of masking tape, write the words "Spiritual Disinfectant." Place the tape on a small spray bottle. Fill the bottle with water and, if you wish, add a drop or two of your favourite essential oil or perfume. When you encounter a negative situation, simply spray the air with the spray bottle, saying, "I now spray all negative thoughts and situations." You can also use this technique to spray away the negative thoughts of others. (Note: Never spray a person in the face.)

Tom goes to his office early each day and sprays around his work area before the other employees arrive. He is careful to avoid contact with the papers and materials in that area. He says he really notices the difference that activity makes in his day. Now co-workers comment that when Tom is absent, things do not run as smoothly in his department. He is convinced this spray method works very effectively. One reader relates how she uses her Spiritual Disinfectant when her husband Greg comes home from work in a negative mood. When he goes into the kitchen, she gets out her Spiritual Disinfectant and sprays around his chair. She swears that 10 minutes later, he is back to his normal, positive self. Greg is totally unaware of this exercise. She is so excited about her wonderful results that she tells all her friends about her success.

To read realtor Merv Wright's delightful letter about his use of Spiritual Disinfectant, please see page 214.

The Angel Letter Process

This is a process whereby you write a letter to someone's higher self— or angel—from your higher self (see sample). Write the Angel Letter out 15 times, because this is the number mystics believe has the power to destroy negative thoughts.

When I do this exercise, I write the original on a 3" x 5" card and keep it in my wallet. I read over the other 14 letters, then burn them. The person whose angel you are writing to never sees the letter. You only need to do the Angel Letter Procedure once! This is a simple, powerful exercise that produces unbelievable, positive results. Do it and see for yourself.

Note: I have done this process writing the letter only three, 10, and 12 times, but the process works best doing it 15 times.

When writing from your angel to another's angel, you are communicating on an angelic or higher level, filled with loving kindness, peace, joy, and happiness.

If you wish to change your Angel Letter, write out a new one and staple the new 3" x 5" card to the original card. On the new one, write "Revised Edition in red ink."

You can even write an Angel Letter to a prospective employer. Write, "To the Angel of the Decision-Maker or Manager: I send you divine wisdom and I thank you for considering my application and for hiring me, to the good of all parties concerned. Thank you from the angel of your prospective employee."

Sample Angel Letter

To the Angel of _____:

I love you or I send you God's love, I bless you, and I thank you for

_____

_____
(State what you wish to ask the Angel to do.)

 to the good of all parties concerned. Thank you, thank you, thank you.

Love from the Angel of _____

(Your signature) _____

Date: _____

The Angel Letter Worked for Me!

When I moved into my second husband's home, it was full of moose and deer antlers, fishing rods, and wading boots. What bothered me the most were the huge, gigantic moose antlers that decorated the fireplace in the living room. I read the engraved inscription below the antlers, which gave his name and the date he acquired them. I sighed and thought, "I am stuck with these."

Then I decided to write an Angel Letter to the antlers.

I wrote:

"To the angel of the antlers of the moose that hangs over the fireplace in the living room of our house: I love you, I bless you, and I thank you for moving yourself to another room, to the good of all parties concerned. Thank you, thank you, thank you. Love from the angel of the lady of the house."
Anne Marie Evers

Every time I passed them, I touched them gently, saying lovingly, "I love you, I bless you, and I thank you for removing yourself." I did this procedure many, many times. I was very careful to say "To the good of all parties concerned" in my angel letter, as I was aware it had to be to my husband's good as well as mine.

I never told anyone and sometimes wondered if I was diverting my energy into an avenue of non-performance. In other words, I really did not believe this could happen, but I kept doing it faithfully. After all, how could an inanimate object jump off the wall and walk into another room? And even if they did fall down, Roy would likely put them back up.

About three months later, my husband said, to my surprise, "When we decorate the living room, those antlers will come down and I don't think they will go back up." I said, "Yes, dear. They are very nice antlers. Would it be possible to put them in another room—you know, a sort of trophy room?"

I thought about this progression of events and came to the conclusion that I had been working with the Law of Attraction. The antlers could not physically remove themselves from the wall, but they could and did work on the mind of the person who placed them there.

He got the message loud and clear and followed through, moving them to another room. My Affirmation manifested, despite my disbelief. Such is the wondrous, magnificent power every human being has within, just waiting to be unleashed and put to work, creating miracles.

The Angel Letter Method has worked in many sticky situations, even with a bothersome bear, barking dogs, unhappy family situations, noisy renters, a friend, co-workers, a future daughter-in-law, and many more—with excellent, almost unbelievable results.

Cijaye DePradine Writes:

"An unpleasant neighbour used to live in my building. He was very rude, played loud music, and was quite violent to my family. After I used the Angel Letter Method, to my complete shock and disbelief, he did a complete turnaround and became kind-hearted, then he moved out. I now have a brand new neighbour who is perfect in so many ways. Angel Letters are magical— there is no other way to describe them!"
Cijaye DePradine
www.cijayecreative.com

Magic Magnetic Circle Procedure

When you get up in the morning, clear your mind of any negative thoughts. Forgive everyone and everything that has ever hurt you. Stand facing the window, slowly turning from left to right (clockwise) with your arms outstretched, saying the following Master Affirmation to yourself.

"I, (your name), now magnetize into my Magic Magnetic Circle (aura) peace, joy, love, health, and happiness to myself, which extends to everyone I meet. (Add your personal requests here, such as your desire for a loving, happy relationship, perfect career, money, health—anything you desire.) We are happy, to the good of all parties concerned. Thank you, thank you, thank you."

Short-Form Affirmation: **Full of powerful, positive magnetism**

No, it is not selfish to magnetize these wonderful things to yourself first, since you cannot give to others without first giving to yourself. You cannot give from an empty cup. You need to love and respect yourself before you can expect others to do so.

Completed Hospice, Port Moody, BC, Canada

Linda Kozina Writes about Creating a Hospice:

"For many years, the Crossroads Hospice Society held the vision of having our own free-standing hospice. After the land was selected, our task was to raise over $1,000,000 in capital funds.

We knew that Affirmations when properly done would produce results. From magazines, Anne Marie and I fashioned a circle of pictures for our Hospice scrapbook, showing the desired colours and the home-like environment we wanted to achieve in the hospice. We wrote the names of the corporations, foundations, and community leaders we wanted to contact and added the positive words that would create the Magic Magnetic Circle.

Over the course of four years, the Magic Circle enlarged. With the efforts of many dedicated community citizens and our

Capital Campaign Chair Tracy Price, we were able to raise the funds to build our free-standing hospice.

Thank you, Anne Marie. You were the catalyst that enabled us to fulfill our dreams."
Linda Kozina, Hospice Manager
Crossroads Inlet Centre Hospice
www.crossroadshospice.bc.ca

A Reader Writes:

"I wish to thank you, Anne Marie, from the bottom of my heart, for all the miracles you have helped me realize. Your book on Affirmations has inspired and comforted me greatly. After you shared the gift of the Magic Magnetic Circle Procedure with me, I practised it every morning for three months and won $10,000 on a scratch and win ticket! I am a single parent of an 11-year-old daughter and a full-time nursing student. I desperately needed the money. It was a Godsend."
Joanne Thiessen
Coquitlam, BC

Affirmations When Properly Done Always Work!

Cards of Life

www.affirmations-doctor.com

Affirmations, Your Passport to Happiness

11 • *Material Wealth & Career and Business*

A.   Becoming a Powerful Money-Magnet

M*oney cannot buy happiness, but it does make a good down payment!*

Make Money Your Friend

Money $$$

The human mind is the creator of all wealth. Money evolved from beads, stones, and shells to the sophisticated, economic tool it is today. Money is so charged with divine intelligence, it seems to have the ability to tune in to whatever you think and say about it. It responds accordingly. Money is a form of energy that can be directed, multiplied, or blocked. It has been called green energy, as green represents growth, change, and action. You can use your wonderful imagination and AMCAM to draw money to you and become abundantly wealthy.

Are You Broke or Poor?

Being broke is a temporary condition; being poor is a state of mind. Now is the time to uproot those old, negative beliefs of poverty. Those fortunate enough to have been born into wealth have developed a prosperity consciousness. This consciousness attracts more thoughts of wealth—and wealth itself—through the Law of Attraction.

If you were poor in your childhood, forgive your parents for being poor and realize they did the best they could with what they had at the time.

Take full responsibility for your life now, knowing you have the power to change your negative financial situation.

Never endorse or cash in on a thought of lack or scarcity in your life or the life of another. Refrain from criticizing money. When you say money is dirty or filthy, guess what happens. It takes on wings and flies away. This is the Law of Attraction working perfectly. You cannot attract what you reject through criticism.

Watch your self-talk. Could this be the reason you are unable to keep money in your possession? Think about it! Make a habit of saying, "Wealth is now mine. I deserve and now have wealth. Riches are forever flowing freely into my life and there is always a surplus."

The secret to making and keeping money in your life is to keep it circulating and use it wisely, to the benefit of all. Never allow the flow of money to become stagnant or blocked. Circulate it freely and lovingly.

How Do You React to Money?

- When bills arrive in the mail, do you suffer from a money anxiety attack?
- How long do you postpone opening the envelopes that hold your unpaid bills and invoices?
- What feelings do you experience when you are purchasing any item?
- Do you feel you are losing money?
- Are you exchanging or recycling it?
- How do you treat money?
- Do you crinkle it up or do you fold it neatly?
- Is your chequebook neat, tidy, and balanced?

When you understand how you think about and react to money issues, you will begin to see how to remedy your thinking.

Take full responsibility for your financial situation. Use your own positive thoughts and powerful mind to get yourself out of debt and stay debt-free. Respect money, bearing in mind it responds as people do. You can consciously change your mind about your thoughts of poverty and make them thoughts of wealth.

Say repeatedly during the day that you attract money and great wealth. Tell yourself you are on the road to prosperity. Accept the money consciousness. What we envision in life is what we get. Our Affirmations, images, concepts, and ideas—whether they are negative or positive—are self-fulfilling prophecies.

It is normal to experience a certain amount of difficulty, insecurity, or even fear about changing and letting go of old, familiar, comfortable, negative beliefs from past programming. But it is important to move with confidence out of your comfort zone into new, exciting, prosperous concepts and beliefs. This process ensures your prosperity.

Concentrate on what you save, not on what you spend. When you are experiencing a shortage of money, stay away from garage sales and swap meets, etc. You can always visit these places when you are flush with money.

Are your debts growing faster than your income? Put yourself on a strict money diet. Start saving small amounts, such as $5, $10, and $20.

Change your spending habits. Leave credit cards and chequebooks at home. Move out of your comfort zone and practise thinking big! Ask yourself how winning $10 million would change your life.

Examine What You Say about Money

- What are your feelings, beliefs, and emotions about it?
- How often have you said money creates unhappiness or greed, that money is evil, or money is scarce and that you do not deserve money?
- Do you believe that to be wealthy, you must be educated?

Substitute your negative ideas about money with the following concepts.

- Love, respect, and approve of money as a divine idea in God's mind.
- Accept your own divine inheritance of prosperity.
- Be open to receiving.
- Look for opportunities to give and be willing to receive and enjoy, in accordance with Universal Laws.

Wise Money-Management

Be aware of get-rich-quick schemes and chain letters promising wealth. It is also wise to be cautious when lending money to friends or family. If you lend a large amount, have the borrower sign a promissory note. If it is for a smaller amount, insist the borrower sign an IOU. If the debt is not repaid, you could lose a friendship or association with a family member.

When you give a gift of money to a friend or family member, however, give it freely and unconditionally, without expectation of return from the person. When people are in need, it may be wise to give a gift of groceries or anonymously pay that person's hydro or telephone bill instead of giving cash.

If you are a shopaholic who just has to shop or a spendaholic who cannot save a penny, you may have unexpressed feelings of inadequacy or low self-esteem. Those who exhibit these compulsive behaviours often feel it is important to dress up the outside because the inside is an empty void.

A friend of mine has a closet full of clothes, yet claims she has nothing to wear. She is driven to buy a new outfit at least every month, even when her finances are overextended. She will never be able to wear all the clothes she has in her closet. So why buy more? She says buying new clothes makes her feel happy and complete.

There are support groups such as Debtors Anonymous and others that can assist you in debt counselling and debt management. Enlist their services, if necessary. Begin the *Personal Contract Affirmation Method* to regain control of your life now!

Your Subconscious Mind Bank

Your subconscious mind is like a bank, magnifying whatever you deposit in it—whether it be thoughts of wealth or thoughts of poverty. Your subconscious never takes a holiday; it is open 24 hours a day.

If you say, "I cannot afford it," your subconscious mind takes you at your word, preventing you from being able to afford what you desire. Instead, say, "I cancel my desire to purchase that item at this time." Or "I choose to distribute my wealth in a different manner." Your subconscious mind is always striving to please you and carry out your instructions to the letter.

Making Money

You can use the power of your mind to create wealth in your life. Bear in mind, however, that whatever is in the mind affects everything else in the mind. If you are doing positive Affirmations and, at the same time, you are reading, thinking, and acting negatively, your positive Affirmations are negated. But if you keep pouring the pure, clean water of positivity into the dirty water of negativity in the mind, it will eventually become sparkling clear and clean.

If you are reading positive material, doing Affirmations, and trying to be positive, but old tapes of lack from the past keep surfacing, concentrate on abundance in every area of your life. Never make money your sole aim. Affirm health, wealth, happiness, peace, and love for all others and self. Radiate loving kindness and goodwill to everyone. Truly wealthy people never focus on money alone.

Be aware of people and things around you. Watch for and be conscious of mini-miracles occurring in your life on a daily basis. There is no lack in the Universe. There is abundance in all things. Reflect on the millions and millions of trees, plants, flowers, blades of grass, mountains, and animals. Does this depict lack or shortage? Start your Affirmations of abundance today!

Love, respect, and approve of yourself. You are a wonderful, worthwhile human being. Life is not only willing to pay, it has no alternative but to pay the exact price you put upon yourself. It can pay no more or no less because it is as impartial as a mirror that reflects your image back to you.

Negative Self-Talk Can Make You Poor!

It is very important to watch your self-talk closely. Never say anything about yourself that you would prefer not manifest in your life. Affirm you have rid yourself of negative feelings. Affirm you are worthy, responsible, and able to handle large sums of money. To help disperse any fears you have about your personal safety, affirm you are safe and protected.

Never say, "I can't afford it, I never have enough money, I hate money," etc. Your subconscious mind—which is your humble servant, always willing to carry out your instructions—will keep you broke and in lack.

It is very important that you never withhold or attempt to withhold wealth from another. If you do, you are automatically withholding it from yourself. What you wish for yourself, wish for everyone else. Always be genuinely happy for others when they receive or have wealth, health, happy, loving relationships, promotions, material things, or any other blessings.

You cannot experience abundance or prosperity without giving appreciation. Say "Thank you," feel thankful, and have and maintain an attitude of gratitude.

Creating Wealth and Abundance

Money and Mind-Power

Seed your sleep with thoughts of prosperity. Lull yourself to sleep, saying, "Great wealth, great wealth." This promotes prosperity consciousness.

Even if you are not wealthy at this present time, "great wealth" will not be rejected or cancelled by your conscious mind because you are not saying that you are wealthy or that you have great wealth. You are merely bringing wealth and prosperity into your consciousness.

When you lull yourself to sleep saying "great wealth," your subconscious mind has all night to locate, assemble, and bring into existence all the material required to make your Affirmation materialize. Once you have fully accepted and worked with the successful blueprint in your mind for making money, you will never again be broke or in need of money.

Bear in mind you never actually make wealth. Wealth comes into the life of those who strongly believe they can be and are now successful and wealthy. This acceptance is the consciousness that prepares the way for wealth.

When you doodle, write dollar signs. Fold your paper money in half, face up toward you. One of my students did this exercise and found $2,000 dollars in an old dresser he was refinishing. One lady said she had to discontinue this practice because she was getting too much overtime. This additional work resulted in her receiving more money. She reported she was becoming overtired.

I told her to rejoice and start another Affirmation that she had an excess of wonderful, healthy energy and was 100 percent healthy, wealthy, and completely balanced.

Ideas Make Money

Create, think, concentrate, and focus on your desire or idea. Every idea begins as a thought in your mind. See it as a tiny bubble and increase and magnify it. Then make it magnify into a bigger bubble; see that bubble burst into the beginnings of the desired object of your Affirmation.

Money has no actual power of its own. You give it power to make you feel secure or insecure, happy or unhappy, rich or poor. Do not make money a god or treat it as if it had a mind of its own. It does not. Money only does what you instruct it to do. It comes when you call it through the proper use of AMCAM. It goes away when you reject it.

Stop thinking negative, outdated thoughts that if you are prosperous, someone else is not or that you should not enjoy money and its luxuries because other people are starving.

Your Very Own Money Tree

The following exercise can be very powerful in helping you manifest abundance in your life. Purchase a small tree and plant it in your backyard. If you are limited for space, plant a small tree in a pot in your home or apartment. Place paper money bills on it, using clothespins or paper clips to attach the bills to the branches or leaves.

If you are unable to do it with real money, take pieces of paper and write out the amounts you wish to see multiplied: $50, $100, $5,000, $100,000, or more. You can also use Monopoly money. Alternatively, you may visualize your own money tree.

See yourself picking all the money you desire—$10s, $20s, $50s, $100s, $1,000s—from your very own money tree.

Renata was a young housewife who was always short of money. No matter how hard she tried, she could not make her husband's paycheque stretch far enough to pay all the bills. Tension over the shortage of money resulted in constant quarrels. When Renata came to see me, I could feel the tension and hostility in her. I told her about the Money Tree Method and she said she was willing to try anything.

She bought a live tree and planted it in her backyard. Every morning, she sat for 20 minutes eyes closed and visualized picking money off the tree. As she brought in all her senses, her visualizations became very clear and real to her.

She imagined:
- *Seeing* the money on the money tree
- *Hearing* the crack of crisp $100 bills
- *Feeling* the money with her fingers
- *Smelling* the new bill and
- *Tasting* a tangy mint.

She also did the following Affirmation.

"I, Renata, deserve to have and now easily pick from my very own money tree in my backyard the sum of $7,000 to pay my immediate debts, pay off the loan on the family car, and to use for spending money. I am not concerned about how this happens. I simply release this request with faith and expectancy into the Universe. Divine Intelligence now puts this money into my hands or my bank account. The power of my subconscious mind now brings it to pass in its own way. I get out of the way and allow it to manifest. I know the answer is appearing now, for which I give thanks. I am content and happy, to the good of all parties concerned. Thank you, thank you, thank you."

Her Short-Form Affirmation: **Great wealth, great wealth**

She lulled herself to sleep saying it. Shortly after she began this process, a friend dropped by for coffee one morning. When Renata served her one of her special muffins, the friend exclaimed, "These are marvellous, you should market them." Two days later, Bill came home from work and mentioned that his company was searching for a new vending company to provide coffee and goodies during the coffee break. As she remembered her friend's words, a light came on in Renata's mind.

The next morning, Bill awoke to the delicious aroma of Renata's muffins. "I have it all figured out," Renata told her husband. "I can use the station wagon, rent a coffee-maker from the church, and put coffee into thermos bottles, serve my muffins, and take over the catering business at your office."

Today, Renata has a flourishing business. She has added soup, salads, and sandwiches to her service and is now catering to several companies. Why did everything fall into place at just the right time? Could it have been because of Renata's Money Tree Affirmation and visualization? By her concentrated thought, action, and focus on money and the Affirmation exercise, Renata generated money consciousness and it manifested into her reality.

You will find a money tree in my home. I find it great for borrowing money and, when I replace it, I always add at least five dollars for the earned interest. You will find that opportunities you never dreamed were possible will come to you. You will be offered positions or business opportunities that will make money for you. New ideas will come to you from your subconscious as you hold the thought of prosperity firmly in your mind.

Become aware of money and how you can use it to help family, others, and self.

When affirming for money, refrain from attempting to figure out where it will come from.

Do not worry about the *modus operandi* (how it happens). It does not matter. Just be certain all your Affirmations contain the safety clause, "To the good of all parties concerned." You are entitled to all the wealth, health, and happiness you desire. You only have to desire it, be specific in your requests, and do AMCAM faithfully.

Multiply Your Money

When paying your bills, put your mind and consciousness in a positive, joyful, thankful mode and say "Thank you" for the opportunity to put money back into circulation in the Universe. Stop and think of the many people you employ daily, just by paying your bills. Bless your employer and your position; be thankful for the opportunity to earn, spend, enjoy, and circulate money.

Write "Thank you" on your Revenue Canada (CRA) or Internal Revenue form when you enclose your remittance cheque. Also bless your purse, wallet, and money and ask them to bring you abundance.

Thank God or the Universal Mind for multiplying your money. Respect, love, and appreciate money for what it can do for you and others.

Make a point of making money for others and you will never be broke. Make money your friend and it will serve you well. Say often how wonderfully blessed you are financially, knowing and accepting the fact that it is your birthright to be rich, happy, and successful.

Expect great wealth and an abundance of money to appear in your life. This way, you are reinforcing this new belief system, step by step.

Should you have problems believing you could receive the sum of $1,000,000, follow this step-by-step process.

- Write yourself a cheque first for $100, then $1,000, then $10,000, later $100,000.
- When your belief system is strong enough and you have developed prosperity consciousness, write yourself that cheque for $1,000,000!

Carry this cheque with you at all times. Look at it often and bless it. Thank it for materializing.

Tell yourself many times daily that you are an irresistible, powerful money-magnet to the right people and circumstances, bearing in mind that wealth and everything else come to you through other people and situations.

One reader told me her mind would not accept the affirmative statements that she was wealthy when she was experiencing money difficulties. Should that be the case with you, you can reword your Affirmations as follows.

"I am becoming wealthy, I am richer and richer every day. Prosperity is coming to me now. I am on the road to prosperity."

Then add an Affirmation that your mind and body now accept this statement as truth for you.

Several years ago, one of my students did an Affirmation to receive money. She simply affirmed she had received the sum of $5,000 to purchase an automobile. She went to a party, drank a little too much, and took a taxi home. She was in a car accident and was injured seriously enough to necessitate being off work for several months. Her settlement turned out to be $5,000—right to the penny!

I asked if she had ended her Affirmation with the safety clause, to the good of all parties concerned, as I had taught her. She admitted to me that she had not.

If she had added this clause to her Affirmation for $5,000, I feel sure she would have received the money in a different manner and been spared the injury. Her story is a good reminder of the utmost importance of adding to all your Affirmations, "To the good of all parties concerned."

Making Pearls Out of Irritations

When you feel sorry for yourself, you narrow your focus. In doing so, you could miss out on the goodness and blessings that are meant for you. Could this be why you are experiencing poverty, lack, and failure?

Refrain from giving power to upsetting, difficult conditions in your life. You have the power to change that. Start this moment making a game of finding good in every person you meet and in every situation you encounter.

Be thankful for all your many blessings and look for qualities to appreciate in others. Feel how blessed you are. Appreciate the miracles in your life, no matter how small and insignificant you may think they are. Appreciating them magnifies them.

When small irritations or problems appear in your life, see them as blessings in disguise. Consider how the oyster takes an irritation and makes a pearl. Take every business, personal, or career problem and make of it a valuable, successful lesson or opportunity.

Master and Short-Form Affirmations

Abundant Wealth

"I, (your name), deserve to be and now am very wealthy. I have supreme power and wisdom and I use it wisely. Money flows to me in avalanches of abundance. Money is my friend and I respect it and it respects me. I write 'Thank you' three times on all my bills and invoices when paying them. I know having money relieves stress. It gives me freedom to pay all my bills and obligations. I now pursue my life-long dream. I believe in myself and in my ability to make money. Money gives me financial security and enables me to help others. I freely circulate my wealth. I take the multi-millionaire's oath to help others. My family and I are safe and protected. I set up trust accounts for members of my family and others striving to help themselves. I am happy, healthy, and wealthy, to the good of all parties concerned. Thank you, thank you, thank you."

Short-Form Affirmation: **I accept the multi-millionaire's oath to help others**

Attracting Wealth

"I, (your name), deserve and now see money already in existence in the Universe. I enjoy being rich and use my money wisely. I see it piled in vaults of the Universal Bank, just waiting for me to withdraw whatever amount I desire. I now withdraw fresh and crisp $20, $50, $100, and $1,000 bills. I am wealthy, safe, and happy, to the good of all parties concerned. Thank you, thank you, thank you."

Short-Form Affirmation: **Abundant wealth**

Multiplying Money

"I, (your name), deserve to have and now have my money multiplied. Every dollar I spend returns to me multiplied, which I use wisely to benefit my family, others, and myself. We are happy, to the good of all parties concerned. Thank you, thank you, thank you."

Short-Form Affirmation: **Money multiplies for me now**

Money Tree

"I, (your name), deserve and now easily pick from my very own money tree, the sum of $_____. I use this money wisely to pay off any debts (be specific here about what bills you desire to pay). Money is good to me. It is constantly circulating in my life. I use it wisely and constructively to help others and myself. I am wealthy, to the good of all parties concerned. Thank you, thank you, thank you."

Short-Form Affirmation: **Abundance of money for all my desires**

Great Wealth

"I, (your name), deserve and now attract in excess of $_____ (net or gross) into my life. I am safe and protected. The world teems with my riches and treasures. I enjoy and use my share of power, money, and possessions, to the good of all. I project my ideas in a radiant stream of mental and physical energy that magnetizes and attracts to me money, power, influential friends, happiness, self-confidence, and peace of mind. I create greater levels of abundance in my life. Money and success now flow to me in waves of prosperity. I use this wealth wisely and constructively, to the good of all parties concerned. Thank you, thank you, thank you."

Short-Form Affirmation: **Great wealth, great wealth**

Dream Home

"I, (your name), deserve and now own the home of my dreams in perfect condition. It has over (specify size) square feet, three bedrooms, office, large recreation room, sauna, hot tub, and elegant furnishings. This home is all paid for or we can easily afford it (whichever your conscious mind can believe). It is situated by the water, in a quiet area, or on a treed lot or acreage. It is in the perfect location. We are happy, safe, and protected in this home, to the good of all parties concerned. Thank you, thank you, thank you."

Short-Form Affirmation: **Ideal home, perfect price, and location**

Overcoming the Shopaholic or Spendaholic Syndrome

"I, (your name), deserve love and respect. I now love and respect myself. I enjoy making wise decisions. I use money wisely and I shop efficiently. I stop and really think about the article I am about to purchase. I know money is important in my life; my self-worth and self-control, however, are more important. It is unnecessary to compete with anyone or measure up to anyone's expectations. I believe in me. I have powerful control over my desires and feelings when spending money. I am happy with my self-image. I concentrate on what I can spend and refrain from dwelling on what I cannot spend. I am debt-free. I am complete, whole, healthy, and at peace, to the good of all parties concerned. Thank you, thank you, thank you."

Lull yourself to sleep at night with these words: happy, debt-free; happy, debt-free.

Short-Form Affirmation: **Normal, healthy spending habits and debt-free**

Use the above Master Affirmation and Short-Form Affirmation process for any item you desire, for example, a brand new vehicle, furniture, clothing, jewellery, etc. Be certain to finish your Short-Form Affirmation with the appropriate symbol. For example, a dollar sign for money, a heart for love, or any other symbol you wish to use.

For more information on Prosperity and Money, please read my companion book, *Affirmations, Your Passport to Prosperity/Money*, available from me or www.amazon.com.

B. Attracting that Perfect, Lasting, Successful Career

The Search

If you are unemployed or short of cash, remember that being broke is just a temporary condition, whereas being poor is a state of mind. What you believe to be true is the key to releasing your old, negative beliefs of unhappiness and lack.

Make positive Affirmations about wealth. To create more abundance in your life, use your thoughts and mind to create the perfect, lasting, successful career for you. A successful, profitable career can bring money, wealth, and security.

- Tell friends and associates that you are looking for that special career. They may help you.
- Check out newspaper advertisements and employment agencies.

- Spend some extra money on having an excellent résumé professionally prepared.
- Have business cards printed to introduce you to your prospective employer in a professional manner.

The Day Before the Interview

Mentally visualize—in vivid Technicolor—exactly how you wish the interview to progress.

Bring the five senses into your creative visualization.

1. *See* your interviewer (just a rough sketch is fine).
2. *Hear* him or her saying, "(Your name), I am so pleased to say I have scheduled you for a second interview with the president. This is just a formality. You have the position."
3. *Feel* the joy and pride at being selected for the position.
4. *Smell* some cologne, flowers, or perfume.
5. *Taste* a tangy mint.

Then step ahead two to three weeks or months and picture yourself in that career. Be certain to put yourself in the picture.

- Before the appointment, find out all you can about the company and, if possible, the person who will be interviewing you. If your prospective interviewer is a golfer, speak about golfing. If he or she likes to fish, talk about fishing, etc.

- Talk about the other person's interest; make the person feel he or she is the most important person in the world at that moment.

I once interviewed a busy multimillionaire executive who informed me at the beginning of the interview that he had only 10 minutes to give me. After two hours, I terminated the interview because I had another appointment. Why did he give me so much time? We were talking about the most important person in his world—him, a subject for which there was no time limit.

The Interview

- Stay calm. Do not allow yourself to become desperate or overanxious.
- Be punctual, neat, clean, and well dressed.
- Be confident. Shake hands firmly and make frequent eye contact with the interviewer.
- Smile and be yourself.
- Speak clearly and professionally and avoid using slang.
- Never speak negatively about previous employers or divulge trade secrets.
- Employers like and appreciate people who are interesting, relaxed, competent, and willing to learn.
- Show your prospective employers you are sincerely interested in working with their company.
- Practise empathetic listening. Really hear what the interviewer is saying.
- Respect the opinions of the interviewer and make comment, when appropriate.
- It is nice to be important, but it is far more important to be nice.
- Concentrate on what you have learned from previous work experiences. Refrain from acting like a know-it-all.

Employer Relationships

Sometimes we transfer our fear from our spouse or family members to our employer.

- Do you fear your employer?
- Is your boss a controlling person?
- Do you experience fear of failure or rejection?

Keep personalities out of the workplace. Personal problems belong at home.

Job Evaluation

When you are about to be evaluated, here are some points to bear in mind.

- Really listen to the comments, concentrating on each word and letting them penetrate your mind.
- Evaluate what the other person is saying.
- Appreciate and value the good comments.
- Give genuine thanks for praise.
- Welcome constructive criticism.
- Ask for clarification (to ensure you understand the statements fully).
- Make suggestions on how to solve problems.
- When applicable, say "No" nicely, with assurance.
- Speak up for yourself. Each time you fail to do so, you take one more dose of no-confidence poison. You lose some of your self-confidence and self-worth. Refuse to be labelled; do not accept unjust, unfair criticism of your work.

The Raise

How do you feel about asking for a raise? If you are unhappy with the way you feel, create a new state of consciousness.

- Do not berate yourself if you feel you are not earning enough money.
- Refrain from comparing your salary to others or trying to compete with them.
- Decide what you want your financial situation to be.
- Choose the exact amount you wish to earn monthly or yearly (net or gross) and prepare the appropriate Master Affirmation.

Assessing Your Current Situation

You may not be able to secure another new position until you have learned how to deal with a particular difficult person or situation at your present place of employment. The workplace is comprised of many varied personalities. It is possible to have a personality conflict with one of your co-workers, your employer, or others. If this happens, start AMCAM immediately.

- Are you expecting too much of your present career, company, or superiors?

- Could you be comparing yourself to fellow employees or competing with them?
- Do you feel you are being treated unjustly?

If this is the case, get to the root of the problem, examine it, discuss it, and then solve it.
- Are you being overly sensitive?
- Is there a legitimate reason for this treatment?
- Why do you feel it is unfair?
- Are you being passed over for promotions?
- Are you attracting this type of treatment by your attitude or actions?
- Does your attitude need to be adjusted or changed?

When you get the answers to these questions, you will be better equipped to look within at the internal problem.

If you are satisfied with your answers and you have been honest, it may be time to secure another position.

Robert's Journey of Discovery

The following story illustrates how important it can be to resolve certain issues before you can move on. Robert was very upset and unhappy in his career. He had been employed at the same company for eight years and had been passed over for promotions on three occasions.

When he called me, he was very depressed and rather grumpy. He assured me he had been doing his Affirmations regularly.

But when I asked how he felt when he began doing his Affirmations, he said, "I can't help thinking how unfair life is. Steven gets more money than I do and he doesn't do half the work. He leaves early and takes time off, while I work overtime every night. I have never missed a day. And Pierre was promoted last week."

It was easy to see why AMCAM was not working for him. He was filling his mind and his being with negative emotions and energy before and while he was doing his Affirmations. The message he was giving his subconscious was, "Poor me, it so unfair. Nobody cares and I am not important." He continued in a complaining voice, saying, "They moved my desk and filing cabinet and never asked me or even told me. I found out when I went to work Monday morning. They do not appreciate or respect me. I hate that place. I want out."

It took several months of counselling before Robert could see that his attitude and actions were keeping him from the success and respect he so deeply and earnestly desired.

He released all resentment and put himself in a positive mood. When he changed his thoughts, emotions, attitudes, and actions, his life changed in a positive way. He decided to make the best of his current career and he introduced and implemented a whole new computer program at work.

He created and taught the program. People really took notice and started treating him with respect. Two months later, completely out of the blue, Robert was offered a new career. When he told his current employer he was leaving, the employer tried to talk him into staying.

Robert moved out of his comfort zone and accepted the new position. He is now very involved and happy in his new career. His whole attitude changed; he realized that doing Affirmations when in a negative, nasty mood or frame of mind, delays, hinders, or stops their positive flow. He now puts himself into a positive, receptive, thankful mood before and during his Affirmation process and the results speak for themselves!

Wording Your Affirmations

Be sure to make your Master Affirmation accurate and specific. Say exactly what you desire. This is your order to the Universe. You cannot expect it to be filled unless you specify exactly what you desire. When doing your Career Master Affirmation, be certain to specify the amount desired in net or gross. It is also important to add the word "lasting" to your Affirmation.

One woman omitted this word and she got exactly what she affirmed. Her career, which was perfect and successful, lasted eight months. Another reader omitted the word "net" to the amount she wished her business to earn. When she deducted her expenses, she was very disappointed with the net figure.

Use separate pages for your Master Affirmations to ensure your intention is crystal clear! Also use colour, add hearts, dollar signs, and happy faces. Make your Master Affirmations colourful, exciting and interesting so you will want to look at them over and over.

Master and Short-Form Affirmations

Perfect, Lasting, Successful Career

"I, (your name), deserve and now have the perfect, lasting, successful career (position) for me. I have a (supervisory) position that I thoroughly enjoy. I am happy with my employers and they are happy with me. I enjoy large bonuses. I am healthy, happy, and balanced. They reward me with $_____ yearly (net or gross). I love my career and am the very best at it, to the good of all parties concerned. Thank you, thank you, thank you."

Short-Form Affirmation: **Perfect, lasting, successful career**

Career, Position, or Business

"I, (your name), deserve and now have the perfect, lasting successful career, position, or business for me. I give myself permission to be successful. I am safe and protected. I earn in excess of $_____yearly (net or gross). I am healthy, happy, and balanced. I have a company car and a large expense account. My company recognizes my excellent work and performance and rewards me accordingly. They respect me and I respect them. I use my time wisely and still have time for my family and interests. Every day is filled with excitement. I am happy, to the good of all parties concerned. Thank you, thank you, thank you."

Short-Form Affirmation: **Perfect business or position**

Achieving Sales Goals

"I, (your name), deserve to achieve and now easily reach my target in the specified timeframe. Nothing deters me from my goals and Affirmations. I give myself permission to be top salesperson in my company. I enjoy perfect balance and a healthy, full social life. I am safe, very successful, and happy, to the good of all parties concerned. Thank you, thank you, thank you."

Short-Form Affirmation: **My target easily reached**

Promotion

"I, (your name), deserve to be guided and now am guided in all my thoughts and actions to do what is required to gain a substantial promotion. I earn in excess of $_____ monthly (net or gross). I am and remain balanced, healthy, and peaceful. I now have that promotion with my company, to the good of all parties concerned. Thank you, thank you, thank you."

Short-Form Affirmation: **Promotion easily attained**

Realtors

You can use the *Personal Contract Affirmation Method* to obtain and sell properties. You can also use it to make your transactions run smoother and increase your self-confidence. Many realtors use Affirmations when handling difficult sellers and hard to-sell properties with remarkable results.

When I sold real estate, I had a situation where an elderly father did not wish to sell the house he had so lovingly and painstakingly built. Due to a serious health problem, however, the father was suffering; his son felt it was in his best interest to sell.

The father resisted, saying, "No, no, this house will never sell. I don't want to move. I won't move. They will have to carry me out." Interestingly, I never did sell that house nor was I instrumental in selling it. I did write two no subject offers on that home that fell apart just before closing. The house did not sell until the elderly gentleman was finally moved into a rest home. Such was the power of his mind.

Success in Real Estate

"I, (your name), deserve to be and now am a successful realtor. It is easy for me to get well-priced listings and sell them quickly. I earn in excess of $_____ yearly (net or gross). I am successful and attract the right clients into my life. I handle ____ listings at all times, confidently. I enjoy balance in my work and social life. I know every transaction must be to the good of all parties. I enjoy giving my clients excellent service. I enjoy helping people and I am happy and successful, to the good of all parties concerned. Thank you, thank you, thank you."

Short-Form Affirmation: **Successful, top realtor**

Selling Property

"My listing at (address) deserves to be and now is sold to the good of all parties concerned. My sellers are happy. The purchasers are happy with the price of their new home. The transaction goes smoothly. I believe in my work and my abilities. I create my future now. Both my company and I are thrilled with the commission and my excellent, professional work. We are happy, to the good of all parties concerned. Thank you, thank you, thank you."

Short-Form Affirmation: **Desired property now sold**

Real Estate Success!

In the 1970s, Merv Wright and I worked in the same real estate office in North Vancouver where we enjoyed a great working relationship. Merv moved to Calgary and we lost touch. Then one day I bumped into him in the bank in North Vancouver and we immediately continued our friendship.

Merv Wright Writes:

"When Anne Marie told me about the books she had written and the work she was doing with Affirmations, I knew I needed to learn more about the power of Affirmations to make positive changes in my life. She invited me to an Affirmation Group that met in her home. I attended and she gave me her book.

As a result of attending that meeting and reading her book, I started doing Affirmations on a daily basis—to my benefit. I used her method to create both personal and business change in my life and I received positive benefits and results.

Every day I walk my dog for 20 minutes and read, review, and say my Affirmations and goals.

I even take her book to church and often find similar and confirming information in the sermons. I use this combined information to create an uplifting, positive environment in my life. It works!!!

Recently I had a challenging business situation. A difficult seller refused to make a price adjustment to bring the selling price of his home into line with other homes in the area to enable me to sell his house.

I decided to try another of the exercises Anne Marie teaches in her book. On a piece of masking tape, I wrote 'Spiritual Disinfectant,' then placed the tape on an empty spray bottle. (I used an empty spray bottle so I wouldn't mark the walls or furniture.)

To create a positive environment conducive to change and to attract the perfect buyer and complete the sale, I went through the motions of spraying the inside of that house. Before holding Open House at the property, when no one was around, I sprayed every corner, saying, 'I now spray any negative thoughts and feelings surrounding the quick sale of this house to the good of all parties concerned. Thank you, thank you, thank you.'

I also did a written Master Affirmation that my listing was now sold for the perfect price. Then I placed a picture of the house at the top of the Affirmation and wrote SOLD across the photo in large red letters.

Well, that process worked, too!!! To my delight, the seller adjusted his price and we received an acceptable offer within 10 days.

So if you are a realtor and have a difficult property to sell, do as I did. W-O-W: Affirmation Selling Success!

This book contains real, powerful information that works. All you need do is access it and use it. I am using it every day in all kinds of situations!"
Merv Wright, Vancouver, BC, Canada

C. Starting Your Own Home-Based Business

Having your own successful business is one of the easiest ways to build your success consciousness with regard to money. You can take this built-in success consciousness and incorporate it into any other type of investments, stocks, bonds, and real estate.

Make your business so much fun that you enjoy every minute. I always say that when you fall in love with what you do, you never have to work again. I have fallen in love with teaching Affirmations and it is true—I never have to work again. Fear of failure, success, or the unknown is what stops many a person from starting a business or being a success.

Today, thousands of home businesses are prospering. They can operate on a minimum amount of money. Many a successful million-dollar business started at the kitchen table with little or no money.

Find an idea for a business venture that is needed and that interests you. As Will Rogers said with regard to real estate, "The secret in real estate is to find out where the people are going and get there first."

Come up with your own idea. Write down what you like to do and brainstorm with others who are supportive of you and your ideas.

One man discovered his friends were always asking him to locate certain car parts, which he did, through auto wreckers, scrap yards, ads, and associates. He provided this needed service to others, too, and it became a thriving business.

Several years ago, four young men rented a truck, bought some tires and equipment, and went to a part of the Alaska Highway that is famous for flat tires and blowouts. They found a need and created their own successful business venture to fill that need. They now have expanded to handling car repairs and other services for motorists.

Do your homework by reading some of the numerous books available on setting up a home business.

Prepare a business plan to take to the financial institution for a loan, if required. When you have your finances in place, start your business.

When starting your own business, be certain to pay yourself a salary, whether your business can afford it or not. Since time is money, it is also important to make wise use of your time and to keep your life and business orderly. Organize your life and learn to delegate. Make your business serve you. Your key to starting and running a successful business is acquiring and using the prosperity consciousness.

Be courageous. Move forward even in the face of fear. You are a survivor, having survived the past and its problems; now you are in celebration of life in the present. Think prosperity and abundant wealth. Think about that perfect, lasting, successful business. Talk to successful businesspeople. Glean, modify, and utilize their good ideas. Read success stories, books, attend self-help lectures, and listen to success tapes.

Live success and be a success. Believe you are successful. Know it is happening to you as you read these words. Embrace the success consciousness; do not overextend yourself or feel like a failure if you do not experience instant success. Lull yourself to sleep saying, "Perfect business; perfect business."

Many people have created successful home-based businesses after taking the Cards of Life Reader's Course. They are now reading the Cards of Life for others and enjoying prosperous, happy, fulfilled careers.

Master and Short-Form Affirmations

Starting Your Own Business

"I, (your name), deserve to be and now am guided in my thoughts and actions in the direction of establishing my own business. I have the experience, education, and knowledge. My business benefits all who come into contact with it. I deserve and now have the sum of $_____ to start my business. I climb to success because of my unselfish motives. My successes enable me to do more for others. I have the funds and necessary education to start my own business. I enjoy perfect balance. I am a successful businessperson, to the good of all parties concerned. Thank you, thank you, thank you."

Short-Form Affirmation: **Perfect, successful, lasting business**

Increasing Business/Sales

"I, (your name), deserve and now attract into my store or place of business a minimum of ____ paying clients or customers daily. This nets me in excess of $_____ monthly. Everyone is totally pleased with my services and products. I believe in myself and my company. My business increases monthly. We are all happy, to the good of all parties concerned. Thank you, thank you, thank you."

Short-Form Affirmation: **Increase in paying customers and clients**

Big Money to Me Now:
Abbreviation Method

Write at the top of a page: "Big Money to Me Now." Below that statement, write the abbreviated form of it using the first letter of each word—"b$tmn." Write "b$tmn" 77 times daily. It is very important to say it as you are writing it so you are focusing on your intention.

Perfect, Lasting, Successful Career For Me Now:
Abbreviation Method

Using the same procedure, at the top of a page write the words: "Perfect, lasting, successful career for me now." Below it, write the abbreviation: "plscfmn." Write "plscfmn" 77 times daily, while saying the words out loud.

Yvonne Writes:

"I just wanted to tell you I wrote out 'Big Money to Me Now,' put it in my purse, and took it to Bingo. That night I won $2,000! Thank you for this wonderful tool. I am telling everyone I meet about it!"

Vic Writes:

"After doing the Big Money to Me method for two weeks, I found a very valuable coin I did not know I had in my coin collection. It turned out to be worth $20,000! It saved my business from going bankrupt. I cannot thank you enough. Your subconscious mind does not differentiate between the real and the imagined. It accepts this statement as true and goes to work immediately to manifest it for you."

Affirmations When Properly Done Always Work!

Nicole Whitney Writes

"I've known Anne Marie for many years and have worked with her in many ways. She's been a regular guest on my radio show. She was a columnist for my 'positive' news newspaper in the earlier years of my broadcasting efforts. And she's been the focus of live events with our networking meetings, as well. It is with awe and amazement that I've watched Anne Marie do all that she can with whatever resources she has at the time, and transform the lives of many in a positive way as a result. And I imagine what a world it would be if everyone did the same. She is an inspiration to many, playing full on at the game of life. I am happy to know Anne Marie—'the affirmations doctor'—a title adopted live and in the moment during one of our broadcasts together on News for the Soul."

Nicole Whitney,
Producer/Host News for the Soul & Life Changing TV
Phone (604) 780 NEWS (6397) email:nicole@newsforthesoul.com

Affirmations, Your Passport to Happiness

Personal Growth

part 3

Love, Happiness, and Meditation

Health and Healing &
Weight Reduction and Control

Retirement

Death

Short-Form Affirmations

The Author's Personal Story:
The Power of Affirmations—
My Story of Disbelief to Belief

Letters from Readers

Feedback from the Media

Resources

Product Information

Kids' Affirmation Program

Order Form and
Feedback

How an Affirmation Created
Affirmations-Doctor.com

Cards of Life

www.affirmations-doctor.com

12 • *Love, Happiness, and Meditation*

Happiness is an Inside Job

Unconditional love is the most powerful force in the Universe. It has the power to transform our deepest fears and phobias and to heal emotional wounds. I remember one day parking my car on the street, with the back end of it protruding over a portion of a homeowner's driveway. There was still sufficient room for the homeowner to get out of his/her driveway, but it would take some effort and manoeuvring.

When I came back to my vehicle a few hours later, there was a note on my windshield that said, "Dear driver: The way you parked is very selfish and unfeeling. If you do this again, I will call the police and have you towed away without further notice." It was signed, "Love, Angelina."

I read and re-read the note; the word that stood out and seemed to vibrate was the single, one-syllable word "Love." This single word motivated me to take action and apologize for my thoughtlessness. I knocked on Angelina's door and apologized with a bouquet of flowers. Never underestimate the power of love!

Three Important Aspects of Love

The first and most important aspect of love is that of being lovable. There must be love from self to self before it can be extended to others. You cannot give from an empty cup. Fill your cup of divine self-love to overflowing. You are loveable in spite of any shortcomings and faults. Learn to love your individuality and your connection with God.

The second aspect of love is that of loving, whereby you give and express love to others and self. Loving others comes naturally and easily when you fully love yourself.

The third aspect of love is that of being loved. You need to allow yourself to be loved and to fully receive love from others.

If you strive daily to achieve these three states, you will come to understand the true meaning of unconditional love. To achieve unconditional love in your life, all three of these aspects must be happening simultaneously.

Everyone needs love no matter how independent, wealthy, or successful a person may be. Without love, there is no self-actualization. Love is an element as essential to our well-being as air or water.

Love of Self

All love begins with self-love. Loving self as you are gives you the permission and the ability to change. Acceptance is the highest form of love. Practising acceptance in your daily life enables you and others to be themselves. On the other hand, envying others or comparing yourself to them inhibits self-love and acceptance.

Say:

> "I, (your name), deserve and now love, respect, and approve of myself, just the way I am."

Some people find it very effective and powerful to say this Affirmation while looking at themselves in the mirror.

An unselfish, divine love of self gives you a mystical power. This unconditional love represents total acceptance without any expectation of return. When you give, the love within expands and you simultaneously receive. You experience inner glorious peace when you are focused on unconditional love and giving to others. Love imparts vitality and fertilizes positive, loving thoughts.

Compassion is love in action. Being compassionate with yourself means giving your body nourishing food, exercise, rest, and relaxation. It also involves listening to your own feelings and feeding your body spiritually, emotionally, and physically.

Master and Short-Form Affirmations

Self-Love

"I, (your name), deserve and now love, respect, and approve of myself, just the way I am. I believe in me. I know thoughts have a powerful effect on my life. I say 'No' easily, when necessary. I enjoy healthy self-respect, self-esteem, and self-love. I count. I respect others and expect respect in return. I am capable, efficient, and fulfilled. I know it is not selfish to love myself. I have confidence in myself and my decisions. I choose happiness, health, and wealth. I easily move out of my comfort zone. I make friends with time and I have all the time there is. Time stands still for me.

I visit the past, on occasion, but I do not linger too long. I am a magnetic, loving person and attract good, faithful friends. I am a faithful, committed friend. I easily eject negative tapes and play powerful, positive new ones. I am happy, to the good of all parties concerned. Thank you, thank you, thank you."

Short-Form Affirmation: **Full of confidence, self-esteem, and self-respect**

Love Affirmation

"I, (your name), deserve to love and now truly do love myself. It is easy for me to love, respect, and approve of myself and others. All my cells and whole body are bathed in love. I love myself with the divine love of God. I am happy, loving, loved, and lovable. We are all happy, to the good of all parties concerned. Thank you, thank you, thank you."

Short-Form Affirmation: **Lovable, loving, and loved**

Self-Love and Acceptance

"I, (your name), deserve to love and now truly love, accept, and approve of myself, just the way I am. I believe in myself and my life. Any fear of rejection immediately leaves my body. I am worthy. I am calm, peaceful, and happy. I am healthy, happy, and peaceful, to the good of all parties concerned. Thank you, thank you, thank you."

Short-Form Affirmation: **Love, acceptance, respect, and approval of self**

Happiness

Happiness is not a destination. It is a journey with stops of interest along the way. It is a state of consciousness or awareness that is not dependent on outside people, places, circumstances, or events. Happiness comes from within you. It is an inside job! If you are unhappy and good things happen to you, you may be viewing these blessings with murky, dirty, negative glasses. You may therefore not recognize them and miss out on your wonderful blessings.

Raise your consciousness and you attract good things to you. Be conscious of your blessings and concentrate on the good things in your life. It is your birthright to be healthy, happy, and prosperous.

Happiness is surrendering to what is and living in the now—the only moment you have. Make happiness your daily habit—look on the bright side, live your faith, and involve yourself in harmonious actions and interactions with self and others.

Happiness appears when the mind is at peace and ceases its search for it.

Certainly, outer conditions and people can contribute to your happiness, but the mere possession of wealth, luxuries, or having a wonderful spouse does not ensure happiness. Many unhappy people are rich in material things and many less fortunate people are extremely happy.

Happiness comes from forgiving, releasing negativity, and accepting, approving of, and loving the self. Try smiling at everyone you meet and make a note of how many people smile back at you. Make a habit of spreading sunshine wherever you go.

A happy person is one who acts purposefully and makes things happen. He or she looks forward to each new day with excitement and happy anticipation.

Don't put off "being happy" until such time as you finally get that dream job, find that perfect relationship, or pay off your mortgage. You may end up wishing your life away.

It is important to enjoy life's journey—not just the highlights. Think, plan, and be constructive and specific about your goals and what you desire in this life. Do your Affirmations daily and faithfully.

Very often, unhappiness is just a bad habit. When you are happy, you don't think about it, but when you are unhappy, you cannot seem to stop thinking about it. Break this negative habit by doing your Affirmations regularly.

Master and Short-Form Affirmations

Generating Happiness

"I, (your name), deserve to be and now am happy. I freely and lovingly share my happiness with others. I radiate happiness! I now choose to be happy. My path in life leads onward and upward. I master all conditions and situations in my life instead of being mastered by them. It gives me happiness to help others and make them happy. I know true happiness comes from within. I am blessed, to the good of all parties concerned. Thank you, thank you, thank you."

Short-Form Affirmation: **Total happiness, peace, and joy**

Enhancing Enjoyment of Life

"I, (your name), deserve to experience and now enjoy life to the fullest. I find joy and happiness in everything and everyone. Happiness is my constant companion. I am too blessed to be stressed. I enjoy spreading happiness to everyone I meet. I am happy for my fulfilled life, my wonderful partner, children, etc. I freely and completely forgive everyone and everything that has ever hurt me. I now forgive myself. I love, respect, accept, and approve of myself just the way I am. I am happy, to the good of all parties concerned. Thank you, thank you, thank you."

Short-Form Affirmation: **Full of happiness**

Meditation/Contemplation and Peace

Meditation is an effort made on the part of the conscious mind to close the gap between itself and the subconscious mind. Meditation is simply a quiet state of mind, a silence of thought. The growth of living things and the movement of the heavens are silent. The dictionary defines meditation thus: "to ponder or to engage in continuous and contemplative thought."

It could also be described as thinking about doing something or planning to do it. Meditation is not daydreaming; it is surrendering, letting go, and sinking deep into relaxation. It is the attuning of the mental body and the spiritual body to its principal source—God. When you meditate, you empty yourself of everything that hinders your creative energies. Meditation sets the foundation for peace of mind and tranquility.

In meditation, you learn to listen to your thoughts and create a space to hear your own voice. Pay close attention to what your mind is saying. Have a pen and paper close by so you can jot down any thoughts or insights that come to you when you still your mind.

Take 15 to 20 minutes from your busy day in the morning and late afternoon or evening to meditate.

- Find a quiet spot.
- Sit or lie down.
- Relax and clear your mind.

Some people can relax by playing music. Do whatever works for you. Tell yourself you will return in 20 minutes, refreshed and full of radiant energy. Setting your own time limit is important so that your subconscious mind will ensure that you observe it. Take several deep breaths, breathing out all negative thoughts, worries, and cares. Then breathe in happy thoughts of peace, joy, love, and happiness.

Concentrate on one two-syllable word to help you focus. If you desire peace, concentrate on the word peaceful. If you desire love, concentrate on the word loving. Keep repeating this one word over and over, to the exclusion of all other thoughts, ideas, and words. Feel yourself going deeper and deeper into relaxation. Find that quiet space within where the real you resides. Let yourself go completely.

There are many excellent books, tapes, and lectures on all types of meditation. As you practise day after day, it will become easier because thoughts will not disturb you as often. Be persistent. Select the time that best suits your busy schedule.

Developing Peace of Mind

Peace of mind is a state of mind. It is not something you acquire, but something you express. It does not come from what you get but how you use what you have. Peace is the condition of mind and body that you reach when you are satisfied with the thoughts you are thinking, the life you are living, and the things you are doing. Peace is the state of your mind when your thoughts are still. It is completeness, totality, awareness, and spiritual growth.

True peace is total acceptance of self. Peace of mind is being glad you have the gift of life. Choose peace instead of conflict and love instead of hate. There can be no spiritual growth without the higher, divine love of self. One cannot attain spiritual growth without practising and living forgiveness of others and self.

Exercising Intense Forgiveness

The following exercise will truly change how you view your life. It is a sure-fire method of curing most, if not all, of life's problems.

Sit quietly every morning for 30 to 35 minutes and mentally forgive everyone and everything that has ever hurt you. Then mentally ask for forgiveness for your negative, hurtful thoughts, feelings, and actions to self and others.

If you have criticized or gossiped about anyone, withdraw those negative words, thoughts, and feelings by asking for forgiveness. See everyone as spirit and send them your strongest, purest, highest quality of love.

Release and let go of hurt from others to achieve peace of mind, love of self, and spiritual growth. You need to take responsibility for your own health, body, and life.

Love yourself and your life. It is the only one you have. Tell yourself you are a wonderful, worthwhile human being and that no one can keep God's blessings from you.

Master and Short-Form Affirmation

Spiritual Growth

"I, (your name), now open up to and deserve higher levels of awareness. I am safe. I now meditate on all that is good, kind, and peaceful. All negativity and fear leave my body now. I attract peace, goodness, and harmony. My mind is free from worry because I am in direct contact with the source of God's power and intelligence. This enables me to dissolve the cause of worry. I am calm and handle any situation. I am free of fear and worry. Spiritual awakening is penetrating every cell, muscle, tissue, and every part of my being. I believe in myself and my life. I experience new levels of spirituality, tranquility, love, peace, and joy. I am happy, to the good of all parties concerned. Thank you, thank you, thank you."

Short-Form Affirmation: **God's perfect peace**

Affirmations When Properly Done Always Work!

Cards of Life

www.affirmations-doctor.com

13 • *Health and Healing &*
Weight Reduction and Control

Health is the Gift:
Happiness is the Journey!

A.   Health and Healing

Sickness begins in the energy field and in the mind about 18 months before it manifests in the physical body. Your body possesses an astonishing ability to restore and recreate itself. You regenerate a completely new liver every six months; many diseases can be reversed with the proper steps.

Every seven years, all the cells in your body are totally renewed. In this continual regeneration of the physical body, you have numerous daily opportunities to stimulate healing and improve your health. This can be accomplished by practising the *Personal Contract Affirmation Method*, exercising, getting enough sleep, meditating, and eating properly.

Use your wonderful mind-power for healing. Your mind holds the power to trigger this fantastic, natural, healing ability. Every thought and emotion you experience causes a chemical response in your organs, bloodstream, and immune system. Repressed negative emotions may trigger disease; positive thoughts and feelings can help facilitate healing.

Members of the medical profession are recognizing the value of mind-power. One acquaintance told me she felt extremely positive and happy after a chiropractic treatment because her chiropractor always had words of encouragement for her. He would say, "Jo-Anne, you can do it. You are a unique and wonderful person. You have the ability to achieve that promotion. Believe in yourself and go for your dream."

Many medical people are adding positive, powerful Affirmations to their patients' prescriptions, with wonderful results. One reader who had chemotherapy treatment for cancer walked out of her doctor's office with the book *Directing the Movies of Your Mind*, by

Adelaide Bry. Her doctor told her to read it and visualize movies in her mind to heal her body.

Your body believes every word you say and your words and thoughts control your health. Conversations with self and others have a lasting impact and impression on how you feel today and how you will feel tomorrow. Words are very powerful. Watch your self-talk!

In the context of health, the term holistic means treating the integrated system of your entire being—mind, body, and spirit. Good health is necessary to enjoy every facet of life. Perfect health should be the natural result of a nutritious diet, sensible exercise, positive thinking, stress management, meditation, positive Affirmations, and high self-esteem.

As my friend Sam from Desert Hot Springs says, "The most perfect diet in the world comes originally from the Garden of Eden—fruit, nuts, seeds, and honey from the bees."

Sickness is not your inheritance! Refrain from referring to any negative health condition in your life as yours. We have all heard people say, "*My* arthritis gets worse in the winter," or "*My* migraine headache is driving me nuts." Why make these negative health problems yours? They are not yours. Give them away.

I have given many headaches, backaches, and other pain to the floor, the table, or a chair, asking that the pain be recycled into positive energy. Visualize pain disappearing from your healthy body. Most disease and pain is caused from negative stress, bad habits, improper eating, and negative emotions.

Some people can relax and let tension seep out of their bodies by watching a fire in a fireplace. Others unwind with a brisk walk in the fresh air among the trees; still others find peace watching the waves caress the shore at some white, sandy beach.

Negative thoughts of pain and disease have no place in your body. Negative thoughts, though invisible, are very powerful, nonetheless.

Be patient when doing your Affirmations. If you are unwell, remember that it may have taken a lifetime to put your body into that unhealthy state.

One of my readers experienced wonderful results with the following exercise. He visualizes his body 100 percent healthy. He focuses on whatever part of his body needs attention, for example, when he has a sore shoulder, he visualizes it being 100 percent healthy and places it inside a fluffy golden cloud. He breathes in an image of vibrant health, holds his breath for a moment or two, then sends it to his unhealthy shoulder. He visualizes the healthy shoulder taking its place. He can actually feel healing energy flowing through it. He then says, "Thank you" three times and goes on to his next Affirmation.

A co-worker does a similar process using the power of colour. If she has a blinding headache, she focuses on the colour blue, closes her eyes, and visualizes that colour clearly in her mind. She then breathes it in and sends that colour, together with its healing power, to her head area.

She holds her breath for a moment or two, then lets it go, instructing it to go to that pain area and release all pain. She then resumes regular breathing. She does this procedure three times and, within 10 minutes, reports wonderful relief. The exercise, she says, requires concentration, faith that it will work, and a strong intent to make it work. Concentrating may be difficult when the pain is very intense but, with persistence, you will get relief. It always works for her.

Glenn Coleman Writes:

"**Dear Anne Marie:**
I was attempting to fend off extreme pain and other symptoms of mercury poisoning when I came across your book on Affirmations. After reading it, I quickly learned that by doing properly worded affirmations, I could actually shut off the pain (torture) for short periods of time. Now I share this important knowledge with other mercury sufferers as an option for relief. I look forward to further discoveries with affirmations."
Glenn Coleman, Internet Power Copywriter
www.LeanMeanSellingMachine.com

Should you experience difficulty with your body accepting the positive statements of health such as "I am 100 percent healthy" when you are not in excellent health or "I am pain-free" when you are hurting, say,

> "I am becoming healthier and healthier every day. My health is improving daily. Pain is now leaving my body. I enjoy becoming pain-free."

Then add an Affirmation that your mind and body now accept this statement as truth for you.

The ABCs of Health

a. *Always* accept responsibility for your health. Learn about and understand the full nature of any disease with which you may have been diagnosed. Always be conscious of what you can do to assist your body in cleansing, healing, and revitalizing.

b. *Be yourself.* Never attempt to copy others. You are unique. Believe disease can be cured and be willing to explore various avenues of healing. Listen to the advice of your healthcare practitioner and other well-meaning people. After careful consideration, make your own decisions. The Internet is a great source of valuable information about virtually every subject.

c. *Cleanse* your mind, emotions, and body of harmful drugs, negative thoughts, emotions, or chemicals. Drugs, prescribed or otherwise, act as poisons in your system. Toxins form a part of every chronic, degenerative disease.

Some doctors now say that taking a form of aspirin every day protects against heart attack and stroke.

You cannot have 100 percent good health if you fill your mind with thoughts of illness, sickness, and all types of negativity. You can choose to be sick or healthy. Two opposing thoughts cannot live under the same mental roof at the same time.

Recurring negative thoughts and emotions set the stage for painful medical conditions. Did you know that prolonged self-criticism may lead to arthritis and other diseases? Anger is now recognized as a bigger factor in heart disease than the other proven culprits, including fatty food and cigarettes.

Speak positively to yourself through Affirmations. Positive, directed spoken words are thoughts that create invisible, wondrous power and work to create your desired result—*perfect health*. Your body, mind, and soul are connected. What your mind thinks, your body feels. Emotional pain causes physical pain and, in time, this can cause disease.

Give Yourself Permission to be Healthy

Permission-to-Be-Healthy Agreement

"I, (your name), hereby give myself permission to be 100 percent healthy. I deserve, create, and have health and happiness in my life. I believe in myself and my abilities. I am safe and protected. I enjoy doing my Affirmations regularly. I take responsibility for learning more about my body and my health. I seek out and employ ways to improve my health daily. I enjoy relaxing, meditating, and exercising. I love myself unconditionally. I accept and approve of myself. I allow myself to be me. I am whole, perfect, strong, powerful, loving, harmonious, and happy, to the good of all parties concerned. Thank you, thank you, thank you."

I Fully Accept:

Signed: _____

Witness: _____

Date of Acceptance: _____

When you sign your name, you say, "Yes, I validate, accept, and agree with this permission slip. I am aware that no one else has a signature just like mine." You have just created a firm and binding document with yourself, your subconscious mind, God, Universal Mind, or whomever you believe in.

"I am whole, perfect, strong, powerful, loving, harmonious, happy, and safe" is a positive statement about your health. If your body is not willing to accept such a positive statement even after you have completed your Permission-to-be-Healthy Agreement, please use one of the following Affirmations.

1. "My health is improving daily."
2. "I am becoming healthier and healthier every day."

Then add an Affirmation that your mind and body now accept this statement as truth for you.

Disease

Disease is the result of a body deprived of the essentials necessary for well-being. Toxins, wastes, unbalanced lifestyles, hormonal imbalances, chemicals, and negative emotions can create a diseased body. Each disease is as personal and individual as a person's fingerprints.

Forgive, release, and let go of toxic people from your past, your present, your workplace, around your neighbourhood, or in your family. Research has shown that toxic emotions can create tension, sickness, physical breakdown, and disease. It has been proven that negative thoughts can contribute to muscular tension, high blood pressure, high cholesterol, heart disease, insomnia, and other weaknesses.

Suppressed anger can dramatically weaken your immune system. Often these physical problems can be helped by simply embracing the positive thoughts, attitudes, behaviours, healthy diets, and lifestyles that lead to good health.

Disease is no more an entity than is darkness, which is simply the absence of light. Disease means not at ease. It is an experience operating through people that does not belong to them at all.

When negative emotions and thoughts inhabit your subconscious mind, all manner of disease and malfunction occur. Your subconscious mind stores your life in memory. This means the things you have experienced in your life are in the cells and organs of your body.

When transplanting organs from one body to another, it has been proven that the person receiving the new organ knows information about the donor, even though no information was ever given to the organ recipient. The recipient may develop a keen interest in a sport or display a talent not evident before the transplant.

Destructive thoughts of hate can actually cook the corpuscles in the blood. Emotions of rage and jealousy release dangerous poisons into the body, causing the cells of the body to harden and interfere with the normal life flow. They also cause hardening of the arteries and other problems.

To improve your health, focus on, forgive, and release any toxic people, situations, and emotions that may be making you sick in the first place.

Rid yourself of resentment. Resentment festers and eats away at your body. This could increase the likelihood of developing tumours and other ailments. You can disarm your immune system when you act out the role of martyr, doormat, or helpless victim.

You do have control over your life. It is time to take that control and work with it to your benefit. If you are ill with toxic and critical thoughts of self and others, emotions, and circumstances, you have the power to change.

Visualize, in vivid Technicolor, a blue or white light pulsating through your body and, with each beat, see it cleansing, energizing, and purifying each cell, tissue, muscle, and organ. As you relax and enjoy this wonderful sensation, the great love and wisdom of the Universe will lift you to new and greater levels of awareness. You will become aware of your body and its powerful built-in healing. Give yourself permission to be healed completely, then relax and allow perfect healing to take place.

AIDS (Acquired Immune Deficiency Syndrome)

This dreaded disease affects every one of us. It can be contracted sexually, by blood transfusions, via needles, and/or through certain forms of human contact. Every one of us is at risk. AIDS, caused by the Human Immunodeficiency Virus (HIV), is a disease of the immune system; the origins of AIDS are not precisely known.

The following Affirmation was co-created with Andrew, the pleasant young man mentioned in Chapter 1, who suffers from this disease.

> "I, Andrew, deserve to be and now am healthier and healthier. My immune system grows stronger every day. I believe in myself and my actions. I have more energy. I am safe. I give myself permission to be 100 percent healthy. My cells become healthy, normal, and energized. I gain more self-respect and self-approval every day. I now forgive everyone and everything that has ever hurt me. I now forgive myself. I am worthy of receiving love and health into my life. I am just human and I am okay. I now release any and all guilt within my body. I have inner peace, joy, and happiness. I release any stress. I feel increased energy flowing throughout my body and I grow stronger every day. I allow my family and friends to love me just the way I am, to the good of all parties concerned. Thank you, thank you, thank you."

Short-Form Affirmation: **Healthy, happy, and guilt-free**

Andrew had experienced many unhappy situations in his life and had attempted suicide. One of the reasons was the deep sense of guilt he experienced over his alcoholic father's suicide. Andrew had been attempting to do healing Affirmations when I met him, but he felt they were not working.

Then he realized he needed to release all these negative feelings. He left with hope in his heart and a spring in his step. I spoke again with Andrew four years later. He told me that as long as he did his Affirmations regularly, the medication worked for him.

Learn from Andrew and take control of your life today.

Master and Short-Form Affirmations

Releasing Guilt

"I, (your name), deserve to and now release the need for blame or guilt. I enjoy being guilt-free. I love, respect, and approve of my body just the way I am. I accept creative intelligence expressing itself through me. I know all transformation of my outer world begins by transforming my thoughts within. I know I make living cells through the imaging power of my thoughts and my mind. My body is capable of healing itself. I invoke this miraculous power in my life now. I am 100 percent healthy and happy, to the good of all parties concerned. Thank you, thank you, thank you."

Short-Form Affirmation: **Happy, healthy, and fulfilled**

Eliminating Headaches

"I, (your name), deserve to be and now am headache-free. I give myself permission to be headache-free. All pain, tension, and stress now leave my body. I think clearly. My head is clear. Any negative tension and stress in any form evaporates from my head, neck, shoulders, and entire body. I am happy and free of pain, to the good of all parties concerned. Thank you, thank you, thank you."

Short-Form Affirmation: **Healthy, happy, and headache-free**

Regaining Total Health

"I, (your name), deserve to be and now am 100 percent healthy. I am safe. I accept and now have perfect health from the life force of God within me. Any undesirable or harmful germ that comes into contact with my body is immediately destroyed. My body and emotions are perfectly balanced. Positive healing energy flows to and through me. My body heals totally and quickly. My whole body is totally bathed in God's healing power. I am healthy, peaceful, and happy, to the good of all parties concerned. Thank you, thank you, thank you."

Short-Form Affirmation: **Whole, perfect, strong, powerful, loving, harmonious, and happy**

Eliminating Pain

"I, (your name), deserve and now have complete freedom from physical, mental or emotional pain. I am safe. I give myself permission to be free of all pain. All aches and pains that have plagued my body are now gone. Every harmful germ that comes into contact with my body is dissolved instantly. I am healthier and healthier every day. I am healed, happy, and pain-free, to the good of all parties concerned. Thank you, thank you, thank you."

Short-Form Affirmation: **Healthy, happy, and pain-free**

Accelerating Recovery from Illness

"I, (your name), deserve to be and now am completely whole and healed. My body heals quickly and completely. I am safe. I give myself permission to accept this wonderful healing. Powerful healing forces and body chemicals are released from my mind. My body heals with incredible speed. The blazing white healing light of God fills my very being, from the top of my head to the tips of my toes. It bathes each cell, nerve, and tissue in its cleansing, healing power. I am completely healed, to the good of all parties concerned. Thank you, thank you, thank you."

Short-Form Affirmation: **Rapid healing, perfect health**

Inducing Peaceful Sleep

"I, (your name), deserve to and now sleep peacefully throughout the night. Angels help enrich my life and guide me on my life journey. I am safe. I give myself permission to sleep peacefully every night. All cells in my body are restored, rejuvenated, and refreshed during my peaceful sleep. I am completely rested, to the good of all parties concerned. Thank you, thank you, thank you."

Short-Form Affirmation: **Refreshing, restful, peaceful sleep**

B.   Weight Reduction and Control

Fat Factors

Metabolism plays a key role in determining our weight. Poor digestion, improper diet, or the natural ageing process can result in a sluggish metabolism, but underlying emotional issues can also be an important factor.

To effectively reduce your weight, you will first need to determine the reasons you are overweight. If purely physical or nutritional factors are involved, you will need to take the necessary steps to remedy any imbalance. Our emotions, however, invariably influence both the quantity and quality of food we ingest; it is therefore crucial to address this aspect in any serious weight-reducing program.

When you eat and drink, you build a thought into your body in accordance with the mood you are in at that moment. To become more conscious of how and what you eat, it is helpful to ask yourself whether you are hungry, why you are eating, and what exactly you are eating. How often do you eat when you are not hungry but are feeling sad, upset, rejected, or lonely? If you eat while emotionally upset, you are unlikely to properly digest your food or make wise choices in what you eat.

If you overeat and become morbidly obese, you may be faced with other issues, such as ridicule, cruel remarks, and discrimination in relationships and in the workplace. You may also be compromising your health.

Some doctors believe a rapid gain or drop in weight can be more harmful to the individual than being somewhat over the calculated ideal weight. It is important to establish your ideal weight, bearing in mind bone structure, height, and hereditary factors. Consult your doctor, nutritionist, or health practitioner to determine the ideal weight for you.

Bulimia and Anorexia

When people—especially teenagers—think they are overweight and unattractive, they can become unhappy, depressed, and obsessed with their weight. They often begin comparing themselves to movie stars or svelte models on magazine covers. In extreme cases, they starve themselves and become anorexic or bulimic, alternately stuffing themselves with food and making themselves vomit. Though they may become very thin, they continue to see themselves as fat because they have never gone within to change the old image.

Beware of the warning signs of this dangerous and destructive cycle.

- Do you have an obsession with looks, food, and dieting?
- Do your conversations always centre around food?
- Do you feel guilty or ashamed when you eat?
- Are you a binge eater?
- Do you abuse laxatives, diuretics, or diet products?
- Do you induce vomiting or have abnormal fluctuations in your weight?
- Do you suffer from depression and irritability?
- Do you refuse to eat and do you avoid social contact?

If you answered "Yes" to some of these questions, it would be advisable to consult your doctor or healthcare practitioner.

Reducing/Releasing Weight

One of my young readers shared with me her secret for reducing weight.

1. First, she drinks a glass of water, then sits in a comfortable position and closes her eyes. She meditates for 10 minutes, putting herself in a state of creative visualization. She forgives herself and everyone and everything that has ever hurt her. She repeatedly tells her body that she loves, respects, and approves of it and that she is in control. She is aware of the fact that her thoughts affect her physical body.

2. She orders her metabolism to speed up and visualizes it as a mini-lawnmower, shaving away her fat cells. She works on each area with her muscles flexed and her hands on that particular area at the same time. She then visualizes the fat cells melting away and sees her body as she would like it to look. (She claims there is scientific proof that when a person goes on a diet or starvation program, the body thinks it is starving and holds that memory in the fat cells.)

3. She tells her body it is strong, efficient, and that it burns fat while she sleeps. She promises her body it will never be starved, therefore there is no reason to hold onto all those reserve fat cells.

4. She states she loves and craves fruit, vegetables, water, and exercise. She affirms she is strong, slim, beautiful, and smart. She visualizes the water she just drank washing away toxins and all the liquefied excess fat in her system. She emerges from her creative visualization exercise refreshed, feeling alive, healthy, and slim.

The following four-step program can greatly assist you in achieving your ideal, healthy weight and, at the same time, in resolving issues that are adversely affecting your self-esteem.

Personal Contract Affirmation Method for Weight Reduction

Step One: Prepare the Soil

Prepare the soil of your subconscious mind by forgiving everyone and everything that has ever hurt you. Forgive anyone who said unkind or cruel remarks about your size or weight. Then forgive yourself for overeating and allowing yourself to become overweight.

Decide on an exact figure for your ideal weight; be realistic in your ability to achieve it. Take into consideration your build, age, and bone structure and any medical challenges you may have.

Step Two: Create Your Master Affirmation (Seed-Thought)

Create your Master Affirmation in the usual manner. You are planting the seed-thought or your Affirmation in the rich, fertile soil of your subconscious mind. Select an old picture of you, taken when you were slim or at the weight you now desire to be. If you do not have one, find a picture of a model or person who has the figure you desire. Cut it out and tape it onto the top of a large sheet of white paper. Below it, write out your Master Affirmation.

Master Affirmation for Achieving and Maintaining Ideal Weight

"I, (your name), deserve and now fully accept the ideal weight or size for me. I enjoy eating fresh fruit and vegetables daily. I reduce my caloric intake and exercise regularly. It is easy for me to achieve and maintain my ideal weight. I am happy and healthy, to the good of all parties concerned. Thank you, thank you, thank you."

Short-Form Affirmation: **Ideal weight for me now**

It is important to date and sign your Master Affirmation, making it a firm and binding agreement with yourself, your subconscious mind and Universal Mind. Also ask someone to witness your signature.

Place your Master Affirmation in a plastic sleeve in your Affirmation Wishes binder, along with the rest of your Master Affirmations. As your Affirmations manifest, place them in your Fulfilled Affirmations binder.

Step Three: Water and Fertilize Your Seed-Thought

Read your Master Affirmation every morning and evening, allowing the words to sink deep into your subconscious mind. Be aware that your subconscious mind is taking in every detail and storing it for all time. You are actually watering and fertilizing the seed (your Master Affirmation).

On a separate piece of paper, jot down your Short-Form Affirmation—"Ideal weight for me now"—three times. You can also say the words "Ideal weight for me now" many times during the day.

Step Four: Visualize the End Result

- Step ahead three to six weeks or months in your mind and see yourself in vivid Technicolor as slim, healthy, and happy. You have already achieved your ideal weight in your mind; it simply has not materialized in your physical reality yet!

- Sit quietly and recall a mental visual image of you at your ideal weight. Engage the five senses.

1. *See* what you were wearing.
2. *Hear* people saying how great you looked.
3. *Feel* how slim and wonderful you looked.
4. *Smell* the perfume you were wearing.
5. Bite into a juicy, delicious apple or pop a sugarless mint into your mouth to engage the sense of *taste*.

The sense of smell can be powerfully engaged in weight reduction and control. People are *sniffing* peppermint to drop weight instead of taking harmful drugs or over-the-counter diet remedies. When you get the urge to munch, *sniff out the problem*.

When you find a scent you feel is right for you, sniff that scent three times up each nostril, as needed. Some people drop weight because they do not feel hungry after the sniffing procedure; others find it helpful in controlling the urge to binge on sweets.

If you are carrying around a fat picture of yourself inside your mind, you will need to change it so it matches the new, slim picture you are visualizing.

This is why it is so important to change your inner picture. Replace old tapes of being fat with this wonderful, inspiring, positive, mental image. Make the inner image of yourself match what you desire the outer image to be, so there will be no opposition. The pictures in the conscious and subconscious mind must agree.

Lull yourself to sleep saying, "Ideal weight for me" repeatedly. You may also wish to place your Short-Form Affirmation under your pillow. People have reported great results with this process.

Watch Your Words

Words have a very powerful impact on your life and the lives of others. Choose your words wisely. You may have noticed I do not refer to *losing* weight. The reason for this is that when we lose something, the first thing we do is try to find it. If, instead, we use words like *burn, melt, drop, give away, release, evaporate,* or *reduce,* the weight does not come back!

This may explain why so many of us become stuck on the weight-loss merry-go-round. We condition ourselves to lose weight by stating our wish to our subconscious mind and we do lose it! The Law of Attraction, however, always working in perfect order, ensures that *we find and regain* that weight, despite our best intentions.

Your subconscious mind is a powerful mechanism that acts as your humble servant, bringing to you what you think, feel, and affirm. But it requires steady programming to ensure continued success. When you go off your diet or stop attending your weight-reducing club, you often regain the weight you took off, plus some extra.

This is why so many diet centres now include a maintenance program. I believe every weight loss program would greatly benefit from the inclusion of a simple set of positive, weight-dropping Affirmations.

Should you discover you feel your body does not believe your Affirmation that you weigh a certain weight (when you don't), do the following Master Affirmation.

> "I, (your name) deserve and now am becoming slimmer, younger, and healthier. I now move closer each day to weighing my ideal weight. It is easy for me to take the steps I need to weigh my ideal weight now. My mind and body now accept this Affirmation as truth, to the good of all parties concerned. Thank you, thank you, thank you."

Short-Form Affirmation: **Slimmer, younger, and healthier**

One of my readers told me of a positive programming method she used with great results. Every day she visualized her excess fat and weight draining from her body into a pail. She then saw herself taking the pail outside, digging a hole in the earth, and pouring the fat into the hole. Then she took a match and burned it. As she visualized it burning, she said to herself, "It is gone forever. It can never come back."

She found this exercise very successful and burned 70 pounds in one year. She also watched her caloric intake, counted her fat consumption, and did a moderate exercise program tailored just for her. She has maintained this weight-drop for the past five years.

Remember Your Safety Net

Be certain to add *to the good of all parties concerned* in your Affirmation. This is a very important part of AMCAM. If there are people in your life who do not feel it is in their best interest for you to be slim, they may try to tempt you with sweets or other rich foods to prevent you from succeeding. An insecure spouse, partner, or lover could be afraid of losing you if you become too slim and attractive; he or she may attempt to sabotage your weight-reduction plan.

Other Proven Methods for Reducing Weight

Write a Letter to Your Own Angel

The following letter may be addressed to your personal angel, affirming the assistance and support you may draw upon from the divine realms.

To My Personal Angel:

"I love you, I bless you and I thank you for assisting me in my weight-releasing program. I also thank you for adjusting my metabolism and my appetite. Thank you for healing my inner child, guiding me to eat nourishing food, fresh fruits and vegetables, and for giving me the strength to avoid sweets, and greasy, fattening, high-fat foods. Thank you for being with me always, loving, guiding, and encouraging me. I am healthy and happy, to the good of all parties concerned. Thank you, thank you, thank you."

Love from (your name).

Dated: _____

Signed: _____

Witness: _____

Encourage Yourself

Post signs of encouragement everywhere. For example, put a *"Weight Reduction in Progress"* sign on your refrigerator to give you a positive jolt of good energy. You can also put a sign in your car, office, bedroom, and bathroom, declaring the ideal weight you wish to achieve. Make your Affirmations fun by singing, chanting, or shouting them out loud with lots of enthusiasm.

Refrain from putting *all* the emphasis on the numbers that appear on the scale. It took time to gain that extra weight, so it will naturally take time to remove it. Some weight-reduction programs suggest that you weigh yourself daily. I find once a week or even once a month to be more realistic when dropping weight. When maintaining your ideal weight, however, do weigh yourself daily.

Another method you can use is to place *red flags* on the fattening food and gooey sweets. Allow your imagination to run wild and have fun with this process. You could even attach small signs. These could say, *"Dangerous to your health,"* or *"Caution: you may break out in bumps of fat."* Have fun developing your own, unique system.

Exercise

Physical exercise slows down the ageing process and reduces excess fat and body weight. Some physical fitness experts say that, with every hour of exercise, you add two-and-a-half hours to your life. The greatest fat loss and muscle gain usually occur with evening exercise. This could be due to the fact that the appetite is reduced for approximately two hours after exercise, at a time when you are likely to eat more. Endorphins, the body's calming chemicals, are released from the brain during exercise. Laughing has the same effect.

Start your exercise program very gradually, tailoring it to your age, shape, weight, and lifestyle. Those who exercise regularly will have more lean muscle fibre to capture and burn fat particles before they have a chance to establish themselves in the body. You may wish to incorporate yoga, meditation, and deep-breathing exercises into your new lifestyle program. It is important to keep healthy while reducing your weight.

A well-balanced vitamin program, in conjunction with a sensible eating regime, is essential to your weight-reduction program.

The hypothalamus gland, the weight-regulating mechanism, is the primary coordinating centre between the nervous system and the endocrine glands. It is your body's set point that tells the pituitary gland when to release hormones. Mentally set your body's thermostat to the ideal weight for you.

Say:

> "I, (your name), now set my set point at _____ pounds, which is the ideal weight for me. I am healthy, happy, and slim, to the good of all parties concerned. Thank you, thank you, thank you."

Get Agreement from Your Body

You may need to ask for, and get, an agreement from the parts of yourself that say, "You could never drop weight" or "You are too fat." Often there is a part of ourselves that is cynical about positive change. It is comfortable with the present condition and afraid to change. Talk to yourself and get all parts to agree that reducing your weight would be beneficial to all.

You may wish to affirm that all parts of your body are in agreement with your weight-reducing program and with you weighing your ideal weight. Give away your "fat person" clothes. Doing this creates a vacuum you can then fill with a new "slim person" wardrobe.

Watch your caloric intake, exercise, drink eight to 10 glasses of water daily, and do your Affirmations faithfully. And remember to love, respect and approve of yourself—just the way your are. This acknowledgement gives you the power to change.

Love Your Excess Away

Love your excess fat and weight away. When you drop a few pounds, reward yourself with a luxurious bath, invigorating stroll, some quiet time, perfume, an article of clothing, etc. Put your arms around yourself and say:

> "Self, I love you, I respect you, I approve of you, just the way you are. You are terrific. Keep up the good work!"

When you drop five pounds, take a five-pound bag of sugar or rice and carry it around for a while, to see how tired it makes you feel. Even a two or three-pound reduction in weight is significant and will definitely make an impression on your subconscious mind.

Becoming aware is the most important key to weight reduction and maintenance.

The habit of overeating has been learned; it can be unlearned by the same process. Loneliness and boredom can lead to overeating, so keep your life involved, interesting, and exciting.

Develop and enjoy a loving, nurturing relationship with yourself (the most important person in your universe) and you will never be lonely. Keep busy doing things that interest you. Help others. Volunteer your time or do whatever you need to do to move out of your "safe, overweight comfort zone."

When you truly love yourself, there is no need to build barriers of excess fat and weight to keep you safe from being hurt by others. You are safe with yourself. Start molding the kind of future and shape you want—today!

The process of getting down to your ideal weight (or becoming the slim person you want to be) is a journey with ups, downs, plateaus, and steps along the way. The first step begins with what you put into your mouth right now! Simple, but true. You are the Master of your Bodyship; you can exercise your willpower to move it out of the safe, overweight port into unknown waters and exciting situations that you only dreamed possible.

If you go off your Weight Reduction Program, stop! Don't start beating yourself up. Just say, *"The next time, I will do it differently."* And then do it!

Make the Next Time Start That Very Second

You have the power and now you need to access it, harness it, and make it work for you. You must change your internal picture to match the ideal weight picture you are affirming. They must both agree to make the Affirmation work and make a difference in your life. Focus all the power of your mind on this one picture. If you don't focus or concentrate on the picture of your desired weight and direct your mind-power, the image moves here and there and scatters its focus.

Create a detailed mental picture of looking and weighing your ideal weight. Make it colourful, bringing in all the five senses.

Did you know diet foods can be exciting and interesting?

Did you know exercise is fun and that, while having fun, you are suppressing your appetite?

Some Helpful Hints

- Do your Affirmations twice daily.
- Always eat breakfast.
- Never skip meals.
- Keep track of what you eat, where you were when you ate it, and with whom you were dining.
- Eat slowly and enjoy each bite.
- Use smaller plates and prepare colourful foods.
- Consciously eat less.
- Never eat while watching TV or reading. Make eating your only activity.
- Say "No" to second helpings.
- Develop new interests.
- Learn to use discipline.

- Put your fork or spoon down after each bite.
- Take the skin off your chicken.
- Make certain your cupboards and fridge are filled with nutritious, low-calorie, interesting foods.
- Keep cold water and low-calorie drinks in the fridge.
- Make food interesting, not boring.
- Never overeat before going to bed.

Have cut-up pieces of your favourite fruit and vegetables in the fridge, ready to fight that sweets or hunger attack. Start making new habits to exercise daily, do your Affirmations, eat healthy, and take your vitamins regularly.

Define Specific Goals

If you say, "I, (your name), deserve to weigh and now weigh 130 pounds," when your present weight is 180 pounds, guess what will happen? Your conscious mind will say, "No, you don't, you weigh 180 pounds!" This will then cancel out your Affirmation. The secret here is to affirm a weight reduction of about two to three pounds per week, until you reach your desired weight.

The first week, you could affirm you weigh three pounds less; each week thereafter, affirm an additional two-pound reduction. If, for example, you weigh 180 pounds and your desired weight is 130 pounds, simply do the following.

First Week: I now weigh 175 pounds.
Second Week: I now weigh 172 pounds.
Third Week: I now weigh 170 pounds.
Fourth Week: I now weigh 168 pounds, etc.

Defining your goals in this way is helpful because your conscious mind can believe in a five-pound drop in weight. To further convince yourself, simply weigh yourself while wearing a pair of boots or a coat. You will see that you weigh three or four pounds more than normal.

In your Affirmation, also be certain to say "*all excess* fat and weight now drops or melts from my body from the right places." When you say excess, you will not drop or melt any necessary fat that is required to maintain your health.

If your timing is off and you don't manage to reduce your weight in accordance with your weekly goals, cut down on your caloric intake and continue to exercise and do your Affirmations. A one-and-a-half-pound reduction in weight each week is ideal. The toxins your body has ingested over the years are absorbed and stored in the fat. If you drop too much fat and weight at once, you release great quantities of poisons into your body for elimination. When you become aware of this fact, you can understand why dropping weight slowly is healthier.

Watch careless self-talk. What you say to or about yourself is very important. Catch yourself when you say, "I am so fat. I hate myself. My body is ugly. I can't wear any decent clothes. I'll never lose weight." Do some serious thought-watching. If you focus on thoughts of how fat you are, your subconscious mind will follow your lead and keep you fat. Remember that it is merely your humble servant, bringing to you whatever you decree.

21-Day Agreement

Make a 21-day agreement with yourself to abstain from sweets or any fattening food. Since it takes 21 days to develop a new habit, this exercise can be very powerful when practised in conjunction with your Affirmations. If you miss a day during the 21-day cycle, start again. Thank your body in advance for assisting you.

Master and Short-Form Affirmations

Ideal Weight

"I, (your name), deserve to weigh and now weigh _____ pounds, which is the perfect weight for me. I am becoming slimmer and slimmer every day. I now incubate a dream of myself being slim, young, and healthy and I now accept that dream as reality. I believe in myself. My body is the place where I live and I love it. I change my inner image of myself to match my desired outer image. I am safe. I give my body permission to weigh the ideal weight for me. I now desire only the foods that are for the highest and best use of my body. I am healthy. I am still powerful. My cells are all healthy and normal. I am happy, to the good of all parties concerned. Thank you, thank you, thank you."

Short-Form Affirmation: **Ideal weight, slimmer, younger, and healthier**

Reducing and Maintaining Weight

"I, (your name), deserve to be and now am slim, healthy, and happy. My body loves burning excess fat and weight. I am safe and in control of what I eat. My metabolism is accelerating and burning up any excess fat and weight in my body. I love, respect, and approve of myself, just the way I am. I now wear a size 8, 10, 12 (whatever size you choose). I set my appestat (the mechanism in the central nervous system that regulates the appetite) at the ideal weight for me. I drop weight easily and steadily until I reach my goal. I believe in me. I am happy and 100 percent healthy, to the good of all parties concerned. Thank you, thank you, thank you."

Short-Form Affirmation: **Ideal weight for me, 100 percent healthy**

Gaining Weight

Use the same procedure as in the weight-reducing Affirmations set out above. Visualize the foods you eat nourishing your entire body, allowing you to gain and maintain your ideal weight. Refrain from eating when you are emotionally upset or under extreme pressure.

When you eat or drink, reflect on the fact that with every mouthful you take, you place and build a thought into yourself in accordance with the mood you are in while eating. Food ingested while under extreme pressure has little or no nourishment value.

Should you wish to gain 20 pounds, do the weekly process, as follows.

First Week:	I now weigh 95 pounds.
Second Week:	I now weigh 98 pounds.
Third Week:	I now weigh 100 pounds.
Fourth Week:	I now weigh 102 pounds, etc.

Master Affirmation for Maintaining Ideal Weight

"I, (your name), deserve to weigh and now weigh the perfect weight for me. I am 100 percent healthy and happy. I enjoy nutritious foods that increase/maintain my weight, which is distributed to the right places in my body. I give myself permission to gain the ideal number of pounds for me. I am safe and balanced. I love, respect, and approve of myself. I am happy, balanced, and secure, to the good of all parties concerned. Thank you, thank you, thank you."

Short-Form Affirmation: **Perfect weight for me**

Affirmations When Properly Done Always Work!

Cards of Life

www.affirmations-doctor.com

Affirmations, Your Passport to Happiness

14 • Retirement

A New Beginning: Scary or Exciting?

Yvou have given many prime years of your life to your family, career, and making money to live. Now it is time for you to pursue your interests and fondest, wildest dreams. Instead of viewing retirement as the golden handshake or the end of your life, look at it as the exciting, fun-filled opportunity for you to do what you desire. Retirement does not mean giving up or the end of life. It heralds a whole new beginning.

It is time to enjoy the rewards of your life's work and harvest the seeds you have sown. Make the latter part of your life exciting and wonderful so that you look forward to every day with enthusiasm, joy, and anticipation.

There are two possible ways to approach retirement. You may experience excitement when you retire, knowing you are now free to do all the things you never had time to do and pursue what really interests you. Or you may be devastated and paralyzed by fear of the unknown, thinking, *"What will I do? My life is finished. There is no reason to live. No one needs me. I am useless without my career."*

Those in the second category have lost their professional identities and are like the *walking dead*. They have given up on their dreams and, without goals or plans, are merely existing.

They have lost their zest for living. Negative, habitual thinking has hypnotized them and they do not know what it is like to really live. They are just waiting to physically die and be buried and forgotten.

Which approach would you choose?

Life is to be lived and enjoyed, not just endured. Assuming that you have budgeted and planned for this time of your life and are financially secure, it is time to enjoy. For those of you less fortunate, it may be necessary to find other types of part-time work to supplement your income. If that is the case, start the *Personal Contract*

Affirmation Method immediately, affirming for that perfect, successful, part-time, lasting career or small business for you.

Moving Out of Your Comfort Zone

I retired from the real estate profession after more than 20 years. When butterflies started flying around in my stomach, I said, "Stop. Listen up, self. I have worked all my life. I am entitled to some relaxation and enjoyment. I give myself permission to do whatever I choose."

When I retired, I visualized placing all the ideas, experiences, business and marketing plans and expertise I had ever used during my business lifetime in a soft, pink cloud. As I visualized it floating up into the blue sky, I said, "I now release every part of this information with loving kindness. I release it to create substance for anyone who wishes to use it to benefit or to further his or her business, career, life, and growing process. I know that when good, positive, constructive ideas are lovingly released into the Universe, anyone may tap into that information and benefit accordingly."

During my business lifetime, I was a school secretary, waitress, restaurant owner, author, legal secretary, and promotion director. I was also a realtor, both in Canada and the United States. I am now Anne Marie—mother, author, lecturer, teacher, and friend. Sometimes we identify with what we do. Being too attached to that identity can make it difficult for us to find another purpose later in life.

If I say I am a realtor, I lose that identity when I retire or am no longer able to do my job. It is therefore better to say, "I am Anne Marie and I am in the real estate profession." This way, I am identifying with myself as a person, not a realtor. As Dr. Wayne Dyer says, "We are not what we do. If we are what we do, when we don't, we aren't."

Since my retirement from real estate, I have been very busy doing what I love to do—writing my Affirmation books, monthly newsletters and columns, counselling, teaching seminars, and conducting workshops on the power of Affirmations. I also have completed my ministerial studies. I make numerous guest appearances on radio and television shows. I thoroughly enjoy visiting, writing, meditating, walking, playing, laughing, reading, and travelling. I can also take advantage of doing absolutely nothing and having fun!

Your Retirement Career

Retirement can be wonderful. Far from being the end of life, it can bring freedom from all the obligations and schedules that restricted and determined your life in the past. It can therefore be a time of great personal fulfillment. The secret to a happy, full retirement is to find something to do that you love. You can leave all the *shoulds* behind and start on the *dreams* of life.

Retirement is just as much a career or livelihood as were your working years. The good news is now you can manage your life the way you desire. This is the time of your life that you can exercise your power as manager, supervisor, and boss over yourself and your life.

You can get up when you want, schedule your appointments to your advantage, and live your day as you desire. To help you get the best out of your retirement career, you can divide it into three segments, as follows.

1.   Inward Part

This is where you go *inward* to focus on loving, respecting, and approving of yourself. Breathe in love, peace, and joy; breathe out worry, fear, or frustration. Find out who you are, why you are here, and where you wish to go. Take long, luxurious baths and meditate, relax, and enjoy the simple things of life.

Get in touch with self and nature.

- *See* the creations of God all around.
- *Hear* the wind blowing through the trees.
- *Feel* its soft, gentle breeze on your face.
- *Stop* and smell that beautiful rose.
- *Taste* a wild strawberry or chew on a blade of grass.

Discover your passion in life, become involved with others, and follow your dream. As I always say, "Fall in love with what you do and you never have to work again." I believe and live this!

2. Outward Part

This aspect of your retirement career involves projecting your good energy out into the Universe and to others. Extend your hand in help and love to those who need it. Visit the lonely and wipe away the tears of the broken-hearted. Share yourself and your talents with others. Give the gift of yourself to a loved one in a healthy sexual relationship.

Give back to the community and the Universe. Nurture old friendships and create new ones. Teach, help, and share with family members and friends. Become involved in charity work, church activities, or fundraising ventures. Create and develop ideas of your own. Start your own home-based business doing what really interests you!

Many senior citizens have become multimillionaires in their 70s, 80s, and even 90s. You are in control. Make it your intention to enjoy this part of your life and do it! And, most important, have *fun*!

3. Action Part

This part involves taking action and seizing every day as precious and filled with exciting opportunities. Do all the things you once only dreamed of doing. Take a trip to somewhere you have always dreamed of visiting. Create a hobby or become that famous artist, writer, or musician.

Do physical things, such as bowling, golfing, knitting, or whatever you desire. Study, read the Bible, self-improvement books and articles, and listen to uplifting shows on television. Keep yourself informed of new experiments and products.

Exercise to improve your health. If you have some health concern, find out all you can about it. If you suffer from pain, find ways to lessen, manage, or get rid of it. Fill your mind with positive thoughts, ideas, and concepts.

Get out and make your dreams come true. This could be the time to share with the world your invention, new book, song, poem, or tape. There are no deadlines being imposed by others. You make the deadlines in your retirement career. You can stay up late at night and *sleep in*, if you desire.

Talk about interesting subjects and positive, happy things; people will love to be in your company. Drop the "Me, me" talk and be interested in the other person and talk about his or her interests.

If you are widowed, lonely, or desire companionship in your life, get busy and meet that special person. Some people prefer to lead the single life; others prefer to be married. This is a matter of personal choice. If you wish to attract that special person into your life, follow the instructions in this book for attracting the perfect partner for you.

You may desire the company of a part-time companion to attend shows, have dinner, travel, go on long walks, or have chats by the fireside. You have learned how thoughts and the mind can change your life for the positive and give you control over your situations. Decide what you want to have happen in your life and make it happen!

Some individuals spend years grieving for a deceased spouse or partner, not realizing they have numerous other opportunities for happiness with other partners. Rather than getting stuck in the past, they could pursue new interests and allow other lonely, single people to have the gift of their companionship.

Find and live your bliss. By doing this, you are giving others permission to do the same. This can be the most exciting time of your life. It is a time for fresh, new beginnings and a time for rejoicing. Become involved 100 percent. Plan something exciting. Take up a hobby you thoroughly enjoy. Make it one that will help others. Become completely involved.

This is your life. Live it to the fullest!

Become Younger by Using Your Mind

Give up all thoughts of ageing. Age can be used as an excuse for not doing certain things. Affirm that your lifespan is in excess of 120+ healthy, active, happy, prosperous years. Intention is a very powerful force. Say often, "It is my intention to grow younger and I do!"

Holding grudges and being unforgiving of self and others can age you far beyond your years. It can also lead to depression, anxiety, and wrinkles, robbing you of your happiness.

Love and respect your body. Meditate and learn to control the stress level in your life. Spend time complimenting and approving of every part of your body. Affirm that every cell, tissue, organ, bone, and every part of your body is now regenerating, rejuvenating, energizing, and becoming younger and younger.

When you exercise, repeat over and over, "Younger and younger. I am becoming younger and younger." Do not buy into the old-age mentality. Watch your self-talk. Refrain from saying, "I'm too old" or "I haven't got many years left, I can't do that at my age." Instead say, "I am growing younger and becoming slimmer and healthier every day. Time stands still for me. I have all the time in the world. Time is my friend. I enjoy and now live a long, healthy, happy life, in excess of 120 years."

Reserve now for your 120th birthday party. Visualize yourself healthy, young-looking, and supple. See your family and friends enjoying the occasion with you and, oh, yes—have fun!

Laugh and have fun. Laughter is one of the best medicines. Laughing and having fun is an important part of my life. I laugh and have fun every day!

Your Choice

Remember, it is all up to you and you alone to determine your degree of happiness. Every person is different; what is right for you may not be right for another. You make the choice and the Laws of the Universe will support whichever path you choose.

Thank the Creator for this wonderful day and for your creative power. You can carve out peace, joy, and happiness for yourself and others.

Master and Short-Form Affirmations
Happy Retirement

"I, (your name), deserve to have and now enjoy a rewarding, happy retirement. I keep busy doing what I want to do. I am safe. I give myself permission to enjoy my retirement. I am fulfilled, happy, and involved. I am now free to pursue all my unfulfilled dreams. I enjoy time spent with loved ones. I believe in my future. I now do things I only dreamed of doing. I enjoy travelling, fishing, golfing, walking on the beach, and just relaxing. I believe in myself and my choices. I choose to be and am healthy, involved in life, and peaceful. I choose to and think positive, uplifting thoughts. I enjoy caring and sharing. I am happy, to the good of all parties concerned. Thank you, thank you, thank you."

Short-Form Affirmation: **Happy, fulfilled retirement**

Growing Younger

"I, (your name), deserve to be and now look, feel, and am 20 years younger. I am forever growing younger. I focus and concentrate on divine life and youth. Any thoughts of the number of years, labels, or excuses for ageing leave my mind and consciousness now. I change my consciousness to that of health, happiness, and longevity. I have fewer and fewer wrinkles. My pituitary gland now produces the wonderful, glorious life hormone. I enjoy a vigorous exercise program that is tailored just for me. The radiance of youth and beauty saturate my whole being. I crave and eat fresh fruit and vegetables daily. I remain in an attitude of gratitude for my many blessings. I am happy, to the good of all parties concerned. Thank you, thank you, thank you."

Short-Form Affirmation: **Growing younger and younger all the time**
Affirmations When Properly Done Always Work!

Cards of Life

www.affirmations-doctor.com

15 • *Death* .

The Final Destination:
The Journey from the Cradle to the Grave

This is the end of the journey. Life's train has taken you from the cradle to the grave. It has been an interesting, intriguing, exciting and, sometimes, a sorrowful and stressful journey. We have all walked on various paths, had our own challenges, and knelt at different graves during our lifetimes.

I absolutely love the way author Maria Dancing Heart Hoaglund, in her book *The Last Adventure of Life: Sacred Resources for Transition*, compares the process of dying to leaves falling off a tree in autumn. She was amazed by the gentle way the leaves naturally let go of the branches that held them. When the time is right or when the wind blows hard enough to disengage the leaf, it slowly and gently floats to the ground, not resisting, secure in the knowledge it is a part of the whole process of nature—living and dying.

A friend told me that the two most important things a person can do are to help someone being born and to help a person die. Death is a fact of life. It is inevitable—the final stage of life as we know it. Are you excited at the birth of a child? Do you rejoice when couples marry? Why is it then, when people die, we try to ignore it, pretend it has not happened, or grieve so deeply?

Bereavement is a loss or event in your life in which someone or something important is taken from you. Any person who has experienced the empty chair syndrome knows the feeling.

We are energy and, as such, we never die; we merely change form. It is like going from one room to another. When you leave the planet, you graduate to a new level. You are then enrolled in the *Heavenly University*!

Grief

To grieve excessively weakens the mind and body. It does not help the person for whom you are grieving and can actually hinder his or her advancement on the other side. Sad thought-forms that reach the deceased can impede his or her spiritual development and growth.

Although grief is a real experience, it may also be an adjustment, a major change, or a transition from what life once was to a new life that is just beginning. Grieving is work and to work through what you are feeling and thinking takes time, energy, and a conscious, directed effort. When you experience too much sadness and constantly dwell on it, you begin a process that corrodes your body's cells.

When you grieve for loved ones who have passed on, you are grieving for yourself, for your own loss, for not being able to see that loved one again in this lifetime. Though you may miss them terribly, it is important to release them so they may get on with their new spiritual life.

Everyone who loses a loved one experiences the pain of grief and loss. This is a normal, healthy process that ultimately leads to healing.

We each react to a loved one's death in a personal way. The timeframe involved is different for every individual. The grieving process could take six to eight months or two, five, 10 years, or more. I once met a widow who was still grieving for her spouse 20 years after his death. Some people never stop grieving. We all grieve in our own ways.

There is a huge difference between grieving and remembering.

My own experience of grief with the death of my two spouses, my mother, father, sister, brother, two business partners, and many friends has taught me that the pain does lessen as time goes by. Time is a great healer.

When you lose that loved one, you lose his or her physical presence, but the relationship still exists. The loved one is still in your heart, mind, and consciousness.

There are several stages involved in handling the death of a loved one.

Shock

- Initial shock or numbness
- Tears or emotional release
- Loneliness
- A desire to die

Denial

- Deep depression
- Anger, confusion
- Pain
- Guilt

Acceptance

- Hope to go on
- Struggle to keep on living
- Plans for the future

Answering the following questions may help you determine what influence your grief has on you.

- What was your relationship with the deceased?
- Do you have regrets and unresolved issues?
- Was the death expected?
- Was the loved one's illness a long one?
- Have you had many losses through death recently?
- Have you resolved grief from past deaths?
- What is the state of your own mental and emotional health?
- Do you have other major stress factors in your life?
- Are you dwelling excessively on death and dying?
- Do you suffer from chronic depression, low-self esteem, guilt, or anger?
- Are you holding on to the deceased's clothing and personal effects too long?
- Do you idolize the one who has died, placing him or her on a pedestal?

I found myself idolizing my first husband following his death. When I spoke or thought about him, I only remembered the good times.

I blocked out all problems or negativity surrounding our marriage. I was able to correct this when it was pointed out to me by a grief counsellor. Then I began to remember both the good and bad times. This created a healthy, acceptable balance and, as a result, I was able to move on with my life.

Tips to Help You Adjust

Refrain from making major changes during the first year or two, such as selling your matrimonial home, moving, or changing professions. Become involved with family members or a group of people who can share and understand your loss. Above all, do not feel guilty when you actually begin to feel better.

- Be good to yourself.
- Eat properly and get plenty of rest and exercise.
- Do something you have always wanted to do.
- Join a new group of people with similar interests, such as writing, or painting.
- If money allows, purchase some new clothes.
- Treat yourself to a massage or reflexology treatment.
- Plan trips (long and short).
- Do not be alarmed if you burst into tears when you hear a favourite song that was special to you and your deceased loved one.
- Show your emotions.
- Be patient and loving with yourself, as you would be with your child.
- Nurture your inner child with gentle loving kindness.

A widowed mother should avoid expecting too much of her children at this time. A young teenage son or daughter should not be given the title and responsibility of being the head of the family. He or she is, and must remain, her child, nothing more. No one is exempt from death. To dwell on a fear of death is to avoid fully living.

Be Prepared

Prepare for death while you are here by creating your own belief system about God. When one door closes, another heavenly door opens. Prepare yourself and live every moment to the fullest.

 Affirmations, Your Passport to Happiness

Be kind to loved ones that will grieve your loss.

1. Have your Last Will and Testament prepared.
2. Place a list of your assets and liabilities with it.
3. If you have stock certificates and shares, record them with their respective numbers.
4. You may also wish to list what personal items you would like to distribute and to name the recipients.
5. List the bank or banks that you do business with, as well as your accounts and account numbers.
6. Keep your personal papers in one place.

Never spend your precious time complaining or dwelling on your illnesses, hurts, or worries. Experience peace by doing AMCAM faithfully. Give thanks every day to God for a glorious, new day.

Master and Short-Form Affirmations

Widowed Father (with Children)

"I, (your name), deserve to be and now am calm and peaceful. I handle all situations with ease and efficiency. I think straight and make appropriate decisions. I realize I now have the role of single father and I accept that role with its new and added responsibilities. I miss my deceased wife. Even though she is no longer here in physical form, her precious memory lives on. She will always be in our hearts and minds. I urge my children to keep her memory alive, to remember the good times and funny incidents, but not to dwell on them excessively. We are alive and well and thank God for each new day. We ask for healing in each of our hearts and the strength to go on. We still love and have each other. I learn to cope with the household duties, as needed. We make it through today and every day, to the good of all parties concerned. Thank you, thank you, thank you."

Short-Form Affirmation: **Healed hearts and lives**

Widowed Mother (with Children)

"I, (your name), deserve to be and now am calm and peaceful. I handle all money and financial matters easily and efficiently. I think clearly and make appropriate decisions. I realize I now have the role of widowed mother and I accept this role with its added responsibilities. I miss my deceased husband and even though he is no longer in our midst, his wonderful memory lives on. He will always be in our hearts and minds. I urge my children to keep his memory alive and to remember the good times and funny incidents, but not to dwell on them excessively. We are peaceful, to the good of all parties concerned. Thank you, thank you, thank you."

Short-Form Affirmation: **Healed hearts and lives**

Accepting Death (of a Female)

"I, (your name), deserve to be able to and now do adapt quickly and easily to life's changes. I know I will miss (person's name). I let her go with love and allow her to grow in her new life experience. I make the appropriate and right decisions and I think clearly. Every day, I am filled with the healing and loving energy of God. I have great inner peace and strength. I give thanks to God for the happy memories of my loved one that I will always cherish. Her gift of love will always be with me. I release the past and that person, and let her go in peace and love, to her highest good. I am free and she is free and released. I give myself permission to live and find happiness. I am peaceful, to the good of all parties concerned. Thank you, thank you, thank you."

Short-Form Affirmation: **Acceptance of another's death**

Accepting Death (of a Male)

"I, (your name), deserve to be able to and now do adapt quickly and easily to life's changes. I know I will miss (person's name). I let him go with love and allow him to grow in his new life experience. I make the appropriate and right decisions and I think clearly. Every day, I am filled with the healing and loving energy of God. I have great inner peace and strength. I give thanks to God for the happy memories of my loved one that I will always cherish. His wonderful gift of love will always be with me. I release the past and that person, and let him go in peace and love, to his highest good. I am free and he is free and released. I give myself permission to live and find happiness. I am peaceful, to the good of all parties concerned. Thank you, thank you, thank you."

Short-Form Affirmation: **Acceptance of another's death**

Releasing Guilt Around the Death of a Loved One

It is normal to find something to feel guilty about when someone you love dies. If you dig, you will uncover all types of negative thoughts along the lines of what you should or could have done differently while your loved one was alive. Release those negative feelings today.

"I, (your name), deserve to start and now start each day fresh. Yesterday and its problems are history. I forgive and absolve myself of all guilt. I make good decisions at the right time. I am free of guilt, worry, and self-condemnation. I heal quickly. All guilt, fear, and worry completely disappear. I keep only positive, loving thoughts, and good memories of my loved one. I am peaceful, to the good of all parties concerned. Thank you, thank you, thank you."

Short-Form Affirmation: **Release of guilt, acceptance, and peace**

Coming to Terms with Your Own Death

"I, (your name), deserve to be able to release and now do release my fear and doubt. I am at peace. I know this is the last period of my life here on earth. I am ready to complete my final journey. When it is time to cross over, I know the angels will be with me. Any fear of dying leaves my body now. I am safe. I ask the Angel of Death to be with me to help me make my transition smooth and peaceful. I am happy, secure, and peaceful. I know that dying is a part of life and I accept that fact and am at peace. I leave a legacy of love and loving kindness for my loved ones and all humanity. I release myself to my Heavenly Father with peace, to the good of all parties concerned. Thank you, thank you, thank you."

Short-Form Affirmation: **Total acceptance and final release with love**

Affirmations When Properly Done Always Work!

Learn about the history of Affirmations, as never seen before, with a behind-the-scenes view of how famous authors and people around the world are using Affirmations to transform their lives at www.affirmations-playground.com.

Short-Form Affirmations

General Affirmations

Affirmations are a major, important part of my life.
I enjoy doing my Affirmations faithfully.
My *Personal Contract Affirmation Method* is clear and specific.
I do my Affirmations easily and joyfully.

Addiction

All cravings for alcohol are gone.
I am drug-free.
I am in complete control of my body.
I enjoy a smoke-free environment.
I am in control of my life.

I eat nourishing food.
I do everything in moderation.
I am balanced and grounded.

Anger

I let go of anger and bask in the sunlight of God's love.
I am free of anger.
I enjoy being in control of any anger in my body.
I am in control of my emotions and life.
I am balanced, peaceful, and happy.

I release anger and negativity in my body.
Anger now leaves my body.
I am full of peace and love.

Balance

I now have and enjoy 100 percent balance.
I am centred and in control of my life.
I am peaceful, calm, and happy.
I am balanced, happy, and centred.

Career

I now have that perfect, lasting, successful career.
I am efficient, happy, and confident.
My employers, colleagues, and friends respect and honour me.
I respect and honour my employers, colleagues, and friends.

I am valued at my career/position.
I am honest and trustworthy.
I love my career.
I move on from one great success to another.

Death

Death is a natural process of life.
I release any fears and doubts about death and dying.
I am thankful for every day and I live it to the fullest.
I honour my loved one's memory and life.
I thank God every day for the gift of life.
I am a Being of great light and beauty that continues on the next phase of my life.

I accept the end of my journey with hope.
I move easily to the next spiritual level.
I place myself into God's loving care.

Family Relations

I am peaceful, confident, and happy.
I now enjoy being free of fear.
I face and deal with my fears and put them in the proper perspective.
I believe in my future and myself.
I enjoy harmonious relationships with my family members.

Fear

I am free of fear.
I am in control.
I release negative fears now.
Fear is gone.

Forgiveness

I now forgive everyone and everything that has ever hurt me.
I forgive myself and am forgiven.
When I forgive, I release all resentment and negativity.
I refrain from dwelling on the past and past hurts.
I attract positive, happy people into my life.
I know that forgiveness frees and benefits me.

Friendship

I am my own best friend.
I am a loyal, sincere friend.
I have an abundance of wonderful, loyal friends.
I listen empathetically to my friends.
I am very popular and have a magnetic personality.

To have a friend, I know I have to be a friend.
People like to be in my company.
People find me interesting and fun.

Happiness

I know happiness is a journey.
Happiness comes from within.
I give myself permission to be happy.
I am happy.
Happiness is an inside job.

I am happy and confident.
I live in the now.
I spread today's jam thick on my bread today.
I am completely balanced and depression-free.
I believe in myself.

I know happiness comes from within.
Happiness is my birthright.

Health

I release all past programming of sickness and disease.
I enjoy 100 percent good health.
It is my birthright to be healthy, wealthy, and happy.
I accept abundant health now and I feel it saturating my body.
I am whole, perfect, strong, powerful, loving, harmonious, happy, and peaceful.

I enjoy perfect eyesight (20/20 vision).
I enjoy weighing the ideal weight for me.
It is easy for me to be healthy and slim.

Love

I love, respect, and approve of myself, just the way I am.
I have a long, lasting, happy relationship with the perfect partner for me.
I love God, creation, and all creatures.
I attract the right people into my life now.
I love life.

I am a powerful love magnet to the right people and circumstances.
I am happily married.
I am a powerful love magnet.

Magic Magnetic Circle

Magnetism is contained in my brain and all body cells.
My Magic Magnetic Circle is my cosmic power.
I magnetize health, wealth, and happiness to me.
I enjoy doing my Magic Magnetic Circle exercise daily.

I magnetize peace, love and happiness to myself, which extends to all I meet.
I use my Magic Magnetic Circle process to the good of all.

Magnetic Personality

I am a powerful love magnet to the right people and circumstances.
I attract positive people and things into my life.
The right people find me irresistible.
I am a powerful money-magnet.
I attract like thoughts to me now.
I attract the right people to me now.
I use my magnetism to the good of all.

Marriage

I enjoy a long, healthy, wealthy marriage with my life partner.
I love and respect my spouse.
I am loved and respected.
I enjoy my long, lasting, healthy marriage.

Memory

My memory improves daily.
I instantly recall memories to my mind.
My memory is healthy and strong.
I have and enjoy a perfect memory.
I am 100 percent healthy.

Material Objects

I now have the perfect vehicle, in excellent condition.
I now have the home of my choice.
I now have jewellery, clothes, computer, etc.

Mind

I use the power of AMCAM to unlock the door to my mind-power.
I use my conscious mind to instruct my subconscious mind.
I easily and effectively use creative visualization.
My mind is creating miracles for me now.
My mind is clear, healthy, and powerful.

Miscellaneous

Time is my friend.
I have all the time I need.
I focus on and live for today.
I accomplish whatever I set out to do.
I am creating my future.
My thoughts today are creating my future tomorrow.

Money

I release all negative tapes of lack and poverty now.
I now am abundantly wealthy.
I am financially independent.
Money is my friend.
I love and respect money.

Money is constantly circulating in my life.
I am a powerful money-magnet.
Great wealth is mine.
Money is flowing to me in avalanches of abundance.

Pain

Any and all pain leaves my body now.
I enjoy being pain-free.
My body heals quickly, without pain.
I now release all pain to the centre of the earth, to be recycled.
I am relaxed and pain-free.

My body moves easily and quickly to perfect health.
My body is becoming pain-free.
Every day the pain lessens.

Parenting

I am a loving, considerate parent.
I make appropriate decisions.
I am balanced and fair in all my decisions and rules.
I love and respect my children.
My children love and respect me.
My children respect others.

Relationships

I am a love magnet to the right people and circumstances.
I am a faithful partner.
All my relationships are built on communication, love, trust, and respect.
I am honest and trustworthy.
I respect and honour others and their opinions.

I respect and honour my relationships.
I do my Affirmations daily for a happy, healthy relationship.

Self-Esteem

I dare to believe in myself.
I release all thoughts of past failure.
I move on from one great success to another.
I say "No" easily and without guilt, whenever I choose.
I overcome negative habits with ease.

I say "No" to any type of abuse.
I speak my mind with ease.
I release all past thoughts of being unloved or unlovable.
I now enjoy loving and respecting me.
I know I can always count on me.

I love me.
I am the most important person in my universe.
I believe in my future and myself.
I love, respect, and approve of myself.

Spiritual Growth

I have faith in God and the faith of God.
I am an open channel for God's love and wisdom.
I am made in God's own image.
God's pure energy and love now flow into my body.
I am secure.
I am peaceful, balanced, and centred.

Study

I deserve and receive high marks on all my exams.
Studying comes easily to me.
When I need to recall some information, I clear my mind and say, "Clear, search, and retrieve."

Thoughts

I am a powerful thought-magnet.
I know thoughts are energy and I use this energy wisely.
My thoughts are creating my present and future.
My thoughts are very powerful.
I enjoy thinking positively.
I know what I think about, I bring about.

Wealth

I am a powerful money-magnet.
I deserve to be and now am wealthy.
I am the loving child of a rich Father.
I love and appreciate money and what it can do for others and me.
I respect money and spend it wisely.
I am a powerful money-magnet.
Money flows to me in avalanches of abundance.
I am on the road to prosperity.

Weight

My body is becoming slimmer and slimmer.
I easily drop excess weight and fat from the right places in my body.
I now weigh the ideal weight for me.
It is easy for me to weigh and maintain my ideal weight.
Food is spiritual and harmonious to my body.
I am completely balanced and peaceful.
I move easily and joyfully toward my ideal weight.

Worry

All worry now leaves me.
I enjoy being worry-free.
I am in control.
I replace worry with hope.
I am happy.
I am fulfilled.
I love being worry-free and peaceful.
I am peaceful and happy.

Youth

I release all misconceptions about ageing.
I enjoy having great health and live life to the fullest.
Age is just a number and I am as young as I feel.
I am becoming younger and younger every day.
I am slimmer, younger, and healthier every day.

I love looking, feeling, and being younger.
Youth is my birthright and I accept it now.
People remark on how young I look.

Affirmations When Properly Done Always Work!

The Author's Personal Story

The Power of Affirmations—My Story of Disbelief to Belief!

To those readers who may be concerned that sometimes Affirmations don't seem to work or turn out as you would like them to or in your timeframe, I would like to share my story with you.

When my second husband, Roy, became suddenly ill, I started doing an Affirmation that he get well. I did it regularly with faith and expectancy, but—he died! I was devastated and became despondent. I thought about throwing out my Affirmation books because I felt they were not working. Thinking like this really shocked me because I had never believed I would ever question the power of Affirmations.

During this time I heard a little voice in my head saying, "What would you tell others?" It kept on until I, with great exasperation, finally exclaimed, "I'd tell them there is hope." Then instead of stopping, the little voice in my head continued, "Why don't you notify yourself?" So I did!

I now know my Affirmation did work. I was careful to say "to the good of all parties concerned." I rationalized it this way. I am not God and I cannot say how long people will live. I was the one doing the Affirmation, not Roy. I realized it was his time to go. I also took strength from the Serenity Prayer:

> God grant me the serenity
> to accept the things I cannot change;
> courage to change the things I can;
> and wisdom to know the difference.
>
> Reinhold Niebuhr

Now I believe Roy is back at the Source where he is 100 percent healthy. I also believe my strong Affirmation of faith helped him cross over. As for me, I have never looked back. Since Roy's passing, I have completed my ministerial studies and am an ordained minister. I have also written two new books and co-authored another children's program: Kids Affirmation Program (KAP).

My faith in the power of Affirmations is even stronger.

So if you feel your Affirmations are not working, know—just know—they are working under the surface and the manifestation is just around the corner. Sometimes Affirmations do not manifest in the way we think they should or in our timeframe, but they do manifest! I do believe that:

Affirmations When Properly Done Always Work!

Letters from Readers

Dear Anne Marie:
Your book, *Affirmations, Your Passport to Happiness*, is truly a wonderful book. I recommend this book to all people who want to attract wealth, love, happiness, and good health into their lives. The Universe is abundant and you can ask for what you want. What you ask for, however, is not always good for you. It is very important just how you ask for it. In Anne Marie's book, she has examples on how to ask for what you want. I am a psychic reader and tell all my clients about this terrific book. It gives me great pleasure when clients have reported back to me how successful their Affirmations were.

Personally, I have used Affirmations for meeting the man I married, for obtaining a house, a car, trips, etc. Most important for me was using Affirmations for healing after having a colon cancer operation. This book should be in every library and bookstore in the country—every person could benefit from properly done Affirmations.

Caroline Ryker, Psychic and Counselor
Bellingham, WA, USA

Dear Anne Marie:
I am an elementary schoolteacher. I purchased a copy of *Affirmations, Your Passport to Happiness*, read it, loved it, and immediately purchased additional copies for my friends. This book is a powerful, positive tool. I lovingly refer to the book as the Mothership!

When you and I got together, I asked if you thought Affirmations could be made into a book to help children. That was the birth of the *Affirm and Learn Enhancement Program*. We incorporated information from the book and my many years of teaching experience and came up with a three-part anti-violence program that empowers students. The first part is the Parent/Partnership, second is the School, and the third part is the Community.

It teaches and empowers children to protect themselves against violence. Now in its fifth year, the School part of the program is being taught in my grade 3 class in Kendall, Washington. You are teaching the Community part—the Think Affirmations Club (TAC)—to a group of fifth and sixth graders (girls) in Vancouver, BC, Canada. We are so excited about this wonderful children's program, that includes Lesson Plans, two Information Books for Parent Partnership and Community, the Affirmation Family, posters, hand puppets, cut-outs, a video, a puzzle, and a CD of music.

Personally, I have used Affirmations in my life and affirmed for the perfect home for me. I just purchased the home of my dreams in a peaceful, wooded area only four minutes from the school where I teach! Doing Affirmations really work!

It is my hope and Affirmation that the power of Affirmations through the *Affirm and Learn Enhancement Program* makes its way into schools throughout the world. We are doing an Affirmation to that effect and as you say in your book, "Affirmations When Properly Done Always Work!"
Marjie Nistad, Elementary Teacher
Co-Author of the *Affirm and Learn Enhancement Program*
Kendall, WA, USA

Dear Anne Marie:
Affirmations work! Thank you, Thank you. Thank you for your teachings and support via your *Affirmations* book. Things have happened that I never thought possible. With my Affirmations and emptying the cup of all that made my life miserable, then using so many things that you teach, life is not half bad. I have been an alcoholic for many, many years and thought I would

die as such, but no, no! Now I can proudly say, "I am a recovering alcoholic."

I had lost my job, but got it back and everyone is very proud of my accomplishment and me. My children came back into my life again. I thought that would never happen, but I still did Affirmations to that effect and they worked! Life still has its up and downs, but they are manageable with the right tools and you, Anne Marie, have given them to me. Keep up the good work and God bless you.
Denise
New York City, USA

Dear Anne Marie:
While relaxing in a store's reading room, I picked up one of your books. It was exactly what I needed at that particular time in my life. I read the part about forgiveness and the tears began to flow, so I know I have work to do in that area. Please mail me a copy as soon as possible. Thanking you in advance.
Lucinda Bigler
Alberta, Canada

Dear Anne Marie:
I am a 36-year-old male who has been in prison for 16 years. I feel it is unfair. I ordered a copy of your book from www.amazon.com. I was very angry and, after reading your book, discovered I needed to forgive, so I started on this forgiveness process. I have also been doing Affirmations for justice in my case and it was recently reviewed with favourable results.

I am so thankful. Now I truly believe I will find happiness and peace and that all of the answers to questions can be found in my subconscious mind. I have read that when a person can relax into a deep state of calmness that the subconscious mind reveals itself. Your article helped me. This state of mind is very important to me. Thank you, Miss Evers, for being a part of my long, rocky but wonderful journey of healing!
Name of person and prison withheld

Dear Anne Marie:
Just a quick note to say hello and let you know your book is fantastic; when Affirmations are done right, they really, really work! I have purchased several copies of your books for my friends and family, as I want them to experience positive things like I have. I am a very strong believer in the phrase: "What the mind can conceive and believe, it can achieve." Having a positive attitude helps you obtain your goals. Wishing you and all of your readers much success.
Sue Henken
Detroit, MI, USA

Dear Anne Marie:
I enjoyed reading your article in the *New Times Newspaper,* Seattle, Washington, about the power of Affirmations. My friend mails me copies of this newspaper because it features many positive, uplifting articles such as yours.

As I am a very positive person, I have used Affirmations all my life. I now realize I was not using them to their fullest potential. I know after reading the article that to be more effective, Affirmations must be more structured, specific, and focused. I also love your suggestion to harness and use the power of the five senses to realize our goals. I enjoy your articles. Keep up the good work!
Mohammed
United Arab Emirates

Dear Anne Marie:
I just finished reading your book on Affirmations. This one is a keeper: practical and, I found, positively affecting, just in the reading of it. The book itself employs the method of reinforcement by the repetition of examples you give. I can clearly see hundreds of people in more confident direction of their lives to the benefit of society at large. Thank you, thank you, thank you.
Jacek
Poland

Dear Anne Marie:

We were just trying to remember how many years it has been since we purchased your book. Lance and I have been thinking back to when your book and your teachings came into our lives. We also think of you often, because your book is on our nightstand all the time and it even goes on all of Lance's out-of-town trips. The information in your book has helped him close many business transactions. Many thanks are in order. Let's catch up soon.
Amber
Bermuda

Dear Anne Marie:

I have a retail metaphysical book and gift store, UTOPIA, located in the Vancouver, BC, area. We have been selling your first book, *Affirmations, Your Passport to Happiness.* for nearly five years. Currently, it is our best-selling book and has been for over two years. This wonderful little book has become very popular by word of mouth; it helps that you make frequent appearances on television and radio, both locally and internationally.

In addition, we also carry your titles, *Affirmations, Your Passport to Prosperity/Money; Affirmations, Your Passport to Lasting, Loving Relationships*; and your Cards of Life—all good sellers in our shop. I wholeheartedly recommend that every store carry these helpful books.
Donna King, Owner of *Utopia Book and Gift Store*
North Vancouver, BC www.utopiagifts.com

Dear Anne Marie:

Your books have inspired me to integrate your teachings, not only in my private life, but in my business, as well. As an artist, I feel integration is the key. I create special pieces of jewelry using a collection of semi-precious stones and consider the buyer's spiritual need to amplify and support this process. Affirmations are matched to the properties of the crystals to help the client to achieve his or her goals with a more powerful focus. Thank you, Anne Marie, for your loving, inspiring presence and uplifting work!
Regina von Wyl

Kid's Review: This Book Rocks!!!

Dear Anne Marie:

I am so lucky my mom gave me a copy of your book on Affirmations to read because I know most people my age don't know about Affirmations. I know you teach how to use the power of positive thoughts. Before I met you or read your book, I used to keep my feelings inside me. But now I know how to get rid of them—I do my Affirmations daily and I love and respect others and myself. You know, I think they should have this *Affirmations* book in all the schools and libraries. I also want to thank you, Anne Marie, for helping me and showing me the way to change my life to live more positively. Thank you, thank you, thank you.
Adrian, Grade 7
North Vancouver, BC, Canada

My dear, lovely Anne Marie:

I'm so very proud to know you. Your book is the most life-altering gift I have ever received and quite serendipitous. It is personal, informative, and completely helpful. It teaches the reader exactly how to do Affirmations properly. I have experienced a lot in my life—things that people would never imagine. That, I think, is how everyone's life goes. What you see is not always what you get. I didn't quite know how to deal with all the knowledge and experiences life had set into my lap. The timing was right. I was ready to learn and the teachings in your book guided me.

This year has been full of lessons and rewards that I have been able to affirm for and accept. Your words helped me express my new outlook on life. With your lessons, I have been able to help so many others. Thank you so much for being an author and writing this amazing book and for being kind enough to give your knowledge to the rest of us.
My kindest, most affectionate blessings,
Zahra

Dear Anne Marie:

Your book on Affirmations has helped me in many aspects of my life, as follows.

- Affirmed for a quick sale of my house for the asking price and it sold within three weeks—above the asking price.
- Affirmed for "Big Money to me Now" and I retired with a great deal more money than I had expected and was even able to pay off the loan on my brand new car.
- Received a large sum of money from an unexpected inheritance.
- Affirmed for the perfect man for me for a loving, lasting, happy relationship and I met the man of my dreams on a cruise. He is financially independent, single, and wonderful. If you are wondering if Affirmations really work—you bet they do! You just have to be very clear about what you are affirming (or ordering up).

So if you are feeling depressed and want to change your life, just use the powerful, proven techniques in this book to make it more positive. I did!
Grace Jensen
Port Moody, BC, Canada

Dear Anne Marie:
In the recent past, I encountered a less than pleasant neighbour in my building. He would blast his music until unacceptable hours to the point where it would shake the foundation of our building. During these times, he was also quite violent to my family due to his overuse of alcohol. I have two very young children and run a business from home. The sleepless nights were difficult and the fear-filled days were worse. Due to the very alarming encounters with him, I became afraid for my children and myself. I wanted to move out of what was the best home we ever had!

Needing a solution, I began writing the Angel Letters. I stopped at 9 and nothing changed. Then upon the next frightening encounter, I finished the letters. To my own shock and disbelief, the man did a complete turnaround; he became kind-hearted then moved out of my building! Now I have a brand new neighbour who is perfect in so many ways. I tell everyone I know about these letters in their times of struggle or need. They are magical! There is no other way to describe them! Thank you, thank you, thank you, Anne Marie!

With love, Blissful Wife, Mother, and Businesswoman
Cijaye DePradine, President
Cijaye Creative: www.cijayecreative.com
and PROJECT Jumpstart: www.jumpstartexperience.com

Feedback from the Media

- "During my years of hosting my online radio show, The Messengerfiles, the Universe has sent me many interesting people to interview and share with my listeners . . . from Ontario, Canada to Greece.

  Anne Marie is one of the most uplifting people I have ever met or shared a microphone with. Her quick wit, boundless energy, and total optimism is what is needed in today's world and through her many books and words of integrity, she has encouraged many people . . . including myself . . . to believe in the power of Affirmations.

  I trust that through this book and her many others, you also will learn that 'Affirmations when done properly work.' THANK YOU, THANK YOU, THANK YOU, Anne Marie, and keep up the good work!"
  Carole Matthews, Intuitive Medium
  Host of The Messengerfiles Radio Show
  CFOS 560AM
  www.carolematthewsintuitive.com

- "Anne Marie, you are the master of Affirmations. You have brought empowerment and happiness to my audience, creating a path of positive living."
  Hehpsehboah, Host of Eye on the Future Radio
  Author of *The Etherean Travellers and The Magical Child*
  www.eyeonthefutureradio.com

- "Anne Marie Evers has been a regular at News for the Soul shows and events for many years. She is truly a Master in her field. She has inspired positive change in the lives of thousands. I believe that everyone following the Affirmation methods in her books and workshops is going to see results in his or her life. I like to call it 'real life magic.' If you are actually doing them, Affirmations HAVE to work!"

Nicole Whitney is founder and co-host of News for the Soul, an online positive news broadcast center, global community, and consciousness movement for like minds and a live life-changing talk radio show airing in Vancouver and around the world. Nicole has officially named Anne Marie Evers as "The Affirmations Doctor."
www.newsforthesoul.com

- "Anne Marie Evers' books and Cards of Life have always and will always be a part of our life as they are very powerful tools to create a life we want. When she comes on the radio, the listeners' feedback is awesome and they always ask for her return. We lovingly call her 'The Affirmations Doctor' because she prescribes Affirmations like a doctor prescribes rest and relaxation."
Blessings to you,
Cameron and Lucia Steele, Contact Talk Radio Hosts
KKNW 1150 AM, Seattle, WA, USA

- "Whenever Anne Marie Evers appears as a guest on my TV show, I get numerous phone calls and letters from viewers saying how her teachings of Affirmations have transformed their lives and have given them the tools and confidence to go out and do something."
David Ingram, Host of the David Ingram Show

- "This book is an essential companion for those who are honest and committed about their growth. It is a powerful tool for fulfilling your dreams."
Olga Sheean
Former Senior Editor of *Shared Vision* magazine

Affirmations When Properly Done Always Work!

Resources

1. *Who's the Matter with Me?* Alice Steadman, DeVorss & Company, 1966.
2. *A Method for Producing Ideas,* James W. Young, Advertising Publications Inc., 1940.
3. *The Law of Success,* Prof. J. H. Kelly, published by Prof. S. A. Weltmer, 1900.
4. *Three Magic Words,* U. S. Andersen, Hal Leighton Printing Company, 1954.
5. *Power Thoughts,* Robert Schuller, Harper Collins Publishers, 1993.
6. *The Creative Power of Thought,* Alice Magnusson, D. W. Friesen & Sons, Ltd., 1981.
7. *The Science of Mind,* Ernest Holmes, G. P. Putnam's Sons, 1938.
8. *The Magic of Believing,* Claude M. Bristol, Prentice-Hall, Inc., 1948.
9. *Perfect Health,* Deepak Chopra, Harmony Books, 1989.
10. *Feel the Fear and Do it Anyway,* Susan Jeffers, Ph.D. Harcourt Brace Jovanovich Publishers, 1987.
11. *Dare to Believe,* May Rowland, Unity School of Christianity, 1961.
12. *How to Change your Life with Affirmations,* Anne Marie Evers, Evers Publishing Company, 1989.
13. *Directing the Movies of Your Mind,* Adelaide Bry with Marjorie Blair, Harper & Row Publishers, 1976.
14. *The Master Key Course,* Og Mandino's University of Success, Og Mandino.
15. *Every Good Desire,* Ernest C. Wilson, Harper & Row Publishers, 1973.
16. *Affirmations, Your Passport to Lasting, Loving Relationships,* Anne Marie Evers, Affirmations International Publishing, 2003.
17. *Affirmations, Your Passport to Prosperity/Money,* Anne Marie Evers, Affirmations International Publishing, 2004.
18. *Affirm and Learn Enhancement Program, Anti-Violence Program for Children,* Anne Marie Evers and Marjie Nistad, Affirmations International Publishing, 2002.

19._Look Who Believes In You: A Guide to Letting Love In_, Tanya Harmon, www.LookWhoBelieves.com.

20._The Last Adventure of Life: Sacred Resources for Transition_, Maria Dancing Heart.

21._AAAGH!! I Think I'm Psychic_, Natasha J. Rosewood, Trafford Publishing, 2004.

22. _Mind, Time & Power!_ Anthony Hamilton, lifeworks@canada.com.

Product Information
Products from Anne Marie Evers' Personal Store

Address: 4559 Underwood Avenue
North Vancouver, BC
Canada V7K 2S3

Email: annemarieevers@shaw.ca

The Cards of Life

Exciting Cards of Life

- Ask questions and receive answers from within.
- The Cards of Life are a set of 72 inspiring, beautiful, colourful cards that represent a powerful personal-growth tool.
- The Cards of Life are divided into 12 sections—Health, Relationships, Career, Money, Forgiveness, Fear, Love, Happiness, Children, Beginnings and Endings, Self-Esteem, and Spiritual Growth.
- The Cards of Life come boxed, with an accompanying instruction booklet.

The Cards of Life On the Go

When I was speaking with one of my dear friends and associates who volunteers in Africa—teaching children how to plant gardens and learn English—she mentioned it would be great to have some flashcards to help the children learn English. I remembered I had some extra blank cards from the Cards of Life. I took 100 of them, put labels on them (Happiness, Sharing, Love, Forgiveness) and shipped them to her in Africa. She showed them to school officials in both India and Africa, with the intent to implement these flashcards into the school system. It is my affirmation that the Cards of Life give love, hope, and help wherever they are led to go.
Visit www.cardsoflife.com.

Affirmations Coaching

Available in Person or Online

Cards of Life Instructional Course

Available in Person or Online
Toll-Free Phone Number: 1-877-923-3476

Affirmation/Prayer Cards

New Workbooks

Attracting Wealth through Affirmations
Attracting Health and Happiness through Affirmations
Attracting Loving, Lasting, Happy Relationships through Affirmations

e-Books

Affirmations, Your Passport to Happiness
Affirmations, Your Passport to Happiness (in German)

Books

Affirmations, Your Passport to Lasting, Loving Relationships
Affirmations, Your Passport to Prosperity/Money
Co-Author of the #1 Best-Selling Series *Wake up—Live The Life You Love* with Dr. Wayne Dyer, Dr. Deepak Chopra and Terry Cole-Whittaker

Programs

KAP: Kids Affirmation Program (www.kidspower.ca)

Ongoing International Internet/Media Show

TV/Internet Monthly Show, Anne Marie & Friends
www.affirmations-media.com

Anne Marie's Personal Interests

- Radio TV/Internet Host
- Chair, International New Thought Alliance World Congress 2006 in Vancouver, BC, Canada

- District President, International New Thought Alliance for Canada (British Columbia)
- Ordained Minister, The World Federation of Unity Churches and Community Church of New Thought Lola Pauline Mays, New Thought Seminary of the Community Church of New Thought, Church of Divine Love, Phoenix, AZ
- Public Lecturer: Strategies for Affirmative Living and Learning
- Lecturer/Workshop Facilitator
- Columnist

Websites

ww.affirmations-doctor.com
www.kidspower.ca
www.strategiesportal.com

New Website

Learn about the history of Affirmations, as never seen before, with a behind-the-scenes view of how famous authors and people around the world are using Affirmations to transform their lives at www.affirmations-playground.com.

Kids' Affirmation Program (KAP)

KAP provides a fun-filled, safe, and secure learning environment that teaches children strategies for positive daily living and learning at school, at home, and at play. This interactive and experimental program affirms and strengthens each child's worth, personal value, and giftedness.

KAP is a Triple E Program—Educational, Entertaining, and Experiential.

Co-authored by:

Anne Marie Evers, Affirmations Author and Coach

Michael Robb, B.A., B.Ed., M.R.E.

To Purchase the KAP Program:

Visit www.kidspower.ca.

Order Form

Anne Marie Evers
4559 Underwood Avenue
North Vancouver, BC Canada   V7K 2S3

Fax: 604 904-1127
Email: annemarieevers@shaw.ca
Tele-Class Program Info: 1-877-923-3476

Please Print

Name _____

Address _____   Apt # _____

City _____

Prov./State _____   Postal/Zip Code _____

Phone _____   Fax _____

Email _____

Product Price	Quantity	Unit Cost	Tax	Total

Signature _____

Comments _____

_____

_____

Method of Payment:
Please send a cheque or money order to the above address.
Make cheque payable to Anne Marie Evers.

"How an Affirmation created Affirmations-Doctor.com!"

This is a powerful story of how my Website Affirmations-Doctor.com came to be. I had been writing books and helping thousands of people around the world for the past 35 years to create what they want in their lives.

I created an Affirmation that stated that I wanted to expand my Affirmations program, to be able to reach more people and generate greater opportunities for people to achieve greater results using the power of multimedia, the Internet, and TV.

Shortly after creating this Affirmation, a young gentleman came into my life, Glenn Coleman, who was suffering from extreme illness from mercury poisoning. He was a big promoter of positive thinking, but was being heavily burdened by this illness. He asked me if I could help him to control the nerve pain in his body. I told him how to create an Affirmation that would train his mind how to shut off the pain.

Shortly after, he responded back to me, elated that he was able to shut off pain on demand, for short periods of time, using Affirmations. This was a huge relief, and that became the seed that launched him forward to overcome his health problems.

He was so impressed with my Affirmations program and told me that he didn't think my book was marketed well enough, given the powerful results that people were getting. He said he was training to become a world-class Website copywriter and that he could send my book to the best-sellers list if given a chance.

Two months after this conversation, we started our journey building this site. Within three months, we had reached the top 3 percent of sites in the world. The site is now reinventing itself about once every three weeks, with new services and features that continually provide new ways for people to transform their lives with Affirmations.

He has identified the golden eggs of Internet marketing that are very inexpensive. These include the most advanced market research system, site builder, and search engine optimization system available.

Now he has people coming from all over the Internet, wanting to know how he was able to achieve such amazing results so quickly.

Part of his secret is that he also created an Affirmation to become a world-class Website copywriter. His Affirmation quickly came true!

Glenn is now building a new site called <u>www.Soaring-Internet-Sales.com</u> to reveal this powerful combination of Internet Marketing Systems.

"Happy Affirming"